Contract, tender the Player a new Standard Player's Contract upon the same terms and conditions (including this Section 18) as this Standard Player's Contract (as the provisions of said contract may be modified from time to .... provisions of any Collective Bargaining Agreement between the member clubs of the League and the NHLP... fixed term may be different. If the Club fails to tender such a contract to the Player on o... provided such option may not be exercised later than August 13th, may elect to become .... vide services under this Contract and as such will have the right to negotiate with any c... obligation on the part of a club which might, under such circumstances, acquire his serv...

(c) Without regard to any action taken by the Club under subsections (a) and (b), the Player may notify .... September 10th of the final year of this Contract that he wishes to sign a Player's Option Contract. If the Player gives such notice, the Club shall no later than September 25th of that year tender the Player a Player's Option Contract, and the Player shall forthwith enter into said contract. The Player's Option Contract shall be on the same terms and conditions, including any and all performance bonuses, as this Contract (as the provisions of said contract may be modified from time to time pursuant to the applicable provisions of any Collective Bargaining Agreement between the member clubs of the League and the NHLPA) except that it shall be for only one additional season at the Player's previous year's salary and shall provide that effective the following July 1st the Player will be a free agent, without any further obligation to provide services under said Player's Option Contract, and as such will have the right, as provided by Section 9A of the League By-Laws, the text of which Section is printed on the reverse side hereof, to negotiate and contract with any club in the League, or with any other club.

(d) If the Club has not taken the action permitted under subsection (a) and the Player has not exercised the option provided by subsection (b) or has not given notice to the Club in accordance with subsection (c), then the parties shall enter into a new Standard Player's Contract by mutual agreement or, failing such agreement, the parties shall, no later than September 25th, enter into a new one-year Standard Player's Contract for the succeeding season upon the same terms and conditions (including this Section 18) as this Standard Player's Contract, except as to salary, which shall be determined by neutral arbitration under the applicable collective bargaining agreement providing a mechanism for such arbitration, provided, however, that if no such collective bargaining agreement is then in effect, the Player's salary shall be the same as his salary, including any and all performance bonuses, for the previous year.

(e) As used in this Section 18, the phrase "final year of this Contract" does not include the "option year".

(f) The Club's notice and tender obligations under this Section 18 shall be deemed fulfilled if the Club delivers the required written notification and/or the proposed contract to the Player in person on or before the applicable deadline date or mails same by registered mail postmarked no later than said deadline date to the Player at the address set forth below his signature hereto. If the Club has elected to use the mail, the Club shall notify the NHLPA of its action in writing, by sending a copy of the transmittal letter or otherwise, at the time of mailing to the Player. The Player's notice and delivery obligations under this Section 18 shall be deemed fulfilled if the Player hand delivers the required written notification or the executed contract on or before the applicable deadline date or mails it by registered mail postmarked no later than said deadline date to the Club at its address set forth below.

19. The Club and the Player severally and mutually promise and agree to be legally bound by the Constitution and By-Laws of the League and by any Collective Bargaining Agreement that has been or may be entered into between the member clubs of the League and the NHLPA, and by all of the terms and provisions thereof, copies of which shall be open and available for inspection by Club, its directors and officers, and the Player, at the main office of the League, the main office of the Club and the main office of the NHLPA.

The Club and the Player further agree that in case of dispute between them, except as to the compensation to be paid to the Player on a new contract, the dispute shall be referred within one year from the date it arose to the President of the League, as an arbitrator and his decision shall be accepted as final by both parties, unless, and to extent that, other arbitration procedures are provided in any Collective Bargaining Agreement between the member clubs of the League and the NHLPA to cover such dispute.

The Club and the Player further agree that all fines imposed upon the Player under the Playing Rules, or under the provisions of the League By-Laws, shall be deducted from the salary of the Player and be remitted by the Club to the N.H.L. Players' Emergency Fund.

20. The parties agree that the rights provided in Section 18 and in any Addendum hereto and the promise of the Player to play hockey only with the Club, or such other club as provided in Sections 2, 11 and 12, and the Club's right to take pictures of and to televise the Player as provided in Section 8 have all been taken into consideration in determining the salary payable to the Player under Section 1 hereof.

21. It is severally and mutually agreed that the only contracts recognized by the President of the League are the Standard Player's Contracts, Player's Termination Contracts, Player's Option Contracts, Post-Option Year Termination Contracts, Standard Contracts (Corporate), Standard Termination Contracts (Corporate), Standard Option Contracts (Corporate) and Post-Option Year Termination Contracts (Corporate) which have been duly executed and filed in the League's office and approved by him (or his designated representative), and that this Agreement contains the entire agreement between the Parties and there are no oral or written inducements, promises or agreements except as provided herein.

In Witness Whereof, the parties have signed this .... day

of .... A.D. 19 ....

WITNESSES:

....

.... *Club*

.... *Address of Club*

.... By ....

.... *President*

....

.... *Player*

.... *Home Address of Player*

I hereby certify that I have, at this date, received, examined and noted of record the within Contract, and that it is in regular form.

Dated .... 19 ....

for the National Hockey League

ON ACTIVE SERVICE

CANADIAN
KNIGHTS OF COLUMBUS
WAR SERVICES

THE SALVATION ARMY
CANADIAN
WAR SERVICES

Dear Hap.

Sorry I haven't answered your letter sooner than this.

I wish you all the luck in the play-offs. I fancy you have the plug in the glass case by the time you get him.

Hap I've been doing little scouting for over here, and I have the best hockey player in this country (He's great) worth (Twenty five) you. His name is Ed Brown, and he is only

4/71 CFA 170   PLEASE WRITE ON BOTH SIDES
                          (over)

Maple Leaf Gardens,
(HOME OF THE TORONTO MAPLE LEAF H...

CORNER
CARLTON & CHURCH
STREETS

IN ACCOUNT WITH

National Hockey League
603 Sun Life B...
Montrea...

April   Montreal Playoff Trip:

Mon. 8 & 9 - 20 returns Toronto to Montreal @ $...
             1 drawing room   "   "   "
            19 lowers Toronto to Montreal @ $ 3...
            19 "   " Montreal to Toronto @ 3...
             1 drawing room Montreal to Toronto

             Players' meals - 20 for 1½ days @ $5...
             Hotel accommodation - 20 men for 1 ...

             Sundry expenses for 3 games @ $60.00

Telephone   Summary
Charges, etc. against
Hockey Players

A. D. Blair	J. J. Boll	F. M. Clancy	C. W. Conacher	...
.20	.30	.40	.10	
.20	.05	.10	.10	
.20	.10	.20	.10	
.10	.15	.05	.15	
.20		.10	.10	
.30	.70	.10	.15	
1.20		.75	.15	
		.37	1.15	
		1.50	4.05	
		3.37	1.05	
			.37	
			.20	
			3.00	
			10.92	

G. Stewart	Wm. Hollett	G. R. Horner	A. M. Jackson	R...
.10	.30	.20	.20	
.10	1.88	.10	.05	
.10	.20	.10	.30	
.10	.05	.10	.55	
.10	.40	.50		
.05	.40	.12		
.10	.60	1.12		
.30	.10	1.74		
.95	3.93	4.56		

A. J. Pirmean	M. D. Thoms	F. Finnigan
.10	1.05	.37
.20	.10	
.20	.15	
.10		
.10		
.30		
1.10		
3.30		
5.40		

6:45 p.m.   — Turnstiles open
6:45 - 7:00   — Usherettes (6) distribut...
7:00 - 7:20   — Leafs on ice for photos
                Side glass removed.
7:20 - 7:30   — Leafs back in room. Gla...
7:30 - 7:45   — Leafs warmup.
7:45 - 7:55   — Resurface ice
7:55 - 8:00   — Leafs return. B. McFarl...
                Welcome. Introduces Bot...
                Introduces Tiny Tim. Me...
                Tin. expresses desire to
                so..SCORES!
                Tim promises to sing dur...
                Tim drops puck for offic...
8:00 p.m.   — Game.

First Intermission: Ice resurfaced

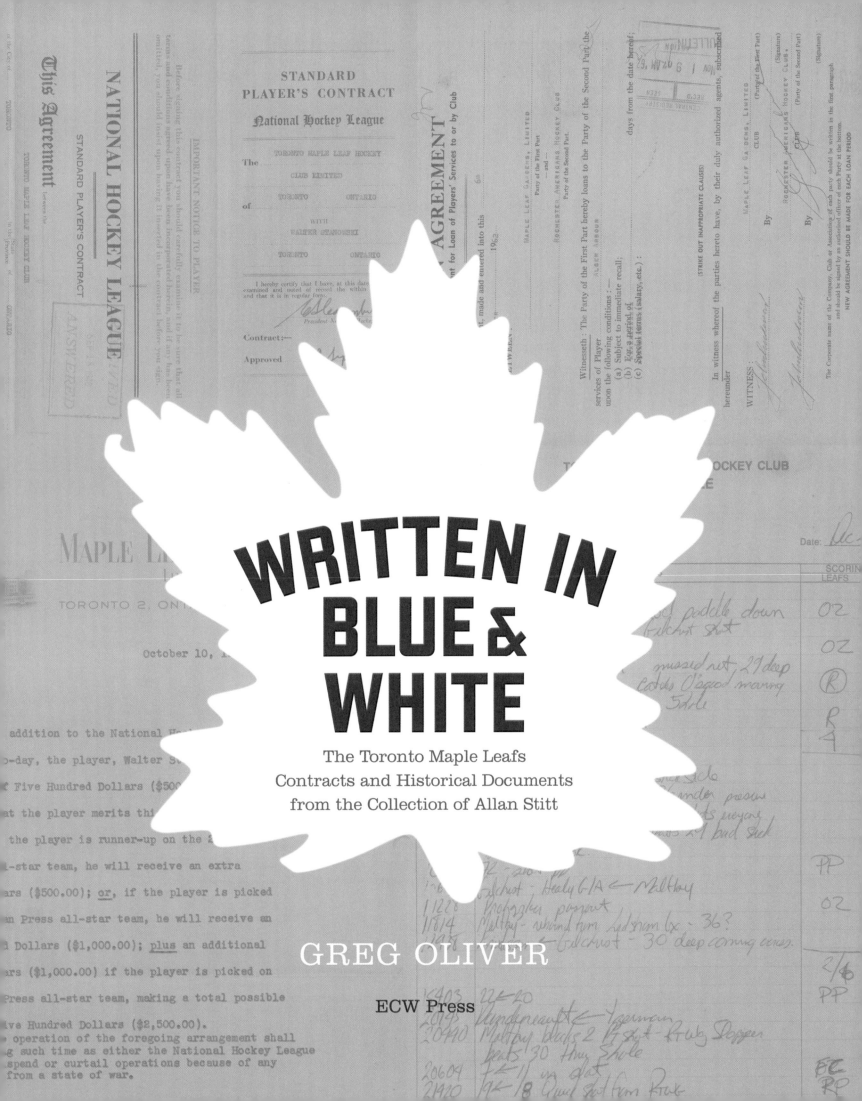

WRITTEN IN BLUE & WHITE

The Toronto Maple Leafs
Contracts and Historical Documents
from the Collection of Allan Stitt

GREG OLIVER

ECW Press

Published by ECW Press
2120 Queen Street East, Suite 200
Toronto, Ontario, Canada M4E 1E2
416-694-3348 / info@ecwpress.com

Library and Archives Canada Cataloguing in Publication

Oliver, Greg, author
Written in blue & white : the Toronto Maple Leafs contracts
and historical documents from the collection of Allan Stitt /
Greg Oliver.

Includes bibliographical references.
ISBN 978-1-77041-215-6
also issued as: 978-1-77090-620-4 (PDF);
978-1-77090-621-1 (epub)

1. Toronto Maple Leafs (Hockey team)—History—Sources.
2. Professional sports contracts—Ontario—Toronto—
History—Sources.
3. Hockey players—Ontario—Toronto—History—Sources.
4. Hockey teams—Ontario—Toronto—History—Sources. 5.
Hockey—Ontario—Toronto—History—Sources.
6. Stitt, Allan J.—Private collections. I. Title. II. Title: Written
in blue and white. III. Title: Toronto Maple Leafs contracts
and historical documents from the collection of Allan Stitt.

GV848.T6O45 2014   796.962'6409713541   C2014-902564-5
C2014-902565-3

Editor for the press: Michael Holmes
Cover and text design: Tania Craan

Cover and interior images from the collection of Allan Stitt,
with the following exceptions: courtesy David Poile page
60; Rochester Americans 118; Hockey Hall of Fame — 5,
19, 22, 23, 24, 26, 30, 44, 66, 70 (top), 72, 74, 96, 115, 124,
130, 132, 134, 140, 145, 160, 162, 164, 168, 174, 178, 184,
186; HHOF–Craig Campbell 12; HHOF–Dave Sandford
Collection 172, 180, 188; HHOF–Frank Prazak Collection 142;
HHOF–Graphic Artists Collection 136, 148, 150, 154; HHOF–
Imperial Oil Turofsky Collection 28, 32, 34, 42, 46, 50, 52, 54,
56, 58, 62, 64, 70 (bottom), 75, 78, 82, 84, 86, 88, 90, 94, 98,
100, 102, 104, 106, 108, 110, 112, 114, 116, 120, 122, 128, back
cover; HHOF–John Hanlon Collection 144; HHOF–Lewis
Portnoy Collection 138, 152, 156, 158, 166; HHOF–Miles
Nadal Collection 170, 176; HHOF–Paul Bereswill Collection
182; HHOF–Steve Poirier 8; Radek Cecha 10, back flap.

Printed and bound in the United States at Lake Book Mfg.
5   4   3   2   1

We acknowledge the financial support of the Government
of Canada through the Canada Book Fund for our publishing
activities, and the contribution of the Government of Ontario
through the Ontario Book Publishing Tax Credit and the
Ontario Media Development Corporation.

Get the
eBook
free!

Purchase the print edition
and receive the eBook free!
For details, go to
ecwpress.com/eBook

in the ...

The summer is really flying by and it will be notime at all before we'll be hearing the old whip crack again

So long for now, Hap sure hope you can use this fellow Roy Kelly

Yours Sincerely

George Boothman.

"Hello to all the girls in the office."

Mr. George Boothman,
620 12th Avenue East,
Calgary, Alberta.

Dear George:

Thanks for your letter of July 3rd.

Kelly apparently has signed an optional agreement with Cleveland as he is on their Contingent Reserve List. This means that no other club can talk terms to him.

Said "hello" to all the girls in the office as you requested and the only reply I received was "who is Boothman?"

Thanks for all your trouble. I hope when the new addition arrives, he looks like his mother with his father's curly hair, and without your singing voice.

Very sincerely,

CHD/LP

To the unheralded secretaries, accountants, and personal assistants, who have helped teams run smoothly through the ages.

George Boothman (Leafs 1942–44), letter to Hap Day, July 3, 1944:
"Hello to all the girls in the office."

Hap Day, letter to George Boothman, July 10, 1944:
"Said 'hello' to all the girls in the office as you requested and the only reply I received was 'who is Boothman?'"

Eddie Shack, the Stanley Cup, and many of the women employees of Maple Leaf Gardens.

CONTENTS

April 26, 1948.

Mr. C. Campbell,
President, National Hockey League,
603 Sun Life Building,
Montreal, Que.

Dear Sir:

Enclosed please find letter signed by Mr. Syl Apps, in which he signifies his intention to retire from hockey, and requests that his name be placed on the V. R. List. We shall, therefore, appreciate it if you will place this player's name on the Voluntarily Retired List of the Toronto Club.

Yours very truly,

CS/McD

Conn Smythe

April 23, 1948.

The President,
Maple Leaf Gardens, Limited,
Toronto, Ontario.

Dear Mr. Smythe:

    I wish to retire

Toronto, Ontario,
April 23, 1948

The President,
Maple Leaf Gardens, Limited,
Toronto, Ontario.

Dear Mr. Smythe:

    I wish to retire from hockey
and would like my name to be placed on the
Voluntarily Retired List of the National Hockey
League.

    Yours very truly,

    S. Apps

Ron Ellis played 16 years with the Toronto Maple Leafs and was a member of the 1967 Stanley Cup winning team and a member of Team Canada '72, the Team of the Century. Ron is now the program director for the Hockey Hall of Fame's Development Association.

FOREWORD

Allan Stitt is a huge sports fan and can hold his own with anyone who wants to talk about his Leafs and Blue Jays. Thankfully, he encouraged me to attend the Vancouver Winter Olympics with him and our sons and it has become the memory of a lifetime, forever cementing our friendship.

The Hockey Hall of Fame has benefitted from Allan's love of hockey and generous spirit. How so, you might ask? Well in my opinion, he is a member of the elite when it comes to expertise as a collector of sports memorabilia. Allan is always on the lookout for artifacts that would be of interest to the Hockey Hall of Fame and upon finding these special items he then donates them to the Hall.

Because of his interest in sports memorabilia, Allan also has numerous hockey jerseys, sticks, and other pieces that were used by professionals during their NHL careers and games played with Team Canada in international competition. If you are fortunate enough to visit his office, you might just get an impressive VIP tour.

In his successful professional life, Allan is a lawyer specializing in mediation and arbitration. No doubt, this is the reason he especially enjoys collecting NHL contracts. More than once, he has given me original copies of contracts I signed with the Toronto Maple Leafs.

In our conversations, I have shared the circumstances of signing my first contract with General Manager Punch Imlach.

As an 18-year-old in 1964, all alone, I sat in a very low chair looking up at Punch in his office. Punch said, "Sign here now or continue going to school." This was the era of the Original Six and there were no player agents on the scene and the Players' Association was still a few years away. There was little negotiation as all first-year players made the same basic salary. I do recall asking for one clause in the contract that prevented the Leafs from sending me to the minors in my first season. This gave me an opportunity to determine if I could play in the NHL and proved to be beneficial to my career.

As you read this book, you will have the opportunity to peruse some of the contracts and other historical documents that Allan has accumulated over the years. Behind each there is a story that describes the circumstance that enabled players to take advantage of opportunities like league expansion or becoming part of a dynasty.

Assembling this book has been a labour of love for Allan.

His willingness to share his unique collection of contracts gives all hockey fans an opportunity to study the history of the NHL from a totally new perspective. Enjoy the read!

Ron Ellis

Allan Stitt in his "Leafs room" at the office.

INTRODUCTION

The Genesis of a Collection

It started with Teeder Kennedy's rookie contract.

Allan Stitt was at a major hockey card show near Toronto's airport when he spotted the old document, listed for $300. The next table over was a Teeder Kennedy hockey card for $100.

Trained as a lawyer, a well-known mediator, and a negotiation specialist, Stitt thought that the prices were wildly incongruous—one was a mass-produced photo with no direct connection to the former Toronto Maple Leafs captain in the Hockey Hall of Fame, and the other was a real piece of Toronto Maple Leafs history.

"I didn't know anything about the value of either, but I thought, 'That's just crazy, that a hockey card they made thousands of, and wasn't really significant in terms of historical NHL memorabilia, could be compared to a document signed by Hap Day, signed by Teeder Kennedy in his rookie year, and signed by Merv Dutton, the league president," said Stitt. "The relative values made no sense to me, so without knowing whether either of them was undervalued or overvalued, I just bought the contract because I thought it was an incredibly cool document. I think too, because of my background in law, I was interested in contracts."

For the record, it was a contract signed on March 3, 1943, that covered the end of the 1942–43 season (two games) and the 1943–44 campaign. The future captain of the Leafs got $1,000 for the remainder of the year, and $3,500 for his full rookie season. In the subsequent bulletin issued by the NHL, it was announced that "Kennedy's number will be 20." (Interestingly, he wore #10 for the first three years, #12 in 1945–46, and #9 until he retired.)

The collection grew from there.

"It turned out that the Kennedy contract wasn't undervalued. That's what the market was," explained Stitt. "So over the years, I did my best to buy as many contracts and documents as I could, as long as I thought they were at market value. Obviously, I didn't get them all. But the more I got, the more I became interested in them. I wanted to get one from every year to see how they evolved. Then I tried to get more and more from different players I liked."

The greats are represented in Stitt's collection in different ways: with "The Rocket" Maurice Richard, it's a lot of contracts relating to life outside hockey—TV shows and endorsements; Jacques Plante's file goes from telegrams relating to his early career, up and down from the minors, to the Leafs renting him an apartment; Brad Park's

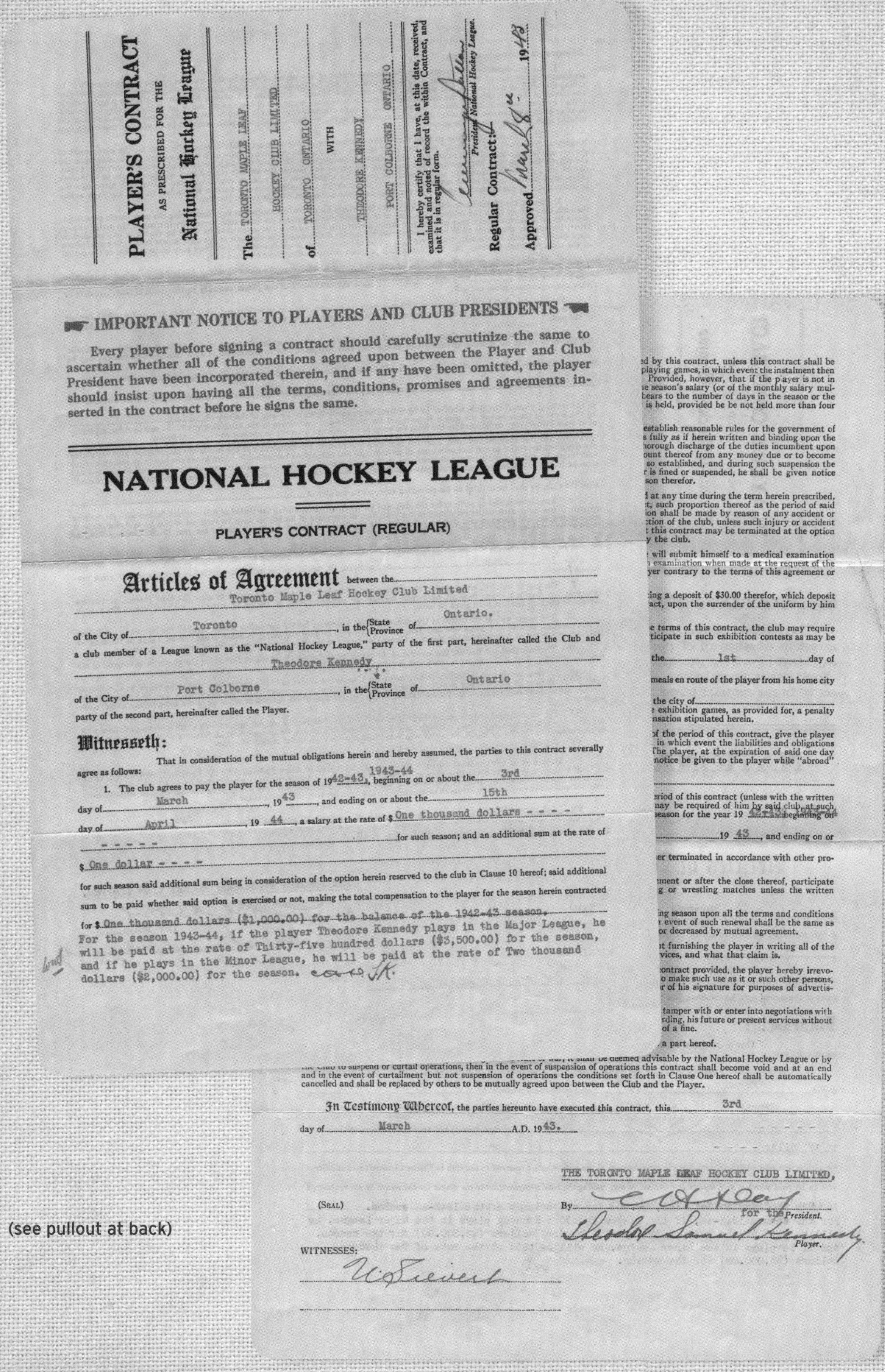

PLAYER'S CONTRACT

AS PRESCRIBED FOR THE

National Hockey League

The TORONTO MAPLE LEAF

HOCKEY CLUB LIMITED

of TORONTO, ONTARIO.

WITH

THEODORE KENNEDY

PORT COLBORNE, ONTARIO

I hereby certify that I have, at this date, received, examined and noted of record the within Contract, and that it is in regular form.

[signature]
President National Hockey League.

March 8 1943

Regular Contract:

Approved

☛ IMPORTANT NOTICE TO PLAYERS AND CLUB PRESIDENTS ☚

Every player before signing a contract should carefully scrutinize the same to ascertain whether all of the conditions agreed upon between the Player and Club President have been incorporated therein, and if any have been omitted, the player should insist upon having all the terms, conditions, promises and agreements inserted in the contract before he signs the same.

NATIONAL HOCKEY LEAGUE

PLAYER'S CONTRACT (REGULAR)

Articles of Agreement between the

Toronto Maple Leaf Hockey Club Limited

of the City of Toronto, in the State/Province of Ontario.

a club member of a League known as the "National Hockey League," party of the first part, hereinafter called the Club and

Theodore Kennedy

of the City of Port Colborne, in the State/Province of Ontario

party of the second part, hereinafter called the Player.

Witnesseth:

That in consideration of the mutual obligations herein and hereby assumed, the parties to this contract severally agree as follows:

1. The club agrees to pay the player for the season of 19 42-43 1943-44, beginning on or about the 3rd

day of March, 19 43, and ending on or about the 15th

day of April, 19 44, a salary at the rate of $ One thousand dollars - - - -

- - - - for such season; and an additional sum at the rate of

$ One dollar - - - -

for such season said additional sum being in consideration of the option herein reserved to the club in Clause 10 hereof; said additional sum to be paid whether said option is exercised or not, making the total compensation to the player for the season herein contracted

for $ One thousand dollars ($1,000.00) for the balance of the 1942-43 season. For the season 1943-44, if the player Theodore Kennedy plays in the Major League, he will be paid at the rate of Thirty-five hundred dollars ($3,500.00) for the season, and if he plays in the Minor League, he will be paid at the rate of Two thousand dollars ($2,000.00) for the season. *C.S.J.K.*

[partial right-hand column text, folded page]

...ed by this contract, unless this contract shall be ...playing games, in which event the instalment then ...Provided, however, that if the player is not in ...he season's salary (or of the monthly salary mul- ...bears to the number of days in the season or the ...is held, provided he be not held more than four

...establish reasonable rules for the government of ...s fully as if herein written and binding upon the ...horough discharge of the duties incumbent upon ...ount thereof from any money due or to become ...so established, and during such suspension the ...r is fined or suspended, he shall be given notice ...son therefor.

...d at any time during the term herein prescribed, ...t, such proportion thereof as the period of said ...ion shall be made by reason of any accident or ...ction of the club, unless such injury or accident ...t this contract may be terminated at the option ...y the club.

...will submit himself to a medical examination ...n examination when made at the request of the ...yer contrary to the terms of this agreement or

...ing a deposit of $30.00 therefor, which deposit ...act, upon the surrender of the uniform by him

...e terms of this contract, the club may require ...ticipate in such exhibition contests as may be

...the 1st day of

...meals en route of the player from his home city

...the city of

...e exhibition games, as provided for, a penalty ...nsation stipulated herein.

...of the period of this contract, give the player ...in which event the liabilities and obligations ...The player, at the expiration of said one day ...notice be given to the player while "abroad"

...period of this contract (unless with the written ...may be required of him by said club, at such ...season for the year 19 beginning on

...19 43, and ending on or

...er terminated in accordance with other pro-

...ement or after the close thereof, participate ...g or wrestling matches unless the written

...ing season upon all the terms and conditions ...e event of such renewal shall be the same as ...or decreased by mutual agreement.

...t furnishing the player in writing all of the ...vices, and what that claim is.

...contract provided, the player hereby irrevo- ...o make such use as it or such other persons, ...r of his signature for purposes of advertis-

...tamper with or enter into negotiations with ...rding, his future or present services without ...of a fine.

...part hereof.

the Club to suspend or curtail operations, then in the event of suspension of operations this contract shall become void and at an end and in the event of curtailment but not suspension of operations the conditions set forth in Clause One hereof shall be automatically cancelled and shall be replaced by others to be mutually agreed upon between the Club and the Player.

In Testimony Whereof, the parties hereunto have executed this contract, this 3rd

day of March A.D. 19 43.

THE TORONTO MAPLE LEAF HOCKEY CLUB LIMITED,

(SEAL)

By *[signature]* for the President.

Theodore Samuel Kennedy Player.

WITNESSES:

[signature]

(see pullout at back)

abandoned negotiations with the World Hockey Association's Ottawa Nationals are interesting; for "The Great One" Wayne Gretzky, his 1977 contract with the Sault Ste. Marie Greyhounds of the Ontario Hockey League is Stitt's pride and joy, though Gretzky's WHA deal with the Edmonton Oilers and owner Peter Pocklington is a close second.

Great games are represented too: the statistical sheets from Game 7 of the 1972 Summit Series is pretty cool, especially because the Canada vs. USSR battle had made such an impression on Stitt. The first piece of memorabilia he bought—even before Kennedy's contract—was a Paul Henderson stick from the series. "Knowing nothing about it and nothing about its value, I bought it—not knowing how to check provenance," said Stitt. "In retrospect, it was just a completely blind, stupid purchase. But I bought it because I thought it was really fantastic. It turned out to be a good stick, but that was more good luck than good management." That stick now hangs in his office, in a custom-made frame, along with photos of Stitt and his son, Jason, with Henderson and the stick. Stitt has dozens of jerseys from the various Team Canada teams through the years, including Dennis Hull's Team Canada '72 jersey and numerous Leafs jerseys.

Many contracts and documents from the Minnesota North Stars are included as well, and give some insight into Wren Blair, the coach/general manager from 1967 to 1970, who will forever be known as the man who discovered Bobby Orr.

"I got them from a guy who worked for the North Stars. When they were cleaning out the North Stars' offices, they threw all the old documents out in boxes," recalled Stitt. Four boxes were saved, and eventually found their way to the Stitt Collection. "The staff were told to take the boxes out and put them in the trash. At the end of the day, before the trash was picked up, a few employees carried these boxes home—and I bought the boxes. Of course, the staff should have taken all of the boxes out of the trash, but I think they could only carry so many."

There is a decent collection from the Edmonton Oilers of the 1980s and 1990s. "I got them because the Oilers sold them off at one point," said Stitt.

Over the years, and even during the course of this book being written, Stitt made copies of old contracts and gave them to the players.

Danny Lewicki, a pro from 1950 to 1963, never got a copy of his own contract. "Being a kid, you never even realize what it's all about," he said. In general, three copies of a contract were made, with one going to the NHL's Central Registry, one

for the player, and one for the team; it seems the team often ended up as the care-taker of the player's copy as well.

Besides the hockey contracts and memorabilia, there are some unique baseball documents, contracts and letters, four World Series trophies, and even a 1917 letter written by James Naismith, who created the game of basketball, to his wife. Oh, and a Tribble and a phaser from *Star Trek* too.

Stitt scours auctions, eBay, and other places for things that catch his interest.

"I tell any dealer who will listen that I'm collecting contracts," he said.

Glen Pye is a Toronto memorabilia dealer who specializes in everything from Hollywood and rock stars to astronauts and sporting legends. He knows Stitt well.

"Most guys collect by player or by team. I deal with a guy in Toronto who just collects Toronto Maple Leafs so he's collecting Leafs contracts just because it's Leafs memorabilia," said Pye. "Allan's unique in the world, I think—there are probably a couple of guys in the States who specialize in baseball contracts, but I've never met them. I find Allan really interesting, because his business is negotiation. He often asks me if I have any interesting documents, because I got many of the personnel files. They all came out from the Gardens, and I ended up with all these great things. I had all the negotiation notes, and he loves them, seeing how the team and the player arrived at the number."

For collectors of autographs, contracts are "the safest autographs to have," said Pye.

"Some people buy the contracts for the autographs," said Stitt. "There's nothing that upsets me more than seeing on eBay that somebody cut an autograph out of a contract and is selling it as an autograph. It makes me want to cry."

Since a lot of what he buys is in lots, Allan picks and chooses what he wants and gives much of the rest to the Hockey Hall of Fame in Toronto. His donations have made him one of the largest donors to the HHOF. Period.

"He's been supporting the Hall of Fame for years. He's quite the collector," said Ron Ellis, an ex-Leaf who now works at the HHOF.

Stitt will call Phil Pritchard and Craig Campbell (the Keepers of the Stanley Cup!) at the HHOF for their opinion on things he is interested in.

"He finds stuff and he asks Craig Campbell and myself, 'What do you think of it?' We have enough knowledge between us, and then we have the Resource Centre archives, so we can start researching for him and see what we can come up with," said Pritchard. "As he's looking for contracts, he comes across other different things, whether it's old equipment, jerseys, or table-top hockey games."

One of the real finds, said Pritchard, is a 1952 women's hockey pinball game. "It's awesome. He sourced it out. He's a very generous guy and thought the Hall was the place for it," said Pritchard. "He's given us old books and old medals from the turn of the century that are probably historically a lot more valuable to the history of hockey, but the women's pinball, it's in the foyer, and every person that comes in thinks it's unbelievable."

In going through the collection with Allan, it is evident that each and every piece means something to him, and one old contract will remind him of a letter tucked away in another binder, and he'll then bring up a name filed in a third.

Calling all pinball wizards!

Eventually, we found one document that he and I had in common—shares in Maple Leaf Gardens. Like Allan, I was a shareholder; my father's stockbroker had a kids day, where investors were encouraged to buy stock in companies that would resonate with children: Disney, Irwin Toy, and the Leafs.

Growing up in Toronto, Stitt played hockey but wasn't very good. He continued to play recreationally with friends over the years. His father, Bert Stitt, is also a lawyer and is a Leafs season ticket holder. Allan's main memory from his first Leafs game: "I remember thinking how cool it was that Allan Stanley spelled his name the same way I did."

Allan got a single share in Maple Leaf Gardens as a gift in 1974. "It's funny, I don't remember any of my Bar Mitzvah gifts, except that one," he said. "Well, the other one I remember is a calculator; it could add, subtract, multiply, and divide—and it was giant. Those were the two gifts I remember."

There was a certain cachet in the neighbourhood, being an investor in such a famous team. The fact that the stock split five-for-one in 1986 made investors look even more brilliant.

"You could say you were a shareholder in Maple Leaf Gardens, but also, they would send you the Christmas card and calendar each year as a shareholder, and they would invite you, as a shareholder, to the annual shareholders' meeting at the Hot Stove Lounge," Stitt said. "I would go every year to that shareholders' meeting, because it was great to go to a shareholders' meeting at the Hot Stove Lounge."

But unlike Allan, when the call went out to sell the stock, I did, without question, without sense of its true worth; minority shareholders were offered $34 a share, and bigger investors like Jimmy Devellano and Harry Ornest fought Steve Stavro to get $49.50 a share. I was more interested in paying the rent and investing the next round at the pub. Allan preferred to keep his share certificate.

With his foresight, Allan can say that he spans the years with the Gardens, since he is also in possession of an original contract created for one of the thousands of workers who erected the House That Smythe Built, and a single share from the Harold Ballard–era Maple Leaf Gardens, as well as an uncashed dividend cheque for a whopping 25 cents.

So the Teeder Kennedy contract spurred the growth, but it all started with a single share of stock in the Blue and White.

Stitt's desire to share his treasures has led to this book. Think of *Written in Blue & White* as a companion piece to the history of the Toronto Maple Leafs. By no means is it meant to be a complete historical overview. The contracts, letters, memos, receipts, and other paperwork offer a window into the past.

Clauses and Their Development through the Years

The evolution of the standard player contract in the National Hockey League is self-evident: the early contracts are a single sheet, while recent ones run dozens of pages. But the changes are far more than just lawyerese mumbo jumbo.

"Contracts represent both the history of the game, and really, the history of North America—certainly the history of Canada," said Stitt. "You can see through the contracts, as the contracts evolve and the clauses evolve, you can see the country growing.

In 1939 they add a clause that says, 'If play is suspended in case of war . . .' And as the NHL Players' Association gains force, you can see what happens to the contracts, and what happens to the documents and letters around the contracts. You can see the country and the game growing."

There are three clauses in particular that demand closer scrutiny.

Up until the 1945–46 season, NHL contracts required players to leave a significant deposit for uniforms:

> The club shall furnish the player with one complete uniform, the player making a deposit of $30.00 therefore, which deposit shall be returned to him at the end of the season or upon termination of this contract, upon the surrender of the uniform by him to the club.

Players were making just a few thousand dollars at the time, and $30 was a significant amount for many.

The older contracts give teams significant flexibility if they don't like how a player is performing. This is from a standard NHL contract from 1928–29:

> The club may, at any time, after the beginning and prior to the completion of the period of this contract, give the player one day's written notice to end and determine all its liabilities and obligations hereunder, in which event the liabilities and obligations, undertaken by the club shall cease and determine at the expiration of said one day. The player, at the expiration of said one day, shall be freed and discharged from all obligations to render service to the club. If such notice be given to the player while "abroad" with the club, he shall be entitled to his travelling expenses to the city of _____ .

By 1947–48, the clause has changed to give the player 30 days' written notice to end the deal, and six years later, the idea of a player being offered around the league is added:

> The Club may terminate this contract upon written notice to the Player (but only after obtaining waivers from all other League clubs) if the player shall at any time:
> (a) fail, refuse or neglect to obey the Club's rules governing training and conduct of players,
> (b) fail, refuse or neglect to render his services hereunder or in any other manner materially breach this contract,
> (c) fail, in the opinion of the Club's management, to exhibit sufficient skill or competitive ability to warrant further employment as a member of the Club's team.

As of the 1977 standard contract, the third choice, (c), is dropped.

With the start of the Second World War, contracts from 1939–40 onward make allowances for any upheaval outside the team or league's control:

> If, because of any condition arising from a state of war, it shall be deemed advisable by the National Hockey League or by the Club to suspend or curtail operations, then in the event of suspension of operations this contract shall become void and at an end and in the event of curtailment but not suspension of operations the conditions set forth in Clause One hereof shall be automatically cancelled and shall be replaced by others to be mutually agreed upon between the Club and the Player.

Following the Second World War, the clause was amended slightly to "any condition arising from a state of war or other cause beyond control of the National Hockey League." The 1953–54 standard NHL contract seems to lay the groundwork for a work stoppage:

> If because of any condition arising from a state of war or other cause beyond control of the League or of the Club, it shall be deemed advisable by the League or the Club to suspend or cease or reduce operations, then:
> (a) in the event of suspension of operations, the Player shall be entitled only to the proportion of salary due at the date of suspension,
> (b) in the event of cessation of operations, the salary stipulated in Section 1 hereof shall be automatically cancelled on the date of cessation, and
> (c) in the event of reduction of operations, the salary stipulated in Section 1 hereof shall be replaced by that mutually agreed upon between the Club and the Player.

The Office and the GMs

Through the years, the offices within Maple Leaf Gardens changed, but one thing was consistent—the files.

"When I was scouting, right in front of me used to be four or five big filing cabinets, with all the old contracts," recalled Gerry McNamara, who was the GM from 1981–88. When time permitted, McNamara would occasionally delve into the past, wading into history. In particular, he can remember reading through an old Charlie Conacher contract. "He's one of the contracts I looked at. I have often thought, 'I would have loved to have taken some of those contracts.' I wouldn't have taken them without asking, but that's something I would have loved."

Jim Gregory, who worked with Punch Imlach and then assumed the role of general manager from his mentor in 1969, put it simply: "We had a file on every player in our organization."

Naturally, with those filing cabinets comes the duty of filing. There was generally a secretary for the team, who took care of much of the typing and correspondence.

Howard Starkman was director of administration and publicity for the hockey club from 1969 to 1976, at which point he joined the new team in town, baseball's Toronto Blue Jays, where he is now a vice-president. Before that he worked in the Leafs ticket office and doing promotions for other events. As there were no sports management courses at the time, he learned on the job. Starkman was tasked with dealing with the paperwork.

"One of the big things back then were, there used to be these emptying-the-benches brawls. When that happened, there'd be fines from the league," said Starkman. "You'd get 17 letters or 20 letters, guys that had been fined. Back then, it wasn't a lot of money. Those fights used to happen probably every 10 games, so there would be a lot of paperwork on that from the league." Those letters from the NHL were filed in players' personnel files and many are now in Stitt's collection.

The paper trail for the Toronto Maple Leafs hockey club begins in 1919–20, when the team was birthed as the Toronto St. Patricks, out of the ashes of the failed Toronto Arenas. The Arenas played in the inaugural NHL season of 1917–18, claiming the Stanley Cup, but faced attendance woes and withdrew before the end of the 1918–19 season. The St. Pats, managed by Charlie Querrie, built a solid foundation in the city. Conn Smythe came along to purchase the team in February 1927, having guided the New York Rangers for a short while, but was replaced with the Blueshirts in favour of Lester Patrick. One of the gems in the Stitt Collection is a May 1926 Rangers contract Smythe okayed with Bill Cook, the future right wing Hall of Famer.

With his military background, the patriotic Smythe renamed the team the Maple Leafs, opting for blue and white uniforms over green and white. "I had a feeling that the new Maple Leaf name was right," wrote Smythe in his posthumously published memoir with Scott Young. "Our Olympic team in 1924 had worn maple leaf crests on their chests. I had worn it on badges and insignia during the war. I thought it meant something across Canada, while St. Patricks didn't."

The Leafs caught on. Smythe proved to be both a capable manager and owner, and the team grew in popularity, outgrowing the Mutual Street Arena, which sat 8,000 spectators. The Major, who also owned a successful gravel company, drew up plans for a new arena at the corner of College and Church Streets, buying the property from the Eaton family. The new facility, Maple Leaf Gardens, was constructed during the Great Depression in just six months, a feat often referred to as a "miracle in engineering."

Smythe was the *de facto* general manager from his purchase of the team until 1957, but coach Clarence "Hap" Day, a former star with the team, would have a lot of influence. Much of the correspondence you will find in

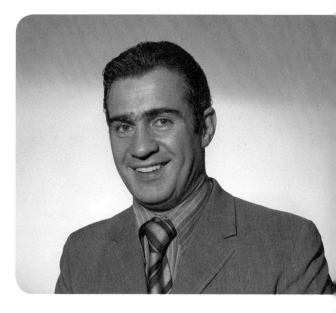

Jim Gregory.

TEL. UNIVERSITY 6-9755

FEB 9 1961 REC'D

NATIONAL HOCKEY LEAGUE
601 SUN LIFE BUILDING
MONTREAL 2, P.Q.

PRESIDENT'S OFFICE

February 8, 1961.

Mr. George Imlach,
Maple Leaf Gardens Limited,
Toronto 2, Ontario.

Re: Horton – Game January 18

Dear Mr. Imlach:

The official penalty record of the above game shows that the above-named player left the Players' Bench to enter an altercation.

Under Rule 66(b) this calls for an automatic fine of $25 which, by Clause 18 of the Player's Contract, you are authorized to deduct from his salary.

Will you please advise him of this fine and remit same to this office, charging it to this player's account?

Yours very truly,

NATIONAL HOCKEY LEAGUE

President

CSC:t

In duplicate

THIS AGREEMENT made in duplicate this

day of May, A. D. 1926,

BETWEEN:-

W.C
C.S.   ~~William Ossar~~ Cook, of the City of Saskatoon,
        in the Province of Saskatchewan,

                        hereinafter called the Party
                        of the First Part,

                -and-

        THE MADISSON SQUARE GARDEN CORPORATION, herein
        represented by Conn Smythe, of the City of
        Toronto, in the Province of Ontario,

                        hereinafter called the Party
                        of the Second Part.

W.C
C.S.
        IN CONSIDERATION of the sum of ~~Fifteen Hundred~~
Three Thousand 00/100
~~($1,500.00)~~ -------- Dollars, now paid by the Party of
the Second Part to the Party of the First Part, (the receipt
whereof is hereby acknowledged), the Party of the First Part
hereby binds and obligates himself to the Party of the Second
Part as follows:-

        (1) To play professional hockey for the Party of
the Second Part or its successors or assigns within the
boundaries of the United States of America, the Dominion of
Canada, or any of the Countries of Europe, for a period of
three years from the 10th day of October, 1926, exclusive of
the usual summer period between the 10th days of April and
October in each year.

        (2) The Party of the First Part agrees to report and
present himself to the Party of the Second Part or its Manager,
or Managers or Nominees, at any place indicated by it, on or
before the 10th day of October in the years 1926, 1927 and
1928, and will submit himself to the rules and regulations of
the Party of the Second Part, its successors or assigns, and
Manager or Managers or Nominees, during the term of this contract.

        (3) The Party of the First Part during the term of
this contract will obey and follow all the rules and regulations
prescribed by the Party of the Second Part, its Manager, Managers or Nominees, in the training of and maintenance of pro-

-2-

fessional hockey players, provided that such rules and regulations
are not incompatible with those laid down by the League or Leagues
in which the Party of the First Part is then playing, and without
limiting the generality of the foregoing, will follow the prescribed rules and regulations of the said Manager, Managers or Nominees
as may be enacted or applied during the term of this contract for
the training of and maintenance of the proper standard of professional hockey players, and failing the observance of such
rules and regulations the Party of the First Part will, in addition to any other remedy of the Party of the Second Part, be
subject to reasonable fines imposed by the said Manager, Managers
or Nominees, said fines to be deducted from any money due or to
become due to the Party of the First Part. The Party of the
Second Part may also suspend the Party of the First Part for
violation of any established rules or regulations and during
such suspension the Party of the First Part shall not be entitled
to any compensation under this contract. In the event of the
Party of the First Part being fined or suspended he shall be
given notice in writing setting out the amount of the fine or
the duration of the suspension, and the reason therefor.

        (4) It is understood that the Party of the Second
Part will conduct and operate a professional hockey club in
the National Hockey League and in the event of the Party of
the First Part becoming a member of the said Club the Party
of the First Part agrees to sign a new contract in the form
then prescribed by the said National Hockey League, it being
understood that the said contract will provide for payment of
the same salary to the Party of the First Part as hereinafter
stated, the same being subject to all the conditions hereof.

        (5) Subject to the provisions herein and in the
event of the true and faithful performance by the Party of
the First Part of this contract the Party of the Second Part
agrees to pay him a salary during the period from October 10th,
1926 to April 10th, 1927, of $5,000.00........., which salary
is to be payable in twelve equal semi-monthly instalments,
commencing such salary on the 10th day of October, 1926; and
during the period from the 10th day of October, 1927 to the 10th

-3-

day of April, 1928 the Party of the Second Part agrees to pay
the said Party of the First Part a salary of $.5,000.00,000--
which salary is to be payable in twelve equal semi-monthly instalments commencing such salary on the 10th day of October,
1927; and during the period from the 10th day of October, 1928,
to the 10th day of April, 1929, the Party of the Second Part
agrees to pay to the Party of the First Part a salary of
$6,000.00 ......-- which salary is to be payable in twelve equal
semi-monthly instalments commencing such salary on the 10th
day of October, 1928.

(6) In addition to the foregoing salary and in the
further consideration of the true and faithful performance of
this contract by the Party of the First Part and provided the
Party of the First Part is considered by the Party of the
Second Part its successors and assigns to be amongst the first
.... players exclusive of the goal-keeper on the
Club hereinbefore referred to during the continuance of this
contract, the Party of the Second Part undertakes to pay him
the additional sum of $...................

IN WITNESS WHEREOF the Parties hereto have hereunto
set their hands and seals the day and year first above
written.

SIGNED, SEALED AND DELIVERED)
    in the presence of   )   W. O. Cook

F.G. Mathers as to
both parties   Conn Smythe

IN WITNESS WHEREOF the Parties hereto have hereunto
set their hands and seals the day and year first above
written.

SIGNED, SEALED AND DELIVERED)
    in the presence of   )   W. O. Cook

F.G. Mathers as to
both parties   Conn Smythe

this book is addressed to him, the day-to-day caretaker of the team in the 1950s, after he'd coached the team during the 1940s.

One of the few surviving members of the Leafs from that era, Wally Stanowski, said that Smythe "dealt with all the players" when it came time to sign a contract, and that his office itself was as intimidating as the man himself.

"It had to be 25 yards long, from the door to where his desk was. That was sort of an empty room there," recalled Stanowski of Smythe's office. "It was strictly psychological, walking from the front and al-l-l-l-l the way down there, and you know the devil is waiting on the other end."

The Leafs of the 1950s fell on some hard times and went through four coaches in the decade alone. Smythe had turned over much of the management of the team to his son, Stafford Smythe.

In 1958, George "Punch" Imlach arrived on the scene. He was a Torontonian who had often played in the Gardens in junior and senior hockey and had gone on to prove his worth as a coach and general manager with the senior-level Quebec Aces before he was recruited by the Boston Bruins to help manage their farm system.

Ambitious and head-strong, Imlach convinced the Leafs to give him a chance as GM. Imlach recalled the negotiations in his memoirs, *Hockey Is a Battle*:

Gerry McNamara.

I met Stafford at his office in the Conn Smythe sand pit, up on Jane Street, headquarters of the building industry part of the Smythe holdings. This time I talked turkey. Being in charge of the farm clubs, I said, the hell with that. I've got the same job offered in Boston. I don't owe Toronto anything, I said. I do owe Boston something. If I'm going to run a farm system I'd do it in Boston.

Then we got down to cases. "As far as I'm concerned," I told Stafford, "you have no general manager. I want that job, or at least the opportunity of getting it."

I was talking to Stafford alone when Conn Smythe walked into the office. His manner is rasping and direct. "How you doing with this fellow, Stafford?" he asked. Stafford said something to the effect that we hadn't got anything settled yet.

Conn Smythe turned to me and said, "What's wrong with you, are you scared of the job?"

I said, "I'm not scared at all. It's just a case of not being offered what I want."

He left after a few more words. I asked Stafford if they had promised the general manager's job to anybody else. He said they hadn't. Apparently they had offered it to Billy Reay, but he'd told them he wanted another year to prove himself as coach. . . .

Stafford finally said they'd give me, not the general manager's job, but the "opportunity"—that was his word—of getting it. The way he put it, I'd have the same chance as anybody else. They'd make me assistant general manager; I'd be responsible for the club. From there I could prove myself or not. He also said they'd have to ask King Clancy, who also was listed as assistant general manager, if he had any objection to me coming in with the same title as he had.

Not only did Clancy have no objection, he would turn out to be Imlach's right-hand man, both with the coaching of the club and in management. The King was the heart and soul of Maple Leaf Gardens until his death in 1986.

When Imlach got to Toronto, he shared an office with coach Billy Reay, whom he soon turfed, taking over the coaching reins himself.

"[Reay] had this little office on the second floor of the Gardens, with a window looking out on Church Street," Imlach wrote. "The whole place has been remodeled since, but then it was just about big enough for two desks, one facing the other. One was his and one was mine."

Player agent Alan Eagleson spent an inordinate amount of time in Maple Leaf Gardens, making deals for his representatives, butting heads with Imlach, smoothing things over with Clancy. He described the offices, as he saw them.

"Their offices were probably 10 x 20 at most, a little dirty window on the second floor, behind the upstairs ticket office—that's where you could pick up tickets before the game," said Eagleson. "Connie used to have a really small office, and so did Stafford, in that building. It wasn't conducive to having palatial offices in a building that even at that time was 50 years old."

It wasn't much better when Gord Stellick was working his way up from press box assistant in 1975 to general manger in 1989. "You came up the escalator on the east side, and as you rounded the escalator to the reds to go up to the greens, there was a door and it said Executive Offices, and it looked like a broom closet," said Stellick. "Behind that was our offices, and Harold's apartment/office was at the back."

Gord Stellick.

Before the growth of the NHL Players' Association, a player generally was offered a take it or leave it deal; if there was anyone else helping the player, it would be a parent or relative. Agents didn't exist.

There were psychological games at work, said Ron Ellis, who signed with the Leafs as an 18-year-old in Imlach's office. "I walked in there, and he's up in this big desk, and he's got you sitting in this low chair, and he's looking down at you. It was quite the experience," said Ellis. "He basically said, 'This is it. This is what we're offering you.'"

Paul Henderson echoed Ellis' recollections. "He had this chair in his office that he wanted you to come in and sit down in, and he cut the legs down. You'd sit down and you're looking up at him. He was such a psychologist. I went over there and geez, I was uncomfortable, so I stood up. He said, 'Sit down in that chair!' It was all psychology, you figured it out after."

Imlach was out by 1968, replaced by his protégé Jim Gregory, who had graduated from the St. Michael's Majors as a trainer and then manager, winning the Memorial Cup in 1961. The Majors dropped from the Junior A ranks, however, and eventually Gregory was tapped to run the Toronto Marlboros, the Leafs' junior team in town. Two more Memorial Cups followed, in 1964 and 1967.

Gregory steered the club for a decade, and shared a bit about the team behind the team.

"I had a secretary, I had Howard Starkman, I had Johnny McClelland as the coach, and then his assistant, and Bob Davidson. I had a lot of people helping me," Gregory said. But when it came to contracts—and a lot of deals he did are in this book—it was him and him alone. "If it was a contract, then I did them, if you're talking about an NHL player. If you're talking about a minor league player, then I had help from whomever was running the minor leagues at that time."

Gregory was there for some of the darkest days of the team as board room battles took over the headlines. Shortly after Harold Ballard wrestled control from the

Smythe family, he was sent to prison in Kingston for tax evasion. But that never stopped Ballard from being involved in the team. "My first contract was actually done through my agent, and he had to go to Kingston and negotiate with Harold," said defenceman Ian Turnbull. "I laughed about it at the time, that that was where he had to go to formalize it."

While Gregory had been hired after an apprenticeship with the local farm teams and the Marlies, Gerry McNamara was a surprise. An ex-goaltender who had briefly played in the NHL for the Leafs, McNamara had been a pro scout for Gregory with no experience running a team—in fact, he had turned down the opportunity to coach the team's farm club in New Brunswick after a one-year stint guiding the CHL Dallas Black Hawks. There was no mentor to help him learn the tricks of contract negotiation. "I never sat in on one negotiation in my life. I just thought that I had some common sense," McNamara explained.

Floyd Smith.

"Contracts, they were hard slogging sometimes, they really were. I just didn't give in easily. I fought," McNamara said. "I spent Mr. Ballard's money like I was spending my own. That's the way I felt, and that's what I did, and that's how I negotiated contracts."

Stellick had paid his dues around the offices and was unofficially McNamara's assistant GM. When Ballard turfed McNamara while the team was on the road in Hartford, he didn't announce a replacement, and instead charged Stellick, coach John Brophy, and long-time Leafs scout/Ballard buddy Dick Duff to work things out as a three-headed monster.

"It was predictable that it didn't work out," said Stellick. From his desk just outside Ballard's office/apartment, Stellick was given the opportunity to pitch what he'd do with the club, a 20-plus-page manifesto. "On the Sunday, it was in Milt Dunnell's column in the *Star* that I was going to be the next general manager, which means that you are going to be the next general manager because he gave Milt Dunnell all the scoops," said Stellick. A year later, in another Dunnell column, he learned that he was on the outs and left for an assistant GM job with the New York Rangers.

Gord Stellick left his brother, Bob, behind with the Leafs, where, like Gord, he would work his way up, from public relations to director of business operations under Fletcher at the Air Canada Centre.

Everything changed substantially when NHLPA boss Bob Goodenough introduced salary disclosure in February 1990. "That's really a key point when you're looking at documents. Before salary disclosure, nobody knew what the other guy was making," said Bob Stellick. "You were not sworn to secrecy, but you were basically, just like people in work don't tell. Your defence partner could play beside you for 10 years, and you'd never know what he made."

When Gord Stellick left for the Rangers, the Leafs elevated former coach Floyd Smith from chief scout to GM. "Life throws you some curve balls every so often. I wasn't prepared to be a general manager. I never, ever dreamt I'd be one," said Smith, who had played for the Leafs in 1968–70 and stuck with the team after Imlach relieved him of coaching duties following a car accident in March 1980.

After scrambling to set up a training camp, and ultimately a team in Toronto and the farm team in Newmarket, Ontario, Smith reigned at a time when Ballard was ailing and ultimately died, which led to the power play for control of Maple Leaf

Gardens. "It was tough times. Everything was all screwed up," admitted Smith. "All in all, my experience was okay. I'm not going to say it was great—because I didn't want the job; I really, truthfully didn't. But I was there and I did it."

Ballard's death in 1990 set off a battle for control of the team. Grocery tycoon Steve Stavro eventually emerged as the boss, but partners that he brought to the table, such as the Ontario Teachers' Pension Plan and developer Larry Tanenbaum, resulted in the team becoming more professional and corporate and not the personal fiefdom it seemed under the attention-seeking Ballard.

Given the growth of the NHL, both with expansion and the strengthening NHLPA with the salary disclosure, the timing was right for the Maple Leafs to become a true corporate entity.

Though there are a few documents in this book post-Ballard, there are just a few. As such, the general managers of concern run from Conn Smythe himself through to Floyd Smith, who was demoted in 1991, when Cliff Fletcher became the first general manager hired from outside the organization since Imlach in 1958. (And Imlach would be brought back for a contentious two years, 1979–81, marked by his health trouble as much as anything.)

"If you look at salaries when Floyd Smith took over, Floyd sort of cleared the deck contract-wise for Cliff Fletcher, but the payroll was not much more than $5 million for the whole team," said Bob Stellick. "Then four years later, it was close to $50 million under Cliff. Big changes."

Though changes in management and ownership took place through the years and salaries skyrocketed, Gregory believes that the actual art of negotiation never changed.

"You just have to be in the business, know what's going on, what kind of budget you have, what the status of a player is—there's a hundred things that go into it," Gregory explained. "It's not something you pick out of the air. It's based on the fellow's position in the team. You can't pay a guy who's the tenth best player the biggest salary."

But the contracts got far more complicated, meaning the Maple Leaf Gardens legal staff became key. "When I first started, signing a contract with a player was just like you were sitting down and shaking hands," said Gregory. The key lawyer during Gregory's time was Bob Sedgwick, who often sat in on the final negotiations. "Then these new contracts started coming in and the legal stuff, everything that we did was checked and approved by him before we did it."

Today, there are teams on both sides carefully working through contracts, the agents and lawyers for the player on one side, and management and its legal squad on the other. Stars are shielded from much of the negotiations and paperwork, and the actual signing is little more than a photo opportunity for the media.

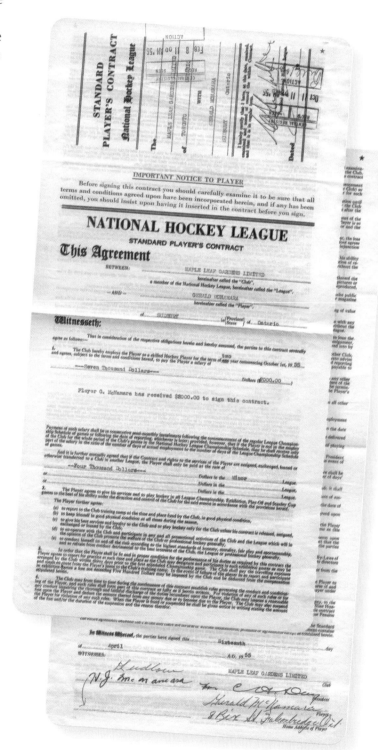

The iconic Maple Leaf Gardens.

CHAPTER 1

THE EARLY YEARS

QUEBEC PROVINCIAL HOCKEY LEAGUE
PLAYERS CONTRACT

Dec 28 _____ 192 /

I, _____ Jacobs _____ hereby bind myself to
play for _____ Voltigeurs _____ Hockey Club during the
season 192/ 192 V. I agree to remain the property of this club after playing season
of 192 / 192 2; unless a written release is granted by the management of the above
named club.

NOTICE.—Should a player sign for two different clubs he will be barred to compete in this league.

Paul C. Jacobs
Player

Approved by _____
President

Witness

Paul Jacobs' Very, Very Brief Career

While the Stitt Collection is primarily about the Leafs, a number of other teams and leagues are represented. In the case of Paul Jacobs, the story still offers mysteries. Hockey historians consider Jacobs the NHL's first aboriginal player, originally from the Kahnawake Mohawk reserve outside Montreal. But his actual on-ice time is questioned, with official records differing from newspaper accounts. Jacobs absolutely was at training camp with the Toronto Arenas in December 1918. The *Toronto Globe* teased his skills: "Paul Jacobs, who starred for the Leaside Indian lacrosse team last summer, was out, and he showed enough to convince the manager that he will be a hard man to keep off the sextette. He is a fairly fast skater, a good stickhandler, and shoots with terrific force." The general manger of the Arenas, Charlie Querrie, knew Jacobs from his other job as president of the Ontario Lacrosse Association. By Christmas, though, Jacobs was back in Montreal, his NHL days—anywhere from zero to five games by most counts—over. But he still played. The Quebec Provincial Hockey League contract reproduced here binds Jacobs to the Quebec Voltigeurs for the 1921–22 season. The only other player to make the NHL from that Quebec squad was Clement Piché, who played just a single game for the Montreal Canadiens.

Hap Day's 1927 Contract

There was little hullabaloo when Leafs captain Clarence "Hap" Day was unsigned just before training camp opened in October 1927. "No trouble is anticipated," reported the *Globe and Mail.* "Day has no grievance and apparently has just neglected to return his contract." After inking his contract on Saturday, October 22, Day reported on Monday to the first day of camp, where the *Toronto Star* reported that Conn Smythe was "a real taskmaster," as his squad played soccer and softball at the Don Flats, followed by relay races and a four kilometre jog back to the Mutual Street Arena. Apparently Day was successful on the diamond as well, and the *Star* said, "'Hap' now wants to follow 'Babe' Dye's example and play pro ball." Fortunately for hockey fans, Day stayed in the game and played defence with the Leafs until 1937, whereupon he was traded to the New York Americans for a single season. Day's contract was certainly one reason he was "Happy." Recruited in 1924–25 from the University of Toronto, where he studied pharmacy and played for the varsity team, he was offered an initial salary of $5,000 by Charlie Querrie, owner of the Toronto St. Pats. It was an incredible wage at the time—especially for a newcomer. Other than Smythe offering him a $500 bonus to serve as captain of the Leafs, his salary was the same three campaigns later (in 1927–28), the first year of the Toronto Maple Leafs. The Hockey Hall of Fame inducted him in 1961.

An unusually dour Clarence "Hap" Day.

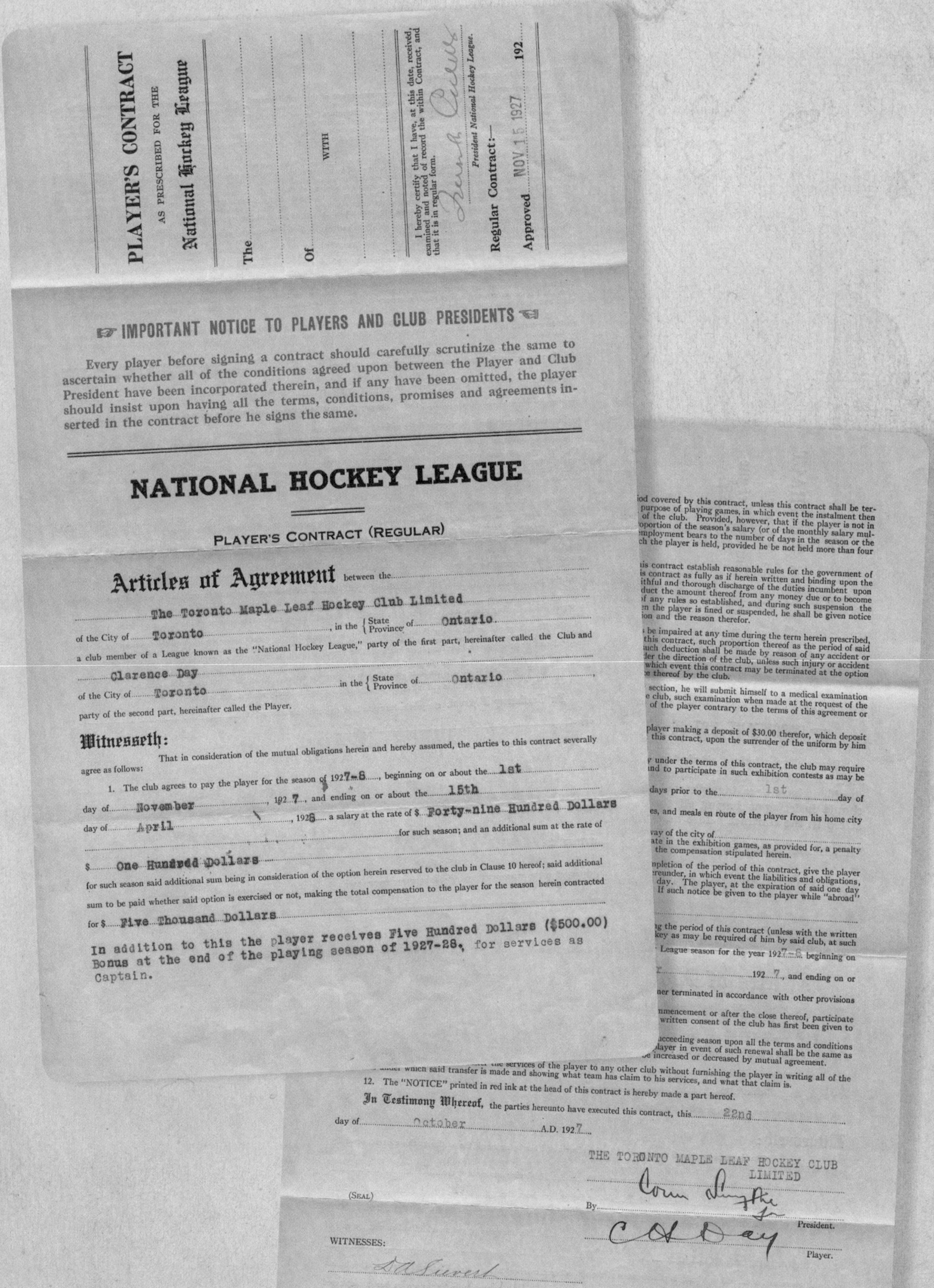

PLAYER'S CONTRACT

AS PRESCRIBED FOR THE

National Hockey League

The ....

Of ....

WITH ....

I hereby certify that I have, at this date, received,
examined and noted of record the within Contract, and
that it is in regular form.

Frank Calder

President National Hockey League.

Regular Contract: ....

Approved NOV 15 1927 192....

☞ IMPORTANT NOTICE TO PLAYERS AND CLUB PRESIDENTS ☜

Every player before signing a contract should carefully scrutinize the same to
ascertain whether all of the conditions agreed upon between the Player and Club
President have been incorporated therein, and if any have been omitted, the player
should insist upon having all the terms, conditions, promises and agreements inserted in the contract before he signs the same.

NATIONAL HOCKEY LEAGUE

PLAYER'S CONTRACT (REGULAR)

Articles of Agreement between the ....

The Toronto Maple Leaf Hockey Club Limited

of the City of ....Toronto......................, in the { State / Province } of ....Ontario.......

a club member of a League known as the "National Hockey League," party of the first part, hereinafter called the Club and

.......Clarence Day.................................. in the { State / Province } of ....Ontario.......,

of the City of ....Toronto..................................

party of the second part, hereinafter called the Player.

Witnesseth:

That in consideration of the mutual obligations herein and hereby assumed, the parties to this contract severally
agree as follows:

1. The club agrees to pay the player for the season of 1927–8...., beginning on or about the ....1st.......

day of.......November......, 192.7., and ending on or about the ....15th.......

day of.......April......, 1928... a salary at the rate of $.......Forty-nine Hundred Dollars.......

.... for such season; and an additional sum at the rate of

$.......One Hundred Dollars...

for such season said additional sum being in consideration of the option herein reserved to the club in Clause 10 hereof; said additional
sum to be paid whether said option is exercised or not, making the total compensation to the player for the season herein contracted

for $.......Five Thousand Dollars.......

In addition to this the player receives Five Hundred Dollars ($500.00)
Bonus at the end of the playing season of 1927-28, for services as
Captain.

[right column, partially visible]

...iod covered by this contract, unless this contract shall be ter-
...purpose of playing games, in which event the instalment then
...of the club. Provided, however, that if the player is not in
...oportion of the season's salary (or of the monthly salary mul-
...employment bears to the number of days in the season or the
...ch player is held, provided he be not held more than four

...is contract establish reasonable rules for the government of
...is contract as fully as if herein written and binding upon the
...ithful and thorough discharge of the duties incumbent upon
...ct the amount thereof from any money due or to become
...f any rules so established, and during such suspension the
...n the player is fined or suspended, he shall be given notice
...ion and the reason therefor.

...be impaired at any time during the term herein prescribed,
...this contract, such proportion thereof as the period of said
...uch deduction shall be made by reason of any accident or
...der the direction of the club, unless such injury or accident
...which event this contract may be terminated at the option
...e thereof by the club.

...section, he will submit himself to a medical examination
...e club, such examination when made at the request of the
...of the player contrary to the terms of this agreement or

...player making a deposit of $30.00 therefor, which deposit
...this contract, upon the surrender of the uniform by him

...y under the terms of this contract, the club may require
...nd to participate in such exhibition contests as may be

...days prior to the ....1st.......................day of
...es, and meals en route of the player from his home city

...way of the city of
...ate in the exhibition games, as provided for, a penalty
...the compensation stipulated herein.

...npletion of the period of this contract, give the player
...reunder, in which event the liabilities and obligations,
...day. The player, at the expiration of said one day
...If such notice be given to the player while "abroad"

...ng the period of this contract (unless with the written
...key as may be required of him by said club, at such

...League season for the year 1927–8. beginning on
..............................., 192.7., and ending on or

...ner terminated in accordance with other provisions

...mmencement or after the close thereof, participate
...written consent of the club has first been given to

...cceeding season upon all the terms and conditions
...layer in event of such renewal shall be the same as
...e increased or decreased by mutual agreement.

...nder which said transfer is made and showing what team has claim to his services, and what that claim is.

12. The "NOTICE" printed in red ink at the head of this contract is hereby made a part hereof.

In Testimony Whereof, the parties hereunto have executed this contract, this.......22nd.......

day of.......October.......A.D. 192.7.

THE TORONTO MAPLE LEAF HOCKEY CLUB
LIMITED

(SEAL)

By *Conn Smythe*
.... President.

C A Day
.... Player.

WITNESSES:

L A Sweet

Maple Leaf Gardens was built in only six months in 1931.

The House That Smythe Built—with Some Help

The numbers on the reverse of this paper—obviously used as scrap—do not calculate how invaluable this document is. When Conn Smythe was constructing Maple Leaf Gardens in 1931 at the corner of Church and Carlton, he ran short on the funds he needed to finish the new arena. "Rather than giving up he was able to convince one of the unions to have their 1,300 or so members take stock in the project in lieu of all cash owed them," said Toronto historian Mike Filey. This one, No. 1393, was never issued, used as scrap paper a few years later, and saved in a ledger that was purchased by Stitt. MLG was built in just six months. "The speed of the site clearing and construction of the new MLG emphasizes how eager people were to work during the awful days of the deepening Depression," said Filey. "City Hall red tape was kept at a minimum to ensure work progressed. Unfortunately, the construction company in charge of the project [Thompson Brothers] cut its margins so severely that it lost money and ultimately went broke." Maple Leaf Gardens turned out to be more than a hockey arena, though, stressed Filey. "At the time the city had no facilities large enough to hold various events, not just hockey but political conventions, religious services, operas, world-renowned big bands, war bond drives, and other sporting events. So in that way the Gardens brought people and organizations to the growing city who would, without the Gardens being there to host these events, never have given Toronto a second thought."

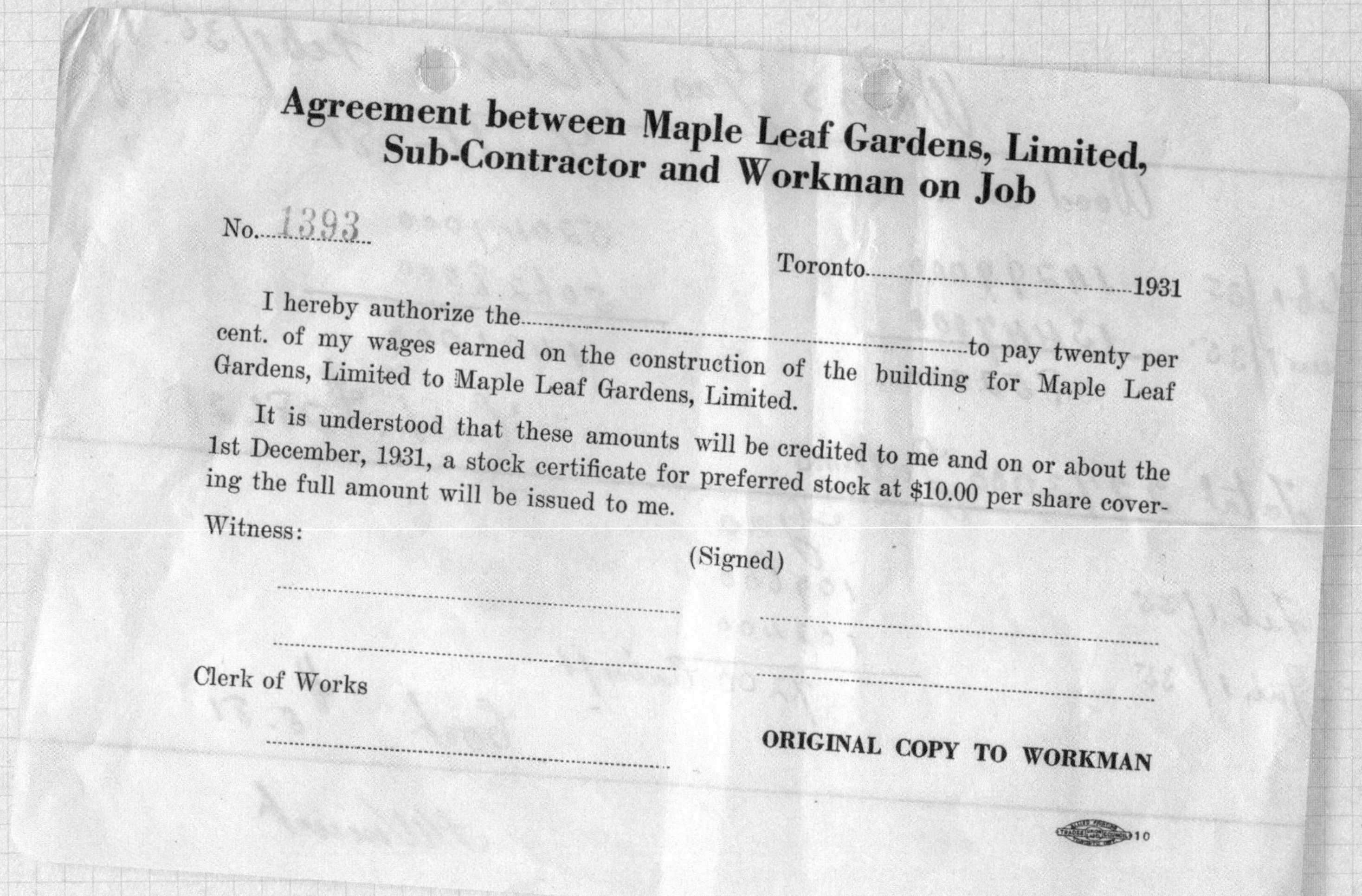

Agreement between Maple Leaf Gardens, Limited, Sub-Contractor and Workman on Job

No. 1393

Toronto...1931

I hereby authorize the...to pay twenty per cent. of my wages earned on the construction of the building for Maple Leaf Gardens, Limited to Maple Leaf Gardens, Limited.

It is understood that these amounts will be credited to me and on or about the 1st December, 1931, a stock certificate for preferred stock at $10.00 per share covering the full amount will be issued to me.

Witness:

(Signed)

....

....

Clerk of Works

....

ORIGINAL COPY TO WORKMAN

Receipts: Pucks, Laundry, Operations

The 1934-35 Toronto Maple Leafs.

Like any business, the Toronto Maple Leafs had to keep track of its expenses, but not every business has to pay to get its underwear cleaned. One of the messy treasures of the Stitt Collection is the receipt book for Maple Leaf Gardens Ltd. for 1935. In a world a long way from computers, there are countless handwritten receipts for food, laundry, baggage delivery, and train fare. On the hockey-related side, how about a dozen pucks for $4.00? Or $1.50 for mending 10 pairs of hockey stockings? Sharpening three pairs of skates with H.F. Dettmer (a Dominion Tire Depot!) in Kitchener set the club back 60 cents. The accrued wages for two days, November 29 and 30, for the special police, building operations, ushers, telephone operators, office staff, and ticket takers was $373.51. Frank Ayerst, the publicist who created the programs, shows up often in the documents. There's a receipt listing the 26 tickets taken by the Shriners on October 31. As for the building, there are details on the city taxes, the gas and water expenses, the allowable deductions for depreciation, and details on what it cost to remove and replace the ice for events like boxing, wrestling, or piano recitals.

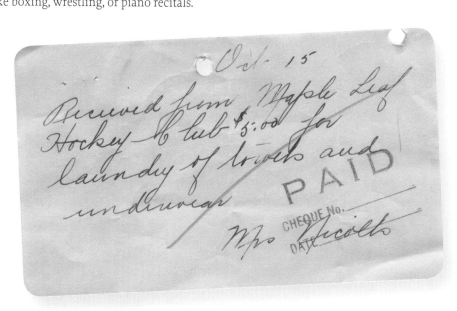

241 YONGE STREET   MONTHLY STATEMENT   PHONE WAV. 4501

TORONTO 2, *March 20th* *April 1st,* 193 *5*

M. Toronto Maple Leaf Hockey Club.
           Toronto.

IN ACCOUNT WITH **TORONTO RADIO & SPORTS**
LIMITED

RADIO AND SPORTING GOODS

ACCOUNTS OVERDUE SUBJECT TO SIGHT DRAFT

FORM NO. T.R.C. 3

1 doz. Hockey Pucks. $4.00

Goods taken March 20th.

This is a duplicate receipt.

Paid Cash
J.K. Dixon

PRICE, WATERHOUSE & CO.
EXAMINED
1935
No. 27
ACCOUNTANTS

Insuring the Leafs

In a time before names on jerseys, it could be hard to tell who was on the ice, even with a program. It was also hard to tell an insured player without a nickname. This Imperial Life Assurance Company policy from 1935 covered three active Maple Leafs: centremen Andy Blair and Joe Primeau and defenceman Hap Day. The fourth player is right winger Irvine Wallace "Ace" Bailey, who hadn't played since a game in Boston on December 12, 1933. In that contest, he was tripped by Eddie Shore and fell to the ice unconscious. Shore would be knocked out in retaliation by Bailey's teammate Red Horner, and both were stretchered off the ice, leaving pools of blood behind. While Shore returned to action after a suspension, Bailey never did, instead coaching at the University of Toronto for a decade. Team owner Conn Smythe was loyal to his Ace, who scored 111 goals in eight seasons and was inducted into the Hockey Hall of Fame in 1975. "When Conn Smythe owned the team, if you produced for him he would never forget," Bailey told the *Toronto Star*'s Paul Hunter in 1988. "When I was unconscious in Boston, Smythe stayed there the whole time. He even brought his family down to celebrate Christmas in Boston." Smythe called Bailey "as fine a gentleman as ever lived" in his autobiography. Bailey's number 6 is one of only two numbers retired by the Leafs. (The other is number 5 for Bill Barilko.)

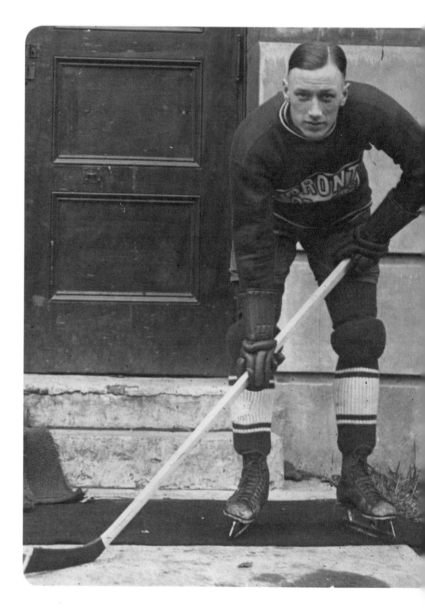

Ace Bailey with the Toronto St. Patricks.

The Imperial Life Assurance Company
of Canada

HEAD OFFICE - IMPERIAL LIFE BUILDING

Toronto, Ont.   January 24, 1935.

The Maple Leaf Gardens Limited,
60 Carlton Street,
Toronto, Ontario.

Gentlemen:

Re Policies Nos. 179,061 - A.D. Blair
                179,062 - I.W. Bailey
                179,063 - C.H. Day
                204,673 - A.J. Primeau

As requested in your letter of the 23rd instant, we are showing below the accumulated value of the dividends that have been left with the Company at interest. The dates shown in the schedule are the dates to which each deposit has been accumulated.

Policy Number	Name	Date	Accumulated Value	Was
179,061	A.D. Blair	2. 1.35	$156.72	153.38
179,062	I.W. Bailey	2. 1.35	331.76	324.65
179,063	C.H. Day	14.12.34	413.02	405.10
204,673	A.J. Primeau	2. 1.35	160.39	156.95

1061.89   1040.08
1040.08
21.81

Yours very truly,

W. B. Strachan
Assistant Actuary,

Per: *R.*

There and Back Again—with Oranges

It's as true today as it was in 1935—the players have a job to do on the ice, but they couldn't do it without help off of it. While it is unclear exactly who filled out this expense report, it does offer some insight into the challenges of travel for a hockey team and all its accompanying equipment. By far the biggest chunk of this expense report goes to transporting the trunks that carried the hockey gear. There's the loading in Toronto and the unloading in Montreal, and then the opposite for the return trip. After that, the uniforms and undergarments need washing. Fortunately, a decent supply of oranges seemed to be on hand to help the people who needed to get the job done— but do the oranges and Coca-Colas taste better after a 1–0 victory over the Montreal Maroons? Food for thought.

Maple Leafs at Montreal Maroons March 12 & /35

Cartage (Duggans) 781 5.00
" (Tompkins) 66 5.00
Oranges .... .60
Checkers Toronto .... .25
Trunk handlers Toronto Depot ....
Taxi 1.00
Meals 1.00
Club house boys 4.00
Checkers Montreal 2.00
Coca Cola .... .25
Trunk Handlers Montreal Depot 2.40
Trunks sent to Depot & return Toronto 1.00
"   "   "   "   "   " Montreal .... .50
                                           Montreal 2.00
                                                    _____
                                                    $ 25.00

Shirts Service Laundry 1.44
                                                    26.44

Oranges Canadian at Toronto .... .50
                                                    26.94

Mrs Nicolls Laundry 7.00
                                                    _____
                                                    $ 33.94
                                                       .15
                                                    _____
Eatons wool 34.09

Taxis, ticket tax Mtl. 2.50
                                                    _____
                                                    $ 36.59

supplies
 .60
2.40   Trav $ 24.50   O.K.
1.44   supplies 12.09
7.50   _____   S.a.S.
 .15   36.59
_____
12.09

PAID
CHEQUE No. 8736
DATE Mar 6/35

PRICE, WATERHOUSE & CO
EXAMINED
1935
No. 27
ACCOUNTANTS

Swept Away

To the winners go the spoils; to the losers, just a bill. It must have been a quiet train ride home after the Montreal Maroons swept the Maple Leafs in three straight games to become NHL champions for the second—and last—time in 1935. "Maroons were much the best!" wrote Lou Marsh in the *Toronto Star* after the final game, April 9. "They whipped the Leafs 4–1 last night down in Montreal and knocked the club which dominated the league all season out of the world's championship, and the Stanley Cup, in three straight, and looked to be distinctly the better team in doing it." The Leafs did finish best in the league at 30–14–4, topping the Maroons in the Canadian division and winning five of six regular-season games. A sidebar to the game recap reported that tickets at the Montreal Forum reached $35—for a pair. Coach Dick Irvin said they were "beaten by a better team tonight—well beaten in a great game." Owner Conn Smythe said the Maroons, starring a young Toe Blake, Lionel Conacher, Herb Cain, Earl Robinson, and ace goaler Alec Connell, were "the greatest professional hockey team I ever saw" and that "there are no alibis or excuses. We were just beaten by a wonder team."

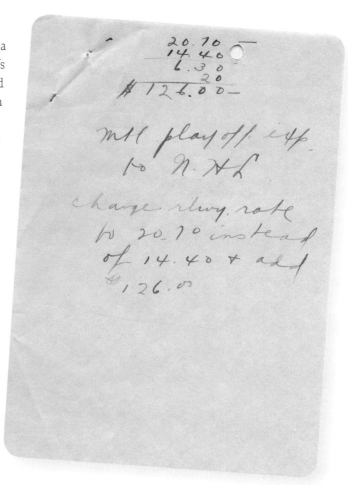

Maple Leaf Gardens, Limited

(HOME OF THE TORONTO MAPLE LEAF HOCKEY TEAM)

CORNER
CARLTON & CHURCH
STREETS

WAVERLEY 1641

TORONTO
ONT. .... April 12 ...., 193 5.

IN ACCOUNT WITH

National Hockey League,
603 Sun Life Bldg.,
Montreal, Que.

	Montreal Playoff Trip:		
April~~Mar.~~ 8 & 9 -	20 returns Toronto to Montreal @ $~~14.40~~ 20.70	~~988 00~~ 414 00	
	1 drawing room " " "	12 10	
	19 lowers Toronto to Montreal @ $ 3.40	64 60	
	19 " Montreal to Toronto @ 3.40	64 60	
	1 drawing room Montreal to Toronto	12 10	
	Players' meals - 20 for 1½ days @ $5.00 per day	150 00	
	Hotel accommodation - 20 men for 1 day at $2.50	50 00	
	Sundry expenses for 3 games @ $50.00 per game	150 00	
		$791 40	
		+ 126 00	
		917.40	

Counting Pennies

A month and a half after losing the finals to the Montreal Maroons, it was time to settle accounts. Detailed notes were kept throughout the 1934–35 season on the players' use of the phone. Some of the players—like Busher Jackson and Charlie Conacher, both among the league leaders in scoring, and both Toronto-born boys—made a lot of calls. Lesser-knowns like Frank Finnigan, Bill Thomas, and Ken Doraty barely called anyone from the company phones. The deductions, as well as a few other outstanding debts, likely cash advances, were taken from the players' playoff payout. Like all the receipts from the 1935 season, there is also a Price Waterhouse & Co. Accountants stamp, the company that verified all the financial transactions for the hockey team.

MAPLE LEAF GARDENS LIMITED

May 28, 1935

	Playoff Pool	Deductions Tel.Calls	Others	Net
				$ 99.80
K. Doraty	$100.00 ✓	.20 ✓		7.78.06
A. D. Blair	779.26 ✓	1.20 ✓		778.56
F. T. Boll	779.26 ✓	.70 ✓		745.89
F. M. Clancy	779.26 ✓	3.37 ✓	30.00 ✓	
C. W. Conacher	100.00 (fine)	7.92 ✓	5.00 ✓	166.34
	779.26 ✓		700.00 ✓	777.33
W. H. Cotton	779.26 ✓	1.93 ✓		775.42
C. H. Day	779.27 ✓	3.85 ✓		778.32
G. Hainsworth	779.27 ✓	.95 ✓		775.34
Wm. Hollett	779.27 ✓	2.05 ✓	1.88 ✓	774.71
G. R. Horner	779.27 ✓	2.82 ✓	1.74 ✓	779.27
J. D. Irvin	779.27 ✓			767.80
R. H. Jackson	779.26 ✓	11.46 ✓		775.83
R. J. Kelly	779.26 ✓	3.43 ✓	1.00 ✓	777.71
H. J. Kilrea	779.26 ✓	.55 ✓	18.50 ✓	755.36
A. J. Primeau	779.26 ✓	5.40 ✓		779.11
Wm. D. Thoms	779.26 ✓	.15 ✓		389.26
F. Finnigan	389.63	.37		389.63
T. M. Daly	389.63			
C. H. Day & A.J. Primeau (for presents)	389.63			389.63
	$13,057.84	$46.35	$758.12	$12,253.37

Pool - 12,957.84

PRICE, WATERHOUSE & CO.
EXAMINED
1935
No. 27
ACCOUNTANTS

F. Daly

Jan. 11/35 - J 56

Supplies	Trav. Exp.
4.00 —	
.50 —	9.00 —
.50 —	7.00 —
.50 —	16.05 —
3.50	24.55 —
$9.00	$56.60
	9.00 —
	$65.60

PRICE, WATERHOUSE & CO.
EXAMINED
1935
No. 27
ACCOUNTANTS

PAID

CHEQUE No. 8078

DATE Jan 11/35

O.K.
A.J. Selke

Foster Hewitt in his gondola.

Foster Hewitt's Radio Revenue

To many Canadians in the 1930s, Foster Hewitt *was* the Toronto Maple Leafs; his voice on the radio brought the team to life and, over time, brought the team to the nation. "I was well aware that the fans were more interested in the excitement and outcome of the game than they were in who told the story. Even so, it was rewarding to know that the hockey broadcasts brought comfort to so many people," wrote Foster in his autobiography. When Conn Smythe took over the Leafs in 1927, he gave Hewitt, whose father was famed newspaperman William A. Hewitt of the *Toronto Star*, exclusive broadcast rights. As Maple Leaf Gardens was being built, Smythe consulted Hewitt on where the broadcast booth should be located, and he settled on a gondola 54 feet above the ice surface. The initial broadcasts were on a station run by the *Star*; when that folded, the games were on CFRB, which is where this receipt from November 1935 comes from. Hewitt received revenue from ad sales. Note that he also broadcast the professional wrestling card on November 7, with a main event of Vic Christy versus Lou Plummer. With the establishment of the CBC in 1936, hockey emerged as a truly national game—and Foster Hewitt emerged as a national icon.

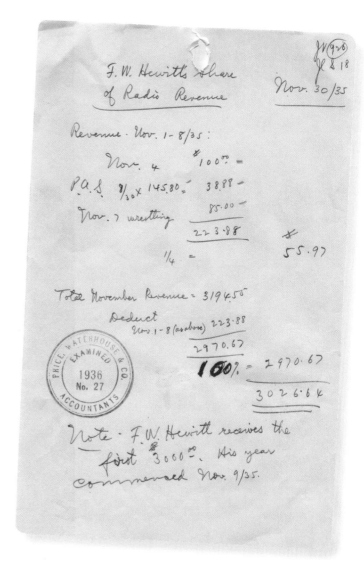

Maple Leaf Gardens, Limited

(HOME OF THE TORONTO MAPLE LEAF HOCKEY TEAM)

CORNER
CARLTON & CHURCH
STREETS

WAVERLEY 1641

IN ACCOUNT WITH

TORONTO
ONT. ...... April 3, ..., 193 5

F. W. Hewitt,

Maple Leaf Gardens,

Toronto, Ont.

Expenses at University Club, Boston. $4.20

Mr. R. T. Coady,
Accountant,
Maple Leaf Gardens,
Toronto.

**Expense Account for trip to New York
by Reginald Stewart on Sept. 8, 1935.**

Train fare	$35.23
Berths	9.90
Hotel	15.00
Tips	5.00
Telephone	1.50
Entertaining	6.00
Taxis	4.00
Loss of time (teaching)	19.00
Meals	5.00
Total...............	$100 .63

PRICE WATERHOUSE & CO.
EXAMINED
1935
No. 27
ACCOUNTANTS

Four Leafs pose for a photo before getting on a train during the 1962–63 season; from left to right: Frank Mahovlich, Johnny Bower, Allan Stanley, and Ron Stewart.

Motoring Along in the Days of Train Travel

The railroad was the primary means of transportation between cities for people in the first half of the 20th century, and hockey teams were no different. Players have many stories of rushing to catch trains to be able to make a game in the next city. In Toronto, the Leafs traditionally played on Saturday nights, with a Sunday game elsewhere—often a home-and-home series. "They kept a car ready for us at the railway station," said Wally Stanowski, who played for the Leafs from 1938 to 1948, when he wasn't serving the country. "We used to have to really hustle after Saturday's game. Of course, our equipment had to be shipped along with us." Those big trunks with equipment had to be dealt with on the train, with the underwear hung up to dry during the journey. "Once in a while, we'd have to put it on completely wet," recalled Stanowski. The players would pass the time playing cards—gin rummy for pocket change was okay, but poker was outlawed, Stanowski said—and sleeping. Rookies got the top berths with the veterans below. Most of the time. When he was a New York Ranger, Stanowski said that goalie Charlie Rayner switched with a rookie for one trip. "The reason for that was he bought a nine-horsepower outboard motor. He put it up and slept on top of it!" laughed Stanowski at the memory. "When the inspector came around there, he poked his nose in, and said, 'Anything to declare?' And Charlie said, 'No, no, let me sleep.' And got away with it—motors were cheaper in the States than they were in Canada."

THE DELAWARE AND HUDSON RAILROAD CORP.

ALBANY, N.Y., October 27, 1948.

File 521.212

Mr. N. J. Ferguson,
G.F.& P.A. - D.&H. R.R. Corp.,
1117 St. Catherine St. W.,
MONTREAL, P.Q.

Dear Sir:

Supplementing my letter to you of October
22nd with regard to holding Train 10 on various
Saturday nights throughout the coming winter season
for the accommodation of hockey teams.

As information, I have been favoured with
a copy of communication dated October 25th, written
by Mr. H. F. Burch, General Superintendent of Transportation, addressed to your Mr. P. P. Connolly in
which he has agreed to hold Train 10 for a maximum
of 50 minutes, if necessary.

You may wish to point out to Mr. Campbell
that holding the train this long is going to seriously
disrupt our service and will undoubtedly cause us
much criticism and that we do not want the train held
for the maximum of 50 minutes, unless it is absolutely
necessary. Under no circumstances will the train be
held for a period greater than 50 minutes and if, on
any of the nights involved, there is any indication
that the game cannot be completed in time to leave
not more than 50 minutes late, we should be advised
as early as possible so that the train can depart on
time.

Yours truly,

(sgd.) E. T. Gillooley

JEH:H   General Passenger Agent

C
  O
    P
      Y

CHAPTER 2

THE WAR YEARS

Shep Mayer, Flying Ace

Shep Mayer played only two NHL games for the Leafs, notching a goal and two assists on right wing in 1942–43. He is, however, Exhibit A on how the Second World War changed the hockey landscape. A native of Sturgeon Falls, Ontario, who worked in the mines and took up boxing, Mayer was a sought-after star on the Guelph Biltmores Junior A team, able to play right wing, centre, or defence. The Leafs landed him, and GM Hap Day praised, "Mayer has thighs like bridge pillars. I think he can take it or hand it out." Such a prize was valued by the armed forces as well. Mayer managed to defer his first call, sticking in Leafs training camp, but not his second, and he was sworn in on November 11, 1942, and posted to a manning depot at Brandon, Manitoba. By January 1944, he was a pilot, stationed in New Brunswick, but still suiting up to compete on the ice with Pennfield Royal Airforce station. Through it all, Mayer kept in touch with the Leaf GM. His first letter on file tells Day about Shep's younger brother, Howard, as a budding prospect. Day and Mayer kept up correspondence, and it seemed that every spring, Day enquired about Mayer's availability for the following season. But it was never to be. After his discharge, Mayer was called back to the air force. "Because he had been a pilot, they called him back; they wanted him to come back and also play hockey," said his widow, Marie. "He didn't go back because of the hockey; he went back because he loved flying." In 1971, Mayer moved from the air force into the Department of Veteran Affairs in Ontario. He died in 2005.

Shep Mayer loved flying more than pro hockey.

Sturgeon Falls, Ont.
April 30th/44

Mr. Hap Day
Toronto 2, Ont

Dear Hap,

I just came back from camp and mother gave me your letter, otherwise I would have answered it sooner.

Here are the things you asked me. I enlisted on Nov. 9th, 1943 and I'm now attached to the R.A.F. ferry command. My category at the time of enlistment was first class as far as I know. My eyes might have been a bit weak but that's all. Now I think I'm just about the same although I haven't had a medical examination for quite some time. I can't see any reason for a discharge in any way. To begin with I was an Aircraftman 2nd class. Then a leading aircraftman and finally my wings and commission as a pilot officer. Anyway I haven't any

pictures that would do for the programme or calendar but if I get one I'll send it to you.

I'm getting along very well in the ferry command except that things are awfully quite and boring. I have gone on a couple of trips since seeing you last. I have been posted to Nassau, in the Bahamas. I expect to be there for a couple or three months and then back up to Dorich Bay.

Well Way I guess this will be all for now.

Wishing you the best in everything

Yours Sincerely,

Skip Mayer

P.S. My present address.

P/o Mayer S.E.

#45 Group A.T.

Montreal Airport

Dorval, P.Q.

Wally Gets His Way

Winnipeg's Wally Stanowski felt he had some negotiating power going into his contract talks for his second season as a Toronto Maple Leaf. "I had a pretty good season in 1940 and I thought I deserved another $500 bonus for the following year," recalled the nonagenarian from his Toronto nursing home. "Eventually, we wound up saying, if I deserved it at the end of the year, if I played well, I would get that extra $500. Hap Day was supposed be the judge of whether I played well enough to deserve the extra bonus." The contract called for a base $4,000, with the rest coming as bonuses. "Well, I made the First All-Star Team, so what's he going to say? I had a bad year?" chuckled the ace defenceman. Other Leafs on the First team were Turk Broda in net and Sweeney Schriner on left wing; Bruins legend Dit Clapper was the other blueliner; and the forwards were Bill Cowley of the Bruins at centre and Bryan Hextall of the Rangers on the right wing. Stanowski's bonuses added up to the maximum $2,500. "I remember Smythe saying, 'This is the biggest bonus we've ever paid out!'"

Wally Stanowski and Turk Broda interviewed by Wes McKnight, with Jack Dennett in the background.

MAPLE LEAF GARDENS
LIMITED

TORONTO 2, ONTARIO, CANADA

CORNER OF CARLTON AND CHURCH STREETS
TELEPHONE   WAVERLEY - 1641

October 10, 1940

In addition to the National Hockey League contract signed to-day, the player, Walter Stanowski, will receive a bonus of Five Hundred Dollars ($500.00), if Mr. C. H. Day says that the player merits this bonus.

If the player is runner-up on the 2nd Canadian Press all-star team, he will receive an extra Five Hundred Dollars ($500.00); or, if the player is picked on the 2nd Canadian Press all-star team, he will receive an extra One Thousand Dollars ($1,000.00); plus an additional One Thousand Dollars ($1,000.00) if the player is picked on the 1st Canadian Press all-star team, making a total possible bonus of Twenty-Five Hundred Dollars ($2,500.00).

The operation of the foregoing arrangement shall be suspended during such time as either the National Hockey League or the Club may suspend or curtail operations because of any condition arising from a state of war.

THE TORONTO MAPLE LEAF HOCKEY CLUB LIMITED

_____
Conn Smythe

_____
Player

HOME OF THE TORONTO MAPLE LEAF HOCKEY CLUB

Jack McLean's Bad Break

Jack McLean was a unique part-time player for the Leafs during the Second World War. Enrolled at the University of Toronto, studying engineering, he was not allowed to cross the border for games in the United States because of his student status. The centre/right winger signed with the NHL team in November 1942, replacing Shep Mayer. He made a big impact in March 1943, scoring the winning goal at 10:18 of the fourth overtime period, as the Leafs beat the Red Wings 3–2, evening their playoff series (though teammate Bud Poile claimed he scored the goal, with McLean not touching it). Limited to action in Toronto and Montreal, McLean got into 27 games in 1942–43 and 32 the following year. In the eighth game of the 1944–45 season, however, it all went wrong. The Leafs were playing Detroit on December 15, 1944, and in the third period, McLean injured his right ankle when he tangled with Jud McAtee while chasing the puck to the sideboards. He was carried off the ice. "It was a tough jolt for young Jackie, just entering Christmas holidays from his university engineering studies," recounted the *Globe and Mail*. "Friday he had obtained permission to make border-crossing trips with the Leafs until schools open in the new year." As evidenced by his letter to GM Hap Day, McLean felt he was a part of the 1945 Stanley Cup–winning squad and felt he deserved a better share of the playoff money. While there is no record of Day's response, he did pessimistically mention McLean's progress to Ike Hildebrand in a letter on January 31, 1945: "McLean is still out injured and I have not many hopes of his playing any more this year. He injured a nerve in his ankle, and has not been responding very quickly to treatment." While McLean never made it back to the NHL, he did play competitive senior-level hockey once he recovered.

Jack McLean.

Mr "Hap" May,
Maple Leaf Gardens
Toronto, Ont.

Dear Sir;

Received my playoff cheque yesterday and also your accompanying note hoping that I was satisfied. Well I'm not exactly that. I would like to know how you can figure my share out as $500 when Jackson, Metz and McCreedy received much more.

After all if it hadn't been for injuries received while playing I would have been available for 33 league

2.

games and all the playoffs. I believe that this should entitle me to as much as Jackson & McCreedy anyway.

Last year when Kiel was out for the season with injuries he, I believe, received his full share plus a nice bonus and I would like to know the reason for the difference in treatment.

Afterall since I had my head injured I haven't felt any too good and haven't been able to work for headaches & dizziness and should be compensated in some way consequently I was expecting a fairer share in the playoff pool to which I believe I am entitled.

3.

When I played for you I always tried to give my best and work my hardest so I would appreciate it very much if you could explain to me about my cheque.

Yours truly
Jack McLean.

appointment for beginning of next week. Be sure & call Mr. May re definite time

George Boothman, Scouting Prospects

Though George Boothman played only two seasons with the Maple Leafs (nine games in 1942–43 and 49 games in 1943–44), he kept in touch with GM Hap Day and always tried to steer players to the Leafs. Since he was a Calgary native, many of the players he recommended were Westerners. Though none signed with the Leafs, he had a decent eye for talent. On Bill Gadsby, who was looking for a junior team and played 1,248 NHL games for the Black Hawks, Rangers, and Red Wings and ended up in the Hall of Fame: "He is 6 ft. tall 185 and only 17, a very aggressive player, and really willing to learn." Another find was Roy Kelly of the Trail Smoke Eaters, who would play a couple hundred games in the AHL. "I have been talking to a young fellow who I thought might be a good prospect for the Leafs. Last summer: that is a year ago he received $50 from Cleveland and apparently signed some kind of agreement. They didn't ask him to camp and he would sure like a tryout. Is this method of tying him down legal or does he have to be on the club's list?" Day shipped Boothman and Don Webster to the Buffalo Bisons of the AHL on October 13, 1944, for the rights to Bill Ezinicki. It is apparent from this letter that Boothman harboured no hard feelings, and that Day thought he might make the NHL again one day—but he never did.

George Boothman.

Dear Hap:-

Just a line to let you know how things are going. I never knew two systems could be so different, especially with two coaches that played in the same span of years. Don Webster and I are both a bit confused so far but we are beginning to catch on to what Shore wants. We have a pretty fair club, but could use a little more experience in goal. I have played both right wing and defence so far, but still think I can play left wing better. Shore was kind of surprised to find out that I played left wing last year.

By the way Hap, Shore said he'd order my other pair of skates from you. I sure could use them as I've only one pair.

Best of luck for the season

Sincerely

George.

November 3, 1944.

Mr. George Boothman,
416 W. Ferry,
Buffalo 13, N.Y.

Dear George:

Thanks a lot for your letter of recent date. Enclosed you will find herewith cheque to cover your expenses.

I note in your letter that you are talking about and comparing the two types of coaching of Shore and myself. This has aroused my interest and curiosity and if at some time you would like to tell me the system that Shore uses I would be very interested in finding out, as no doubt, as I told you, he has lots of good points that may be I can use which would improve our team.

I hope that you and Don are doing well, and that you like it in Buffalo, but not so much that you will not want to get back into the big league. Wishing you both the best of luck for the rest of the schedule, I am,

Yours sincerely,

When Bodnar Bested Durnan

Right from the start, Gus Bodnar could say that he had Bill Durnan's number. The rookie lined up with the Maple Leafs for the 1943–44 season and was named the Calder Trophy winner as the best newcomer. "It certainly is a surprise, a most welcome surprise. I figured that perhaps Durnan would get it," Bodnar is quoted as saying at the time. Bodnar centred the Leafs' first line, between Bob Davidson and Lorne Carr, and finished with 22 goals, 40 assists. It was a close vote, with Bodnar receiving 583 out of a possible 756 points; Durnan had 511. Of course, history has shown that a Calder win is not a guarantee of a Hall of Fame career. Bodnar would play until 1955, 667 games for the Leafs, Black Hawks, and Bruins. Durnan was a reluctant entrant into the pros, joining the Canadiens at 27, after years of success in the senior leagues. He claimed the Vezina instead of the Calder in his "rookie" year and proceeded to win the top goaltending trophy again in 1945, '46, '47, '49, and '50, the year he walked away from the game. The Hockey Hall of Fame inducted Durnan in 1964. For the record, the third and fourth leader vote-getters in the Calder race were Leafs defencemen Elwyn Morris (135 NHL games) and forward Ted Kennedy (who played 14 seasons in the NHL, became known as Teeder, and entered the HHOF in 1966).

NHL President Red Dutton presents Gus Bodnar with the Calder Memorial Trophy.

June 1, 1944.

Mr. Gus Bodnar,
110 West Gore,
Fort William, Ontario.

Dear Gus:

Mr. Selke has asked me if I would contact you and ask you to get for him a picture of yourself and the Rookie Award. I understand that all he wants is the upper part of your body with you holding the cup in your right hand and looking down at it, but not enough that it would obscure your face from your loving public. It might be a good idea to have two or three shots taken, and let us pick out the one best suited. If you would do this as soon as possible and send it along, I would appreciate it very much, and I know it won't be necessary for me to tell you to keep track of the expense so I can repay you.

Squib Walker advises me that your right arm went lame shortly after your arrival home from having so many people shake your hand. I hope you are fully recovered from this type of exercise and have started to take some that will put some weight and muscle on that skinny frame of yours, so that I will have something to work on next winter.

With kindest personal regards, I am,

Yours sincerely,

CHD/LF

1100 W. Gore St.
Fort William Ont.
Sept 10. 1944.

Dear Hap:

I have recieved your letter yesterday, which had a hard time getting here, my address is. 1100 W. Gore you always keep making it 110.

In your letter you are asking for Rejection paper, I have a Mobilization Form issued by my District Registrar.

Well how are the hockey prospects for this season, have you lost any of last years players, I also read in our daily news old smooths Sweeney is coming back.

My employer is granting me a leave of absents till the hockey season closes. Right now I'm on my vacation for a few weeks. I guess I'm just waiting for my okay to go down east again, its plenty dead around home, and talk about the weather when having its rains practicly every second day, I have to do some of my golfing in the rain. My brother just come back from the east he said he couldn't sleep at nights its gets to warm, it never cools off from one day to another like up here in the bush as you would call it. I hope to hear from you soon.

Yours sincerely

Gus Bodnar

Carr Plays It McCool

Lorne Carr played for the Leafs from 1941 to 1946, winning Stanley Cups in 1942 and 1945. His contribution to the second victory extends far beyond what he did as a right winger. It was Carr, back home in Calgary in the summer of 1944, who convinced Frank McCool to give the NHL a whirl. "He is working very hard for a dry cleaning outfit here, outside all of the time and looks quite fit," Carr wrote to Hap Day on July 31, 1944. Nine days later, Carr sent McCool's tryout papers to Day. "He wanted fifty bucks to sign them, but I talked him out of it, saying Toronto didn't do such things," said the loyal soldier. McCool wrote directly to Day, asking for money. Day countered: "[We] are quite willing to forward you $100 if you will give us an option on your services. In a nut shell, this means that if you turn pro you will sign for the Maple Leafs. I might reassure you that a player could not sign with a better pro team or be treated with more consideration." McCool did, and "Ulcers" McCool was rookie of the year on the rag-tag, military-depleted squad of Leafs that had made the playoffs in third place and stoned the mighty Canadiens in the semi-finals. In the finals against Detroit, McCool threw three consecutive shutouts (1–0, 2–0, 1–0) in the first three games, and the Leafs won the Cup in seven. The next year, McCool played just 22 games and was done. He went to work at the *Calgary Albertan* newspaper, rising to assistant publisher by the time of his death in 1973.

Frank McCool signs with the Leafs as Hap Day looks on.

721 - Fifth Avenue West,
Calgary, Alberta.

Mr Happy Day,
c/o Toronto Hockey Club.

Dear Mr Day:

I have been in contact with Lorne Carr for the past few weeks and through him have the opportunity to report to your training camp this fall. Before signing the try-out slip I asked him if there was any remuneration for signing and he informed me that it was out of the question.

In explanation of the request I would like you to know that I was only recently married and due to the high expense of going through the motions, I am now in a position where I have no money to leave with my wife when I go away as we are just now getting on our feet once more by means of my weekly pay-check. If this form of income is abruptly cut off due to my absence from work, an advance from your organization would be very much appreciated.

Hoping you do not think I am too brazen in this request, I remain,

Yours hopefully,

Frank McCool

Western Canada's Largest Billiard Parlor
18 Tables

Helmer's Billiard Parlor
"YOUR DOWN-TOWN CLUB"

210 Eighth Avenue West
CALGARY
ALBERTA

RECEIVED
AUG 14 1944

August 9th/44

Hello Hap:—

Please find enclosed
the signed tryout papers
for McLeod. He wanted
fifty bucks to sign them,
but I talked him out of it,
saying Toronto didn't do
such things. So if I hear
of any player getting anything for signing these papers,
I'll be clunking your frame.

Dave's attitude remains
the same. I bidding
Fredrick abou[t]
him for a
you were
another ha[lf]

3

Western Canada's Largest Billiard Parlor
18 Tables

Helmer's Billiard Parlor
"YOUR DOWN-TOWN CLUB"

210 Eighth Avenue West
CALGARY
ALBERTA

Gee, another six
weeks or so and the
old grind will be on
again. This summer is
really going by.

Best regards, and
good hunting (players not
ducks) and I'll be see—
ing you soon.

Sincerely
Lorne.

"Hitler will rue the day that he started this war"

The hockey career of Bud Poile was interrupted by the Second World War. He wrote to Hap Day from Europe on October 19, 1944: "Well, Hap, I finally got down to writing you and letting you know I'm still alive." In the letter, Poile asks for hockey tickets for his wife and vows to try to find Leafs owner Conn Smythe, who was stationed in England. His son, David Poile, the general manager of the Nashville Predators, was fascinated to learn more about his father's tour of duty. "My dad was 20 years old when that was written," said Poile. "I don't know the sequence of events, how he went to war, had to go to war." Bud Poile played hockey for military teams and also rowed while abroad. A native of Fort William, Ontario, Bud Poile burst onto the scene with the Leafs in 1942–43 and notched 16 goals and 35 assists for a solid rookie season. The next year was interrupted by his military service. He was a part of the 1947 Stanley Cup–winning Leafs team and was traded to Chicago in the Max Bentley deal. Later he was in Detroit, New York, and Boston. "His career didn't last that long after that, because he started coaching pretty early," said his son. Indeed, Bud Poile's 1990 induction into the Hockey Hall of Fame was in the Builder category—he coached in the Western Hockey League for 13 seasons, was the first general manager of both the Philadelphia Flyers and Vancouver Canucks, and was commissioner of the Central Hockey League and then the International Hockey League.

Bud Poile.

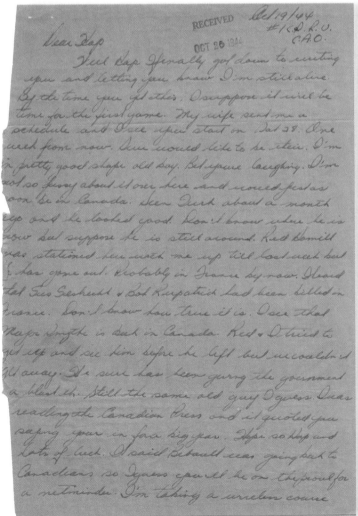

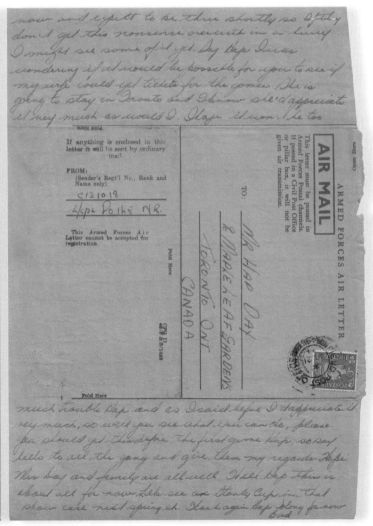

October 26, 1944.

C121018,
L/Cpl. Poile, N.R.,
#1 C.P.R.U.,
C.A.O.

Dear Buddy:

Thanks very much for your letter of October
19th.

I am glad to know that you are getting along
so well in your course, and I am sure that if you ever
get to France, Hitler will rue the day that he started
this war. You can see that I have plenty of confidence
in your ability as a soldier, even if I questioned it
as a hockey player.

I have taken the matter up re tickets for Mrs.
Poile with Mr. Selke and he assures me that they will be
provided as requested. For this consideration, I hope
sometime when you are back playing hockey for us that
you will let me do all the master-minding, and do as
requested, instead of trying to prove the old coach wrong
all the time.

I want to wish you the very best of luck, and
sincerely hope that you will soon be back with us again
trying to catch a position as a centre man. The competition is going to be tough.

With kindest personal regards, I am,

Yours truly,

CHD/LP

Wally Stanowski reads his
fan mail in February 1941.

Stanowski, Buddies, and Beer

When he went to serve his country, Wally Stanowski's dream
of being a pilot was dashed upon learning he was colour blind.
Instead, he served as a physical fitness instructor in Winnipeg
and skated for the Winnipeg RCAF Bombers. Back in the NHL
for the end of the 1944–45 season, Stanowski found his wallet
$100 lighter. He was fined under Clause 2 of the standard NHL
contract—a pretty vague clause that gave the club the right to
"establish reasonable rules for the governance of its players."
Though it was more than 50 years ago, Stanowski's recollection
of the incident is crystal clear. He was plagued by dehydration
early in his career and used to try to replenish with cola or ginger
ale. Back from the war, he moved up to something stronger for
the train ride to the next game. Stanowski picked up the story: "I
sneaked on some beer. We had the whole train, and next door to
Hap's private room was the washroom. It was a fair size. There
were about five or six of us in there. I don't remember who, but
someone went over to the next car and picked up two girls and
brought them back. So they were in there, and now we're making a lot of noise and Hap Day could hear. Hap Day entered the
washroom and the only guy to get away from it was Windy
O'Neill—he was separate. He didn't get busted, and everyone
was fined $100."

January 23, 1945.

Mr. Walter Stanowski,
578 Bathurst Street,
Toronto, Ontario.

Dear Wally:

This is to advise you that you have been
fined One Hundred Dollars ($100.00) for breaking Clause
2 of your N.H.L. Contract. This amount will be duly
deducted from your salary and any further violations
will call for suspension without pay.

Yours truly,

CHD/LP

STANDARD
PLAYER'S CONTRACT

National Hockey League

The ....

TORONTO MAPLE LEAF HOCKEY
CLUB LIMITED
TORONTO ONTARIO

WITH

WALTER STANOWSKI
of
TORONTO ONTARIO

I hereby certify that I have, at this date, received,
examined and noted of record the within Contract,
and that it is in regular form.

....
President National Hockey League.

Contract:— ....

Approved .... 18 Sep 1946

IMPORTANT NOTICE TO PLAYER

Before signing this contract you should carefully examine it to be sure that all
terms and conditions agreed upon have been incorporated herein, and if any has been
omitted, you should insist upon having it inserted in the contract before you sign.

NATIONAL HOCKEY LEAGUE

STANDARD PLAYER'S CONTRACT

This Agreement between the ....

TORONTO MAPLE LEAF HOCKEY CLUB

of the City of .... TORONTO ...., in the State/Province of ...... ONTARIO

a member of the National Hockey League, hereinafter called the "Club", Party of the First Part, and..............

WALTER STANOWSKI

of.......... TORONTO ...., in the State/Province of ...... ONTARIO

hereinafter called the "Player", Party of the Second Part.

Witnesseth:

That in consideration of the respective obligations herein and hereby assumed, the parties to this contract severally

agree as follows:

1. The Club agrees to pay the Player for the season of 19.46–47..., being the period commencing on.........................

16th day of October .... at rate

and ending on the completion of the National Hockey League Schedule, Play-Off and Stanley Cup Games, a salary of $ 5,900.00———

————Fifty-nine Hundred Dollars—————

and an additional sum of $One Hundred Dollars

in consideration of the option granted to the Club in Section 9 hereof; said additional sum to be paid whether such option is exercised or

not, making the total compensation to the Player for the period herein contracted for $ 6,000.00 (Six Thousand Dollars)————

Should the Player, Walter Stanowski, make the second National Hockey League All-Star
Team, he will receive a bonus of $1,000.00 (One Thousand Dollars), and if he makes
the National Hockey League First All-Star Team he will receive an additional bonus of
One Thousand Dollars ($1,000.00), making a total of $2,000.00 (Two Thousand Dollars)
if he makes the National Hockey League First All-Star Team.

In Witness Whereof, the parties have signed this .... tenth

day of .... July .... A.D. 19 46

TORONTO MAPLE LEAF HOCKEY CLUB LIMITED

(Seal)   By .... for the
                                                      President.
                          ....
                                                      Player.

WITNESSES:

R. M. LeBage

Johnny McCreedy's Many Trophies

When Alan Eagleson, the long-time power behind the NHL Players'
Association, got a chance to look through Allan Stitt's files—
Eagleson went to law school with Allan's father, Bert—he didn't
request copies of all the contracts he was involved with. Instead, he
asked for a copy of the correspondence between Winnipeg native
Johnny McCreedy and Hap Day. What's the connection? "Johnny
McCreedy was a great hockey player in the old days. He won the
Allan Cup, the Memorial Cup, the Stanley Cup, and the World
Championship. . . . At the time, he was the only one in the world to
have accomplished that feat," said Eagleson. McCreedy bookended
military service with Stanley Cups with the Leafs in 1942 and 1945,
for 64 total NHL regular season games, plus 21 more in the playoffs.
After his hockey career, he took a job with INCO, rising through the
ranks of the massive mining company to become vice-chairman
in 1979. "INCO, with John McCreedy's help, figured out how to
get the nickel to make the Canada Cup," said Eagleson. "We were
friends a little bit before that, but that really cemented our friendship." For the record, the rest of McCreedy's feats were Memorial
Cup, Winnipeg Monarchs, 1937; Allan Cup winner and World
Champion with the Trail Smoke Eaters, 1938; Allan Cup, Kirkland
Lake Blue Devils, 1940. McCreedy Park in Thompson, Manitoba, is
named in his honour.

Johnny McCreedy.

R.C.A.F. OFFICERS' MESS
TRENTON, ONT.

1 F.I.S.
Trenton.

Dear Hap,

I've enquired more fully into the resignation question. We have been officially told that applications for retirement to the reserve would be very welcome. The Air Training Plan is coming to a halt and there is a great surplus of instructors. Overseas the situation is even worse. They just won't give us postings these.

I, therefore, could be free to go back to work for the Gardens in about two weeks time, if you could use me.

Could you let me know as soon as possible if you want me and what my services would be worth.

Yours truly.

Johnny McCreedy
F/O

Family Learns Something New About Doc Prentice

When the brother and the son of Eric "Doc" Prentice got a copy of the letter that the Leaf had sent to Hap Day on May 12, 1945, they learned something new: that Eric had been rejected for military service. "I never knew that he tried to get into the army. There's about seven years difference in our age, so back in '44, I was only 12 or so. My parents never said anything about it," said Dean Prentice, the veteran NHLer who played from 1952 to 1974. "It was a real shocker." Doc's son, Jim Prentice, was a prominent politician with the Canadian Conservative party, running for its leadership, and is now involved in banking. The letter brought back some great memories of his father and best friend, who died in 2002 after battling Lou Gehrig's disease for 15 years. "My heart jumped when I read it. He would have been just 17 years old," said Jim Prentice, guessing that the rejection would have been over bad knees. Unlike his little brother Dean, Eric only played five NHL games, and he remains the youngest-ever Leafs player. "He was quite slight of build. He was six feet tall, but his playing weight was 145 pounds, 150 pounds," said his son. "They called him the Splendid Sliver actually in Northern Ontario." Doc played in the AHL and the Pacific Coast league before moving back to Schumacher, Ontario, where he worked in the gold mine and literally rose from the depths to the office as an accountant. He played in various northern leagues until 1959. Dean Prentice wonders about the request for pay in the letter. (The note in top right is a calculation, 5/42 of $3,000.) "I don't know if he ever got the money!"

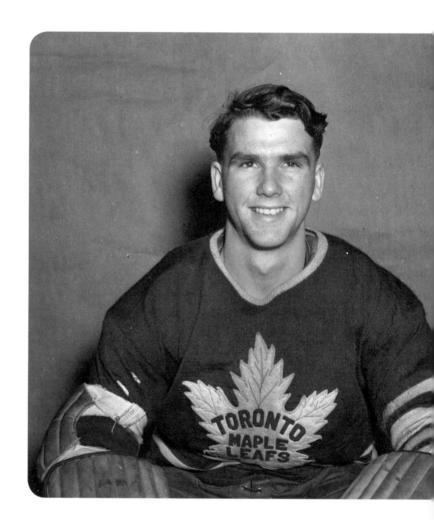

Doc Prentice.

12/5/45

Dear Hap.

Am writing to inform you as to how I stand with the Army. I was rejected for Military Service on May 10th. at #2 District Depot in Toronto.

I believe Hap, the Gardens has neglected in forwarding me wages for five days that I was up in Toronto in March.

Am inclosing my Special Border Permit as I was requested to do.

I suppose I am a little late in congratulating you and the team. I spent two days with Reg & Bob up here, but I don't think they like this north country.

So until I hear from you later on I wish to thank you Hap for all you have done for me,

Yours sincerely

Eric Prentice.

Too Small for Hockey, Perfect for Lacrosse

Ike Hildebrand played just 41 NHL games for the Black Hawks and the Rangers, and never one for the Maple Leafs. But he is in five different halls of fame for lacrosse: Canada's Lacrosse Hall of Fame (1972); Sports Halls of Fame in Peterborough (1978), Belleville (1989), and Oshawa (1993); and Canada's Sports Hall of Fame (1985). Back when this letter was written, he was a 17-year-old kid playing hockey out west for the Pacific Coast Hockey League's Seattle Ironmen, where future great Al Rollins was tending net. In the letter, he brazenly asks Hap Day for a pair of skates, as his had been stolen. "Could you send me a pair of Tackaberrys, size 6 1/2 or 7?" asks Hildebrand. "I would be very willing to pay for them, or I could bring them with me when I come to your camp next fall." Day declined the request, but stayed in touch, and when Hildebrand played junior in Oshawa, he did attend Leaf camp. Instead of Toronto, the 5-foot-7, 150-pound right winger ended up with the Los Angeles Monarchs. "I'd love to be able to play with the Leafs, but I'm afraid I'm a little too small," Hildebrand said in 1949. "And if I can't get into the National League I'd rather stay here in Los Angeles than go to some club like Pittsburgh of the American League." Aside from his legendary lacrosse career, Hildebrand's other major contribution was as player/coach of the 1958 Allan Cup–winning Belleville McFarlands, which won the World Championship for Canada in Prague in March 1959.

ISAACSON IRONMEN		PORTLAND EAGLES	
1. Al. Rollins	Goal	1. Jerry Foday	Goal
2. Walt McIntyre	Defense	2. Bill Irwin	Defense
3. Frank Warshowski	Defense	13. Phil Dalgleish	Defense
10.	Defense	11. Art Schuman	Defense
4.	Defense	5. Aubrey Webster	Defense
14. Scoop Bentley	Defense	4. Ed Shamlock	Forward
5. Ralph Blyth	Forward	8. Bob Morin	Forward
6. Frank Dotten	Forward	6. Ed Vigneau	Forward
7. Shorty Coombs	Forward	15. John Millard	Forward
8. John Ursaki	Forward	7. Andre Bouvrette	Forward
9. Bert Yesowick	Forward	10. Joe Gonn	Forward
11. Ed. Downey	Forward	12. Red Carr	Forward
12. Ike Hildebrandt	Forward		

1212 - Hamilton St.
New Westminster, B.C.
Jan. 27, 1945.

Dear Hap,

I received your letter of Jan. 13. Since then, I have checked with the teams and I don't think there is a player by the name of Planche, unless he is one of the three ex-juvenile players that was kicked off the Portland team. I'm sending you the Portland Eagles line-up.

Our senior team is still on top of league but our junior team is now on the bottom. The lost three games in a row. Our regular goalie Al Rollins, is out with an old back injury.

That's all for now, except you'll be playing to-nite & I hope you win. I listen to all the games. Don't forget to write.

Sincerely Yours,

Ike
Hildebrand.

Ed Brown.

Broda's Find Loses Right Eye

Legendary Leafs goaltender Turk Broda wrote to Hap Day on March 22, 1945, while on active service overseas. He wished the Leafs well in the playoffs (the Leafs would win the Stanley Cup with Frank McCool in net) and mentioned a player that Day should consider, Colonel Ed Brown of South Porcupine, Ontario. "Hap, write him if it's possible to get a tryout with the club. You won't regret it, Hap. He is all yours for the asking," suggested Broda. Brown served in England during the war and laced up the skates for the Algonquin Regiment. In a freak accident on January 6, 1946, while playing for the AHL's St. Louis Flyers against the New Haven Eagles, Brown lost his right eye. He collided with Bob Dawes and fell onto the tip of Dawes' skate, resulting in a one-inch gash. Doctors tried to save his eyesight but could not. St. Louis coach Bouncer Taylor noted the irony, that Brown had served five years in the infantry "and never got a scratch." A couple of days later, Brown was making noise about returning to the game he loved. "I certainly want to get back to the Flyers and in time for the playoffs too, because we're going to be in them," he said after the operation. The defenceman left the hospital on January 18, and the team covered his expenses, paid him for the rest of the season, and raised $7,586 from the proceeds of a benefit game on January 30. Brown never made the big leagues again, but continued to play hockey, including a run to the Allan Cup finals with the Penticton Vees in 1953.

Turk Broda models a different uniform in October 1943—the Canadian Army.

Mar. 22.

Dear Hap:

Sorry I haven't answered your letter sooner than this. I wish you all the luck in the play-offs. Hoping you have the Cup in the glass case by the time I get home.

Hap I've been doing a little scouting for you here, and I have the best hockey player in this country. He probably be worth (Twenty five (Gs)) to you. His name is Ed. Brown, and he is only

2

twenty two on 24. of this month. He is going home soon, probably with a discharge. He is like Apps — and shoots like "Chuck" Con. So Hap write him if its possible to get a try out with the club. You won't regret it Hap. He is all yours for the asking.

Major Dan Campbell from Montreal wants him to go there. But I said he was wasting his time there. And also there is another Davidson here by the name of Valinto from North Bay. I think he is twenty five but he probably won't be home till its over. So Hap if you care to write

one of us for your answer. His address is Ed. Brown #2 C.T.R.

Thanks a million for the lovely parcels I've been getting also the cigarettes.

Hope Major Smythe is feeling much better. Give him my regards. And also the rest of the fellows.

There isn't much news I can write about that you don't get there. So I'll close for the present time. Hoping to hear soon. again

luck + the Stanley cup. yours.

Jack.

B.1807.
#2 C.A.R.C.

(see pullout at back)

Bob Davidson, Super Scout

As the Second World War was winding down, Bob Davidson knew that his on-ice career was almost at an end. He'd loyally served the Toronto Maple Leafs for a decade and acted as the team's captain. Davidson took over as head coach of the AHL's St. Louis Flyers during the 1946–47 season and then guided the AHL's Pittsburgh Hornets (1947–50) and the Ontario Hockey Association's Toronto Marlboros for two campaigns. But it turns out that Davidson's real skill came not behind the bench but in spotting talent. Replacing the ageing Squib Walker as head scout for the Leafs, Davidson became one of the best judges of talent in NHL history. "Davidson's uncanny ability to secure much of the finest junior talent in the country was nothing short of incredible," wrote Kevin Shea in *Toronto Maple Leafs: Diary of a Dynasty 1957–1967*. "He was the best one in the business," said Jim Gregory. Davidson was a scout for 40 years, often the *only* scout the Leafs employed on a full-time basis. "He scouted hockey players when you had to go and talk to them individually and try to sign them to a junior card—there was no draft in those days," added Gregory. "But he was a very knowledgeable, hard-working guy who the Maple Leafs were very lucky to have." Needless to say, Davidson's name appears all over Leafs documentation, with these two 14 years apart.

Bob Davidson.

PLAYER FILL IN

Height..6' 2"

Weight..190

March 28th, 1956.
Date

RECEIVED FROM MAPLE LEAF GARDENS, LIMITED, the sum of One Hundred Dollars ($100.00) for renewal of Form "C" Agreement.

R. E. Davidson
Witness

Kerry M. Namara
Player
Gerry McNamara

Form "C" Agreement dated ......April 16, 1955.......

Renewed to ......April 16, 1957.......

Date of birth ......September 22, 1934.......

TRY-OUT AGREEMENT

(NEW FORM)

Date ....

**MEMORANDUM
OF AGREEMENT**

BETWEEN: JAN POPIEL
....
                hereinafter called the "Player"

— and —   MAPLE LEAF GARDENS, LTD.
....
                hereinafter called the "Club"

In consideration of the agreement by the Club to pay the expenses (including hotel room,

meals and railroad fare) from: ....
                                            (Place of residence or other base of Player)

and return, the Player agrees to present himself, when called upon to do so, at the Club's
training camp for the purpose of demonstrating, to the best of his ability, his qualifications
as a hockey player; and further agrees that if such qualifications, in the opinion of the Club,
justify the Club in offering him a contract as a professional hockey player, he will sign such
contract on terms to be mutually agreed upon.

R. E. Davidson ....   _Jan Popiel_ ....
WITNESS: **PLAYER**

                                        ....
                                                            ADDRESS

Howard Starkman ....
WITNESS: **CITY**   **PROVINCE OR STATE**

                                        MAPLE LEAF GARDENS, LTD.
                                        ....
                                                                    CLUB

                                        PER _Jim Gregory_ ....

FOR PLAYER ONLY

NAME IN FULL..JAN POPIEL..........

PLACE OF BIRTH...VIRUM., DENMARK....

DAY....9th......MONTH...OCT......YEAR..1947....

HEIGHT....5'9"......WEIGHT....180 LBS....

POSITION...LEFT WING....SHOOTS.......L.....
                                        (R. OR L.)

CENTRAL REGISTRY	
REC'D	SEEN

Aug 31 8 39 AM '70

ACTION
noted

(Read instructions for completion and registration on reverse side.)

CHAPTER 3

POST-WAR and the 1950s

Meeker's Rookie Deal—and Rookie Mistake

Golly gee, Howie Meeker can't quite remember actually signing his first NHL contract—but he does remember the advice he got before going in to negotiate with the owner/GM Conn Smythe. His manager on the Stratford Indians of Ontario's Senior League, Dave Pinkney, told the right winger to shoot for the moon. "He said, 'Howard, for what you're doing, $20,000 is cheap, with the cash flow that you're creating and the other players are creating,'" recalled Meeker. "I ended up with $5,000 for two years, and a promise from Smythe of $1,000 if I won any major award for the Toronto Maple Leafs." That $1,000 bonus is not spelled out in the contract, and Meeker was named Rookie of the Year. "He told me that verbally twice and we shook hands on the deal," insisted Meeker. But Smythe never paid Meeker the money. "When the time came around, his excuse was 'You got $1,000, but it was from the NHL.' I was pissed off for a long time." Meeker would play another seven seasons with the Maple Leafs, including time serving double duty as a Member of Parliament, before getting into coaching and suiting up in Newfoundland's senior league. He also ran hockey camps for three decades. Meeker's national fame, of course, came on *Hockey Night in Canada*, and later on TSN, explaining the game to the nation with a passion few could ever match.

Howie Meeker recieves the Calder Memorial Trophy from W.A.H. McBrien, vice-president of Maple Leaf Gardens.

Newly arrived to Toronto from Chicago in November 1947, Max Bentley admires his new uniform.

AGREEMENT

Memorandum of Agreement between.................Howie Meeker.................of

.......New Hamburg, Ont............hereafter spoken of as "the

player" and the TORONTO MAPLE LEAF HOCKEY CLUB LIMITED of

Toronto, Ontario, hereafter spoken of as "the club."

In consideration of..........Two hundred and fifty dollars................

($250.00), which the player hereby acknowledges to have

received, the player will, at the option of the club, enter

into a contract for the season selected by the club upon all

the terms and conditions of the National Hockey League regular

contract, said terms and conditions to be reached by mutual

agreement. In addition, the player agrees to play amateur

hockey with a senior club designated by the Club.

If this contract is not entered into for the....1943-44....

season, the club can extend all conditions for one year upon

additional payment of...........Two hundred and fifty dollars....($250.00   )

to the player.

.....*U. Sievert*............   .....*Howie Meeker*............
Witness   Player

                                    ....
                                    Street No.   Street Name
                                    ...*New Hamburg*.....*Ont.*
                                    City   Province

                                    MAPLE LEAF HOCKEY CLUB

   October 6, 1942......   .....*C. Hap Day*......
....
Date

IMPORTANT NOTICE TO PLAYER

Before signing this contract you should carefully examine it to be sure that all
terms and conditions agreed upon have been incorporated herein, and if any has been
omitted, you should insist upon having it inserted in the contract before you sign.

NATIONAL HOCKEY LEAGUE

STANDARD PLAYER'S CONTRACT

This Agreement between the _____

TORONTO MAPLE LEAF HOCKEY CLUB

of the City of .... TORONTO ...., in the State/Province of .... ONTARIO ....

a member of the National Hockey League, hereinafter called the "Club", Party of the First Part, and

.... HOWARD MEEKER ....

of .... NEW HAMBURG ...., in the State/Province of .... ONTARIO ....

hereinafter called the "Player", Party of the Second Part.

Witnesseth:

That in consideration of the respective obligations herein and hereby assumed, the parties to this contract severally

agree as follows:

1. The Club agrees to pay the Player for the season of 19...47..., being the period commencing on ....

.... 16th day of October ....

and ending on the completion of the National Hockey League Schedule, Play-Off and Stanley Cup Games, a salary of $..4,900.00..

.... (Forty-nine Hundred Dollars) .... —————

and an additional sum of $..One Hundred Dollars.. —————

in consideration of the option granted to the Club in Section 9 hereof; said additional sum to be paid whether such option is exercised or

not, making the total compensation to the Player for the period herein contracted for $..5,000.00 (Five Thousand Dollars)..—————

Should the player, Howard Meeker, make the National Hockey League Second All-Star
Team he will receive a bonus of One Thousand Dollars ($1,000.00) and if he makes
the National Hockey League First All-Star Team he will receive an additional
sum of One Thousand Dollars ($1,000.00) making a total of Two Thousand Dollars
($2,000.00) if he makes the National Hockey League First All-Star Team.

Payments shall be in semi-monthly instalments following the commencement of the said period unless this contract shall be
terminated by the Club while the Player is "away" with the Club for the purpose of playing games, in which event the instalment then
falling due shall be paid on the first week-day after the return "home" of the Club. Provided, however, that if the Player is not in the
service of the Club for the entire period, then he shall receive such proportion of the salary as the number of days of actual employment
bears to the number of days in the said period.

Nevertheless, if the Player is loaned, sold, exchanged or transferred to a club of another League, the Player shall only be paid at the

rate of $.......... or the maximum salary paid in such League, whichever is less.

2. The Player agrees to give his services and to play hockey to the best of his ability under the direction and control of the Club
for the said period in accordance with the provisions hereof; and furthermore agrees that at all times during such period he will maintain
himself in fit and proper condition therefor.

3. The Club may from time to time during the continuance of this contract establish rules for the government, conduct and
conditioning of its players and such rules shall form part of this contract as fully as if herein written and binding upon the Player; and
for violation of any such rules or for any conduct impairing the faithful and thorough discharge of the duties incumbent upon the player,
the Club may impose a reasonable fine upon the Player and deduct the amount thereof from any money due or to become due to the
Player. The Club may also suspend the Player for violation of any such rules and during such suspension the Player shall not be entitled
to any compensation whatsoever under this contract. When the Player is fined or suspended, he shall be given notice in writing stating
the amount of the fine or the duration of the suspension and the reason therefor.

4. Should the Player be disabled or his ability to perform his duties be impaired at any time during the said period, the Club
may deduct from the amount then due or to become due under this contract such proportion thereof as the duration of said disability
or impairment may bear to the said period; but no such deduction shall be made by reason of any accident or injury received by the
Player while playing under the direction of the Club.

5. Should the Player be disabled or unable to perform his duties, he shall submit himself to a medical examination and treatment
by a physician selected by the Club, and such examination and treatment when made at the request of the Club shall be at its expense
unless made necessary by some act or conduct of the Player contrary to the terms and provisions of this contract or the said rules.

6. In order that the Player be fit and in proper condition for the performance of his duties as required by this contract, he shall
report for practice at such time and at such place as the Club may designate and participate in such exhibition games as may be
arranged by the Club within thirty days prior to the first game of the National Hockey League Schedule, the Club to pay the travelling
expenses and meals en route of the Player from his home to the training place of the Club, whether he be ordered to go there direct or by
way of the "home" city of the Club. In the event of the failure of the Player to so report for practice and participate in exhibition games,
a penalty not exceeding $500.00 may be imposed by the Club to be deducted from the compensation stipulated herein.

7. The Club may at any time give the Player thirty days' written notice to terminate this contract, in which event this contract
shall terminate on the expiration of said thirty days and the Player shall be entitled only to the proportion of the salary due at the
date of termination. If such notice be given while the Player is "away" with the Club, he shall be entitled to his travelling expenses
to the "home" city of the Club.

8. The player hereby represents that he has special and exceptional or unique knowledge and skill and ability as a hockey player, the
loss of which cannot be estimated with any certainty and cannot be fairly or adequately compensated by damages. The Player therefore
agrees that the Club shall have the right, in addition to any other rights which the Club may possess, to enjoin him by appropriate
injunction proceedings from playing hockey for any other team and/or for any breach of any of the other provisions of this contract.

9. It is mutually agreed that the Club shall have the right to sell, exchange, assign or otherwise transfer this contract and the
Player's services to any other professional hockey club and the Player agrees to accept and be bound by such sale, exchange assignment
or transfer. Thereafter this contract shall have the same force and effect as if it had been entered into by the Player and the assignee Club.

10. The Player shall not either during the period of this contract or before the commencement or after the end thereof participate
in any hockey, baseball, indoor baseball, basketball, lacrosse or football games or boxing or wrestling matches unless the written consent
of the Club has first been given to him.

11. The Player undertakes that he will at the option of the Club enter into a contract for the following playing season upon the
same terms and conditions of this contract, save as to salary, which will be determined by mutual agreement, and failing which, by the
President of the National Hockey League and the parties agree to accept his decision as final.

12. The Player hereby irrevocably grants the Club the exclusive right to permit or authorize any person, firm or corporation to
make use of his photograph or of his likeness or of his signature for purposes of advertising or publicity. The Player
undertakes to make no radio broadcast without the permission of the Club.

13. The Player agrees and covenants that during the period of this contract or any extension thereof he will not tamper with or
enter into negotiations with any player under contract or reservation to any club of the National Hockey League for or regarding such
player's present or future services, without the written consent of the club with which the player is connected, under penalty of a fine
to be imposed by the President of the National Hockey League.

14. The Player agrees to conform and be subject to the provisions of the By-laws of the National Hockey League insofar as they
concern or affect players and to be subject to any fines or penalties which may be imposed by reason of any contraventions thereof by
him; and he hereby authorizes the Club to take from any salary or compensation due or to become due to him hereunder the amount of
any such fine or penalty and to pay the same to the National Hockey League.

15. The Player furthermore agrees that the Club may carry out and put into effect any order or ruling by the National Hockey
League or its President for his suspension or expulsion and that in the event of suspension his salary shall cease for the duration thereof
and that in the event of expulsion this contract, at the option of the Club, shall terminate forthwith.

16. If because of any condition arising from a state of war or other cause beyond control of the National Hockey League or of
the Club it shall be deemed advisable by the National Hockey League or by the Club to suspend or curtail operations, then in the
event of suspension of operations, the Player shall be entitled only to the proportion of the salary due at the date of suspension, and in
the event of curtailment but not suspension of operations, the salary stipulated in Section 1 hereof shall be automatically cancelled
and shall be replaced by that mutually agreed upon between the Club and the Player.

In Witness Whereof, the parties have signed this .... 5th ....

day of .... November .... A.D. 19 46

WITNESSES:

R. M. LeBage

_____
TORONTO MAPLE LEAF HOCKEY CLUB LIMITED
Club

By _____ for the President.

"Howard Meeker"
_____
Player.

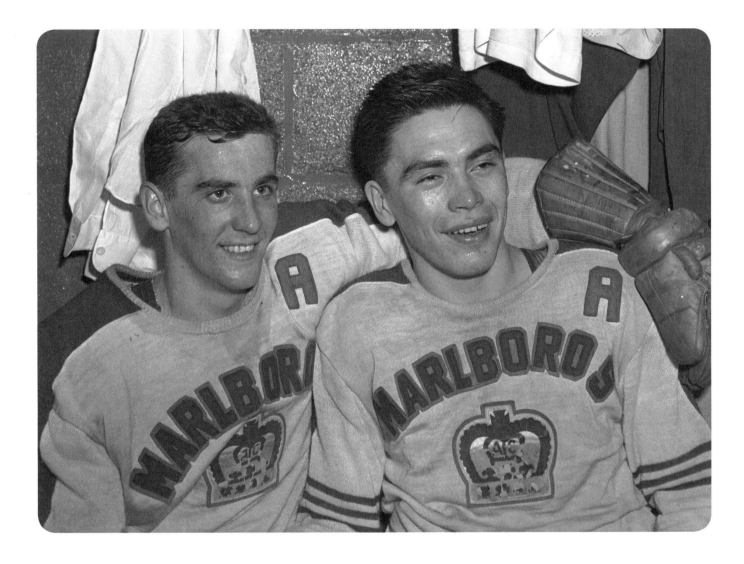

The Battle for George Armstrong

Toronto Marlboros Danny Lewicki and George Armstrong.

"The Chief" George Armstrong, captain of the last Leafs Stanley Cup winner in 1967, was almost a Detroit Red Wing. In a time before email or even fax machines, sometimes things got lost in the mail or delayed at the telegram office. Jack Adams, GM of the Red Wings, thought he had Armstrong on Detroit's negotiation list. But a clerical error in the office of the AHL's Pittsburgh Hornets resulted in, well, a hornet's nest. In the terms of the day, Armstrong, Tim Horton, and Lawrence Regan were "removed" from the Pittsburgh reserve list when they should have been "transferred." Adams demanded a hearing; Frank J. Selke of the Canadiens and Art Ross of the Bruins were arbitrators. "At no time has Armstrong been off the Toronto list in Toronto," wrote Conn Smythe on April 30, 1948, blaming the clerical error made by the AHL. "The Toronto Club is under no necessity to prove anything. They have the player on their list and we cannot understand Detroit's desire to take one of our players knowing the circumstances as they do." The whole process of back and forth between the Wings, Leafs, NHL, and AHL took six months, and it was ruled that Armstrong was still Toronto property.

FORM "C"

A G R E E M E N T

MEMORANDUM OF AGREEMENT between __George Edward Armstrong__

_____,of the __town__ _____ of __Falconbridge,__ _____, in the

Province of __Ontario__ _____, hereinafter called "The Player" and the

__Toronto Maple Leafs__ _____, hereinafter called "The Club".

IN CONSIDERATION OF the sum of __One Hundred__ _____

_____ Dollars now paid by the Club to the Player, the receipt whereof is hereby acknowledged, the Player covenants and agrees with the Club that he will on the request of the Club made within one year from the date hereof sign a contract with the Club to serve the Club as a Hockey Player for a period of __one__ years, and subject to such terms and conditions of employment as are set out in the National Hockey League form of Player Contract (a copy of which has been shown to and examined by the Player) for the following remuneration payable to the Player by the Club:

        __$100.00__ _____ payable forthwith upon signing such contract,

- and -   __$2500.00__ _____ per Hockey season should the Player be assigned to play for a Club operating in the United States Hockey League,

- or -   __$3000.00__ _____ per Hockey season should the Player be assigned to play for a Club operating in the American Hockey League,

- or -   __$4500.00__ _____ per Hockey season should the Player be assigned to play for a Club operating in the National Hockey League.

ALL such payments excepting the _____,payable upon signing shall be pro rated according to the proportion of the hockey season for which the Player is employed in each of such Leagues.

DURING THE TERM of this Agreement and any extension hereof the Player covenants and agrees with the Club that he will play hockey only for such hockey team as may be designated by the Club.

THIS AGREEMENT may be extended for further periods of one year each upon payment by the Club to the Player before the expiration of this Agreement or any extension thereof of the sum of __$100.00__ _____, for each such extension.

DATED at __North Bay, Ont.__ this __21st__ day of __January__ , 19__47__.

Fred J. Armstrong
WITNESS

George Armstrong
PLAYER

__Falconbridge, Ontario.__
ADDRESS

CITY   PROVINCE OR STATE

__Copper Cliff Juniors__
CLUB

H. J. McNamara
WITNESS

PER _R. D. Wilson_

FOR PLAYER ONLY

NAME IN FULL _George Edward Armstrong_
PLACE OF BIRTH _Skead_
DAY _July 6_ MONTH _July 6_ YEAR _1930_
HEIGHT _6 ft. 1_ WEIGHT _170_
POSITION _Centre_ RIGHT OR LEFT _right_

NATIONAL HOCKEY LEAGUE

603 Sun Life Building
MONTREAL

TEL. MARQUETTE 3438

PRESIDENT'S OFFICE

Nov. 20th, 1947.

Mr. Conn Smythe,
Maple Leaf Gardens Ltd.,
Toronto, 2, Ont.

Files A-37, H-104 and R-82
Re: Geo. Armstrong, Myles Horton and
Larry Regan - Pittsburgh

Dear Mr. Smythe:

This will acknowledge receipt of your favour of November 19th, reference the above named players amongst others, with which you enclose copies of your correspondence of November 18th with this office and a copy of your letters to Pittsburgh, under date of November 11th, reference Mitchell and Lee.

Until the telephone conversation yesterday between Miss McDonald and Miss Pinard we had no advice that you were re-purchasing these players from Pittsburgh, and we acted on the advice of the American Hockey League that their names had been removed from the Pittsburgh List on the instructions of Pittsburgh.

This is another case in which, if we had had a copy of your original letter of instructions to Pittsburgh with reference to the re-purchase, no difficulty could possibly have arisen.

Mr. Podoloff has sent us a wire, text of which is as follows:-

"TRANSACTION INVOLVING PLAYERS ARMSTRONG HORTON AND REGAN WAS TRANSFER PITTSBURG TO TORONTO AS INDICATED BY DOCUMENTS DATED NOV TENTH. WIRE OF NOV THIRTEENTH APPARENTLY INDICATING OTHERWISE WAS IN ERROR"

This will be the basis of a cancellation of the original entry on Bulletin No. 391 and removing their names from the Pittsburgh List and substituting therefor this entry transferring them to the Toronto Reserve List.

I have endeavoured to get in touch with Jack Adams of Detroit to advise him of this development, so that there will be no unnecessary friction about Armstrong's

<u>Mr. Conn Smythe</u>   <u>Nov. 20th, 1947.</u>

removal from the Detroit Negotiation List, but he
will not be available until later this afternoon.

It is my intention to send out a memorandum
to all clubs, calling attention to the risk involved with respect to players put out to clubs
in other leagues with option to re-purchase, and
will change the office drill so that no transaction
affecting players belonging to National Hockey
League Clubs can be made without some clear indication of the concurrence of the real owners of the
contract.

Yours very truly,

NATIONAL HOCKEY LEAGUE

President

CSC/PK

"Sudden Death" Hill

Mel "Sudden Death" Hill, who earned his nickname by scoring three overtime goals for the Bruins in a 1939 playoff series against the Rangers, was faced with a decision in the summer of 1948—report for another season with the AHL's Pittsburgh Hornets or call it quits and move on. Claimed by the Leafs when the Brooklyn Americans folded in 1942, Hill played in Toronto from 1942 to 1946. After two more years as Leafs property in Pittsburgh, Hill told Conn Smythe that he was done, and the appropriate paperwork was filed. The diminutive right winger (5-foot-10, 175 pounds) with three Stanley Cups (one with Boston, two with Toronto) and an Allan Cup (1937 Sudbury Frood Tigers) on his résumé kept in the game in Saskatchewan, suiting up another four years in the Western Canada Senior Hockey League with the Regina Caps. Allen Abel of the *Globe and Mail* tracked down Hill in 1983, in Fort Qu'Appelle, Saskatchewan, and learned that Sudden Death, who died in 1996 at age 82, had no regrets. "I was happy being a businessman," Hill said. "I had my own soft-drink plant. I did all right for myself, but I always feel sorry for the fellows from our time who got out of the game and haven't got a nickel today.... I've got to say that I achieved every ambition in life I ever had. My wife and I have the land now, our four children are grown... You know, if I didn't score those goals back then, nobody would know I'm alive."

Bill Ezinicki, Mel Hill, and Bob Davidson.

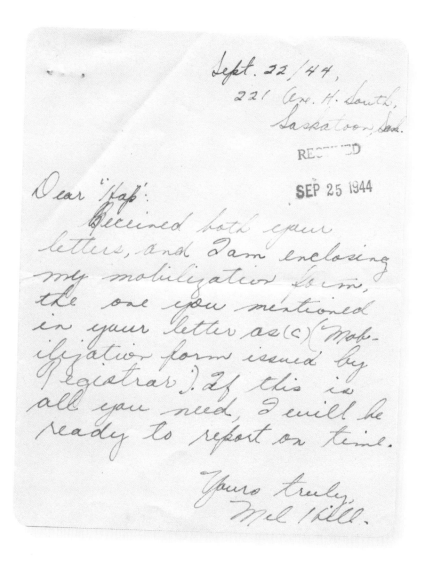

June 17, 1948.

Miss D. Pinard,
National Hockey League,
603 Sun Life Building,
Montreal, Que.

Dear Miss Pinard:

Confirming our telephone conversation of this afternoon, I wish to advise that we are today sending you papers covering the retirement of Mel Hill from hockey. This will provide a space on the Pittsburgh list for the completion of the deal with New York.

We have also requested Pittsburgh by wire to remove Brayshaw from their list and transfer him to the Los Angeles list and this will provide the second space required by you to complete the New York deal.

Yours very truly,

McD   Secretary to
                                             Mr. C. Smythe

The Apps Retirement Plan

Hap Day, Syl Apps, and Conn Smythe after the 1947 Stanley Cup win.

The wooing of Syl Apps began in November 1935, when Conn Smythe invited him to come to a game at the Gardens. Smythe had been enamoured seeing Apps suit up for Hamilton's McMaster University against the University of Toronto. "It was seeing you play against Varsity that made me get in touch with you again," wrote Smythe. Apps would sign in September 1936 and was named NHL Rookie of the Year for 1936–37. Smythe never lost that love for Apps, who played for the Leafs, less time in the military, until the end of the 1947–48 season, when he made $8,000 as captain. "He had a goal to score 200 goals, and he did that by one over," said his son, Syl Apps Jr., who also made the NHL. "He always used to say to me, 'There is life after hockey.'" Post-hockey, Apps served as a member of the Ontario Provincial Parliament for a dozen years, representing Kingston, and spent time in Cabinet as Minister of Correctional Services. One thing he didn't do was dwell on his successes in hockey. "We never talked about hockey," said his son, whose own son, Syl Apps III, made the NHL, and whose daughter, Gillian Apps, is part of the Canadian women's Olympic squad. "I didn't even know he played hockey until I was seven or eight. There was nothing around our house that would indicate it."

MINISTER OF CORRECTIONAL SERVICES

Parliament Buildings,
Queen's Park,
Toronto 182, Ontario,
March 25, 1971.

Mr. L. J. "Sparky" Weiler,
c/o The Carling Breweries Limited,
20 Colborne Street,
P. O. Box 425,
Walkerton, Ontario.

Dear Sparky:

Many thanks for your card in connection with
my recent appointment as Minister of Correctional
Services.

It was very good of you to drop me a line and
your best wishes were very much appreciated.

Yours sincerely,

C.J.S. Apps,
Minister.

CJSA/1h

STANDARD PLAYER'S CONTRACT
National Hockey League

The TORONTO MAPLE LEAF HOCKEY CLUB
of TORONTO ONTARIO
WITH
C.J. SYLVANUS APPS
TORONTO ONTARIO

I hereby certify that I have, at this date, received,
examined and noted of record the within Contract,
and that it is in regular form.

President, National Hockey League.

Dated _____ 19

Oct 16 12 05 PM '47

ACTION 1st
Registered
Oct-Feb 16/47

IMPORTANT NOTICE TO PLAYER

Before signing this contract you should carefully examine it to be sure that all
terms and conditions agreed upon have been incorporated herein, and if any has been
omitted, you should insist upon having it inserted in the contract before you sign.

NATIONAL HOCKEY LEAGUE

STANDARD PLAYER'S CONTRACT

This Agreement between the _____

the TORONTO MAPLE LEAF HOCKEY CLUB

the City of TORONTO, in the State/Province of ONTARIO

member of the National Hockey League, hereinafter called the "Club", Party of the First Part, and

C.J. SYLVANUS APPS

TORONTO, in the State/Province of ONTARIO

hereinafter called the "Player", Party of the Second Part.

Witnesseth:

That in consideration of the respective obligations herein and hereby assumed, the parties to this contract severally
as follows:

1. The Club agrees to pay the Player for the season of 1947-48, being the period commencing on

about middle of October

and ending on the completion of the National Hockey League Schedule, Play-Off and Stanley Cup Games, a salary of $6,900.00 at rate

Sixty-nine Hundred Dollars

and an additional sum of $ One Hundred Dollars

in consideration of the option granted to the Club in Section 9 hereof; said additional sum to be paid whether such option is exercised or
not, making the total compensation to the Player for the period herein contracted for $7,000.00 (Seven Thousand Dollars)

The Player, Sylvanus Apps is to receive One Thousand Dollars for being Captain of the
Maple Leaf Hockey Team, making a total of $8,000.00 (Eight Thousand Dollars)

If the Player, Sylvanus Apps makes the National Hockey League Second All-Star Team, he
will receive a bonus of One Thousand Dollars ($1,000.00), and if he makes the National
Hockey League First All-Star Team, he will receive an additional sum of One Thousand
Dollars ($1,000.00) making a total of Two Thousand Dollars ($2,000.00) if the Player
makes the National Hockey League First All-Star Team.

Payments shall be in semi-monthly instalments following the commencement of the said period unless this contract shall be
terminated by the Club while the Player is "away" with the Club for the purpose of playing games, in which event the instalment then
falling due shall be paid on the first week-day after the return "home" of the Club. Provided, however, that if the Player is not in the
service of the Club for the entire period, then he shall receive such proportion of the salary as the number of days of actual employment
bears to the number of days in the said period.

Nevertheless, if the Player is loaned, sold, exchanged or transferred to a club of another League, the Player shall only be paid at the
rate of $ _____
or the maximum salary paid in such League, whichever is less.

16. If because of any condition arising _____
the Club it shall be deemed advisable by the National Hockey League or by the Club _____
event of suspension of operations, the Player shall be entitled only to the proportion of the salary due at the date of suspension, and in
the event of curtailment but not suspension of operations, the salary stipulated in Section 1 hereof shall be automatically cancelled
and shall be replaced by that mutually agreed upon between the Club and the Player.

In Witness Whereof, the parties have signed this ____19th____

day of ____May____ A.D. 19 47

WITNESSES: THE TORONTO MAPLE LEAF HOCKEY CLUB

M. McDonald   Club

M. McDonald   By _____ for the   President.

                                         C. J. Apps   Player.

Mr. and Mrs. Armstrong: Hockey Parents

George Armstrong's parents figure prominently in the early days of his hockey career, and a lot of it is documented in the Stitt Collection. "I love that correspondence. The story behind that is, George was a great athlete and he was living up north. His mom in particular didn't want him to leave," said Bob Stellick, the former Leafs jack-of-all-trades in the office. Born of Irish-Algonquin heritage, Armstrong grew up in Falconbridge, Ontario, just outside Sudbury, where his father worked in the nickel mines. The young centre was with the Copper Cliff Jr. Redmen when the Leafs inked him to a "C" form and sent him to the Leafs Junior A affiliate in Stratford. His parents were none too pleased with Stratford GM Dave Pinkney. "I didn't think Mr. Pinkney would try to ruin his career. We blame Stratford more than George," his parents wrote to Conn Smythe. The Leafs brought George to the Toronto Marlboros of the OHA for the 1948–49 season and he never left town, though it took a couple of seasons to stick with the big club. George's parents wrote Smythe: "We know from his letters he is broken hearted" by being demoted back to junior. Smythe assured the Armstrongs that "he is in good hands." Aside from brief AHL stints in Pittsburgh, "The Chief" played for the Leafs until 1971, and then coached and scouted for the team. The letters are "a fascinating glimpse into a different era," said Stellick. Armstrong was inducted into the Hall of Fame in 1975.

George Armstrong, accompanied by his mother, signs a contract with Conn Smythe and the Leafs.

Falconbridge Ont.
Thus. Sept 30/48

Mr. Conn Smythe,
Maple Leaf Gardens,
Toronto,

Sir.

We are quite agreeable
for George to go to Toronto
& play for Marlboros. But
we dont like the way Stratford
is holding him. I didn't think
Mr. Pinkney would try to ruin
his career. We blame Stratford
more than George. We think
it would be a good idea
for you to speak to Mr. Pinkney.
I'm sending a copy of
a telegram we received from
George to day.
        We remain
    Mr & Mrs G. Armstrong.

Stratford Ont
Sept. 30/48

Falconbridge, Ont.

Dave found Mr. Smythe
could not suspend me. But
is phoning Clarence Campbell
in morning. Send my blue
suit to nite I need it.

        George.

Watch Your Language

When Conn Smythe received this letter from NHL President Clarence Campbell about obscene language, he passed it down to the Leafs coach—"Copy given to Mr. Day for team" reads the handwriting on the left side. Evidently it didn't make an impact. "The continual haranguing of referees . . . has become synonymous with big-time hockey. President Campbell finally was pressurized into silencing the players during the Detroit-Toronto playoffs last spring," wrote *Globe and Mail* sports editor Jim Vipond in September 1950. "Of course, the players cannot be blamed when their managers and coaches set a bad example. Conn Smythe was once the best referee-baiter in the league and last season we had [Chicago Black Hawks coach] Charlie Conacher spitting expletives at referee George Gravel, and [Montreal Canadiens coach] Dick Irvin making like Little Eva in an attempt to get at referee Hugh McLean." As for Hap Day, famed sportswriter Jim Coleman noted that he could keep himself in check, for a while: "Mr. Day has a fairly modest stock of expletives at his disposal and he prefers to save them until the playoffs."

AHL President Maurice Podoloff, NHL President Clarence Campbell and Cleveland Barons General Manager Jim Hendy at a meeting during the 1951–52 season.

TEL. MARQUETTE 3438

NATIONAL HOCKEY LEAGUE

603 SUN LIFE BUILDING

MONTREAL

PRESIDENT'S OFFICE

December 22, 1948.

Read
Dec 23/48

Copy queue
to mr Day
for team

Mr. Conn Smythe,
Toronto Maple Leaf Hockey Club Ltd.,
Maple Leaf Gardens,
Toronto, Ont.

Dear Mr. Smythe:

Re: Obscene Language

At various times in the past two seasons I have had occasion to speak to most of the Managers in the League about the foul and abusive language of players, both on the ice and on the bench. Sometimes this foul language has been directed to the officials and sometimes to other players, and frequently it has been indiscriminate profanity.

Recently several incidents have occurred which show that this condition is getting worse instead of better, and it cannot possibly have any other than an adverse effect on the spectator reaction. In our game the best and most high-priced seats are located in the vicinity of the players benches and closest to the ice. It is very offensive indeed, particularly to women, and contributes absolutely nothing to our spectacle and will inevitably drive some people out of the rinks.

Some clubs are worse offenders than others and this abuse is not confined to players but extends to trainers and coaches as well.

There is a provision in the Rule Book which gives the referee authority to impose misconduct penalties for foul and abusive language to spectators and other players, but in practice the referees have confined the use of this rule to cases where it was incidental to some threat or challenge to their own authority by players. It may be that instructions should be

---

Mr. Boucher - page 2   December 22, 1948.

given for them to be more strict in this respect, but it seems to me that the referees already have plenty to do without being called upon to deal with a matter which is primarily the responsibility of the club management. I think, in general, it would create a bad fan reaction for the referee to impose misconduct penalties for foul language. Furthermore, the referees have schooled themselves to try to avoid having "rabbits' ears" in respect to critical comment on their own work, and, in addition, their movements all over the rink would make it impossible for them to deal with all the infractions because they would not hear them. Before giving them instructions to crack down on this abuse, I am appealing to the managers of the clubs to try and clean up the situation themselves.

If the situation does not improve then there will be no alternative than to have the referees clamp down on this increasing menace to the support of our game.

Yours very truly,

NATIONAL HOCKEY LEAGUE

President

CSC/PK

Encl. cc.

Davidson Has His Eyes on Horton

The Tim Horton file runs from discovery to doughnuts. This note comes from a Mr. R.D. Wilson, who contacted the Leafs about Horton's play in Sudbury. Leafs scout Bob Davidson went to the next game, Horton's Copper Cliff Jr. Redmen against the Porcupine Combines in the Northern playoffs. Davidson sent GM Hap Day a letter on Hotel Coulson stationery, misspelling Horton's given name as "Miles." The 165-pound Horton got hurt in the first period, "so could not tell much about him," wrote Davidson. He did visit Myles' eye doctor, and "he tells me he needs glasses to read and in school, but he don't need glasses to play hockey." Because Horton didn't play much of the game, Davidson was more intrigued by Elwood Small, a left winger, who scored two goals. "One thing I have done in the past is not make any snap decisions, but this is one boy I say should be tied up," Davidson said about Small. The Leafs, however, would be too late, and Small ended up on Detroit's negotiation list. As for Horton, he signed a contract on October 4, 1947, attended St. Michael's College, and was added to Toronto's payroll on December 7, 1951.

Tim Horton.

Feb.21/47

Mr. R. D. Wilson 'Phoned in following information:

Myles Horton - Copper Cliff Redmen Jrs.

Born Jan. 12, 1930. Shoots right, plays defence.

Attends Sudbury High School

The reason Mr. Wilson hadn't said anything about this player, was that he seems to have something the matter with one of his eyes. Wears glasses. Mr. Wilson thought he seemed to have trouble taking passes on the ice. Watched him last winter, and has seen him three times this year. Same team as Armstrong plays for.

Copper Cliff Redmen are playing Sault Ste Marie Team in Sudbury next week, and Mr. Wilson will see that game.

Questioned

Put on neglect Feb 20/47

dropped Feb 22/47

FORM "C"

A G R E E M E N T

MEMORANDUM OF AGREEMENT between ___Myles Horton___

_____, of the ___City___ of ___Sudbury, Ontario___, in the

Province of ___Ontario___, hereinafter called "The Player" and the

___TORONTO MAPLE LEAF HOCKEY CLUB LIMITED___, hereinafter called "The Club".

IN CONSIDERATION OF the sum of ___One Hundred Dollars___

Dollars now paid by the Club to the Player, the receipt whereof is hereby acknowledged, the Player covenants and agrees with the Club that he will on the request of the Club made within one year from the date hereof sign a contract with the Club to serve the Club as a Hockey Player for a period of _____ years, and subject to such terms and conditions of employment as are set out in the National Hockey League form of Player Contract (a copy of which has been shown to and examined by the Player) for the following remuneration payable to the Player by the Club:

($1000.00) ONE THOUSAND DOLLARS _____ payable forthwith upon signing such contract,

- and $3000.00 THREE THOUSAND DOLLARS _____ per Hockey season should the Player be assigned to play for a Club operating in the United States Hockey League,

- or $3500.00 THIRTY FIVE HUNDRED DOLLARS _____ per Hockey season should the Player be assigned to play for a Club operating in the American Hockey League,

- or $5000.00 FIVE THOUSAND DOLLARS _____ per Hockey season should the Player be assigned to play for a Club operating in the National Hockey League.

ALL such payments excepting the ___One Thousand Dollars___ _____, payable upon signing shall be pro rated according to the proportion of the hockey season for which the Player is employed in each of such Leagues.

DURING THE TERM of this Agreement and any extension hereof the Player covenants and agrees with the Club that he will play hockey only for such hockey team as may be designated by the Club.

THIS AGREEMENT may be extended for further periods of one year each upon payment by the Club to the Player before the expiration of this Agreement or any extension thereof of the sum of ___One Hundred Dollars___ _____, for each such extension.

DATED at ___Toronto___ this ___4th___ day of ___October___, 19___47___.

WITNESS _G. E. Walker_   _Tim Horton_
                                                PLAYER

                                        497 McLeod Street
                                        _____
                                        ADDRESS

                                        Sudbury, Ontario
                                        CITY   PROVINCE OR STATE

                                        TORONTO MAPLE LEAF HOCKEY CLUB LIMITED

M. McDonald   PER _____
WITNESS   CLUB

FOR PLAYER ONLY

NAME IN FULL ___Myles Gilbert Horton___
PLACE OF BIRTH ___Cochrane, Ontario___
DAY ___12___ MONTH ___January___ YEAR ___1930___
HEIGHT ___5'10"___ WEIGHT ___164 lbs.___
POSITION ___Defence___ RIGHT OR LEFT ___Right___

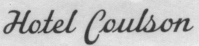

Hotel Coulson
OWNED AND OPERATED BY
HOTEL COULSON LIMITED

Sudbury, Ont.
CANADA

OPERATED UNDER SAME MANAGEMENT

HOTEL COULSON
BOURLAMAQUE, QUE.
50 ROOMS
WITH BATHS AND SHOWERS

ALEXANDRA HOTEL
OTTAWA, ONT.
125 ROOMS
WITH BATHS AND SHOWERS

March 10-47

Mr. C. H. Day
Maple Leaf Gardens
Toronto.

Dear Hap.

I came up here to-day to see
Copper Cliff Redmen and Porcupine Combines
play the first game of the Northern playoffs.

I inquired from a eye Dr. here
about this boy Miles Horton, he tells me
he needs glasses to read and in school,
but he don't need glasses to play hockey.
he was born Jan 12 – 1930 and weights 165 –
plays defence and shoots right, in the
game here to-nite he got hurt in the first period
so could not tell much about him. On Omaha Res.

The boy that took my eye is Elwood
Small born May 19 – 1928 weights 185 lbs
and 5' 10" tall plays on left wing and
shoots left, he scored 2 goals to-nite and
is very strong and fast skater, a good stick

Hotel Coulson

OWNED AND OPERATED BY
HOTEL COULSON LIMITED

▼

Sudbury, Ont.
CANADA

OPERATED UNDER SAME MANAGEMENT

HOTEL COULSON
BOURLAMAQUE, QUE.
50 ROOMS
WITH BATHS AND SHOWERS

ALEXANDRA HOTEL
OTTAWA, ONT.
125 ROOMS
WITH BATHS AND SHOWERS

handler and very aggressive.

One thing I have done in the past is not make any snap decisions, but this is one boy I say should be tied up.

I am going back to North Bay to-nite but will be seeing Small on Wed 12 on his way back up north.

If you want him signed to a form C. please advise.

Lots of luck Hope from here in

Bob.

Tim Horton's 1954-55 contract

Horton was as hard-headed and determined in negotiations as he was on the ice. Hap Day carefully spelled out in a secondary memo, dated August 19, 1954, that the jump from $9,500 to $10,000 in salary "in no way is to be considered a bonus for making the N.H.L. Second All-Star team, but is to be considered part of his salary." For the 1956–57 season, the Leafs defenceman added a $500 contractual bonus if he amassed 30 points. Another clause was put in the following year—an additional $500 if he was among the "first six in the Norris Trophy Selection." Equally hard-headed was Leafs management. GM Punch Imlach wrote to Horton on May 30, 1960, saying, "I feel that you received ample reward for your work last year and believe that with a little extra effort you can probably do better and then be in a position to ask for an increase."

Trainer Tim Daly looks at Tim Horton's previously fractured right leg in October 1955.

August 17th, 1954

Mr. Smythe:

Tim Horton and I had quite a go this a.m.

He was determined to get $10,000. for this year. Last week I offered him $8500. plus a $500. bonus if we had four home playoff games. This morning I offered him $9000. plus a $1000. bonus if we get into the second round of the playoffs. He was still determined to get $10,000., but finally decided to accept the offer I made this morning under the condition that if you thought his play warranted more for this season, then you would give him what you thought he was worth.

This, of course, is all subject to your approval.

C. H. Day

Mr Smythe spoke to Mr. Day about this & told him to give Horton 9000⁰⁰ & if he got 2nd All-Star it is understood his pay would be 10 000 for year. no all star clause MC

August 19th, 1954

Memorandum of agreement between Maple Leaf Gardens, Limited
and Tim Horton.

In a discussion with Tim Horton re his salary for
1954-55, he stated he thought he was worth a straight salary
of $10,000.00. However, he agreed to sign for a salary
of $9500.00 and if he makes the National Hockey League
Second All Star team, he is to be paid a salary of $10,000.00.

This, in no way is to be considered a bonus
for making the N. H. L. Second All Star team, but is to be
considered part of his salary.

Maple Leaf Gardens, Limited

per. ....

....
witness

....
witness

Tim Horton
Tim Horton

IMPORTANT NOTICE TO PLAYER

Before signing this contract you should carefully examine it to be sure that all
terms and conditions agreed upon have been incorporated herein, and if any has been
omitted, you should insist upon having it inserted in the contract before you sign.

NATIONAL HOCKEY LEAGUE
STANDARD PLAYER'S CONTRACT

This Agreement

BETWEEN: MAPLE LEAF GARDENS LIMITED

hereinafter called the "Club",
a member of the National Hockey League, hereinafter called the "League".

— AND —   MYLES (Tim) HORTON

hereinafter called the "Player".

of   Wexford   in {Province/State} of   Ontario

Witnesseth:

That in consideration of the respective obligations herein and hereby assumed, the parties to this contract severally
agree as follows:—

1.   The Club hereby employs the Player as a skilled Hockey Player for the term of one year commencing October 1st, 1954
and agrees, subject to the terms and conditions hereof, to pay the Player a salary of

—=Nine Thousand Five Hundred Dollars—=   Dollars ($ 9500.00   ).

Payment of such salary shall be in consecutive semi-monthly instalments following the commencement of the regular League Championship Schedule of games or following the date of reporting, whichever is later; provided, however, that if the Player is not in the employ
of the Club for the whole period of the Club's games in the National Hockey League Championship Schedule, then he shall receive only
part of the salary in the ratio of the number of days of actual employment to the number of days of the League Championship Schedule
of games.

And it is further mutually agreed that if the Contract and rights to the services of the Player are assigned, exchanged, loaned or
otherwise transferred to a Club in another League, the Player shall only be paid at the rate of

....   Dollars in the .... League,
or..   Dollars in the .... League,
or..   Dollars in the .... League.

2.   The Player agrees to give his services and to play hockey in all League Championship, Exhibition, Play-Off and Stanley Cup
games to the best of his ability under the direction and control of the Club for the said season in accordance with the provisions hereof.

The Player further agrees:

(a)   to report to the Club training camp at the time and place fixed by the Club, in good physical condition,
(b)   to keep himself in good physical condition at all times during the season,
(c)   to give his best services and loyalty to the Club and to play hockey only for the Club unless his contract is released, assigned,
exchanged or loaned by the Club,
(d)   to co-operate with the Club and participate in any and all promotional activities of the Club and the League which will in
the opinion of the Club promote the welfare of the Club or professional hockey generally,
(e)   to conduct himself on and off the rink according to the highest standards of honesty, morality, fair play and sportsmanship,
and to refrain from conduct detrimental to the best interests of the Club, the League or professional hockey generally.

3.   In order that the Player shall be fit and in proper condition for the performance of his duties as required by this contract the
Player agrees to report for practice at such time and place as the Club may designate and participate in such exhibition games as may be
arranged by the Club within thirty days prior to the first scheduled Championship game. The Club shall pay the travelling expenses
and meals en route from the Player's home to the Club's training camp. In the event of failure of the player to so report and participate
in exhibition games a fine not exceeding Five Hundred Dollars may be imposed by the Club and be deducted from the compensation
stipulated herein.

4.   The Club may from time to time during the continuance of this contract establish rules governing the conduct and conditioning of the Player, and such rules shall form part of this contract as fully as if herein written. For violation of any of such rules or for
any conduct impairing the thorough and faithful discharge of the duties incumbent upon the Player, the Club may impose a reasonable
fine upon the Player and deduct the amount thereof from any money due or to become due to the Player. The Club may also suspend
the Player for violation of any such rules. When the Player is fined or suspended he shall be given notice in writing stating the amount
of the fine and/or the duration of the suspension and the reason therefor.

19.   The Player agrees ....
play hockey only with the Club, or such other club as provided in Section 2 and Section 11, and ....
to televise the Player as provided in section 8 have all been taken into consideration in determining the salary payable to the Player under
Section 1 hereof.

20.   The Player hereby authorizes and directs the Club to deduct and pay, and the Club hereby agrees to deduct and pay, to the
National Hockey League Pension Society, out of the salary stipulated in Section 1 hereof on behalf of the Player the sum of Nine Hundred Dollars ($900.00) or such lesser proportion thereof as the number of days' service of the Player with the Club under this contract
bears to the number of days of the League Championship Schedule of games, and to obtain from the National Hockey League Pension
Society a proper receipt for such sum in the name of the Player.

21.   It is severally and mutually agreed that the only contracts recognized by the President of the League are the Standard
Player's Contracts which have been duly executed and filed in the League's office and approved by him, and that this Agreement contains
the entire agreement between the Parties and there are no oral or written inducements, promises or agreements except as contained herein.

In Witness Whereof, the parties have signed this   19th   day

of   August   A.D. 19   54

WITNESSES:

MAPLE LEAF GARDENS LIMITED
                                                Club

....   per ....
                                                President

1382 Warden Avenue   ....
Wexford, Ontario.   Player

....
Home Address of Player

Danny Lewicki Is Conn-ed, Sees Reds

In the Original Six era, teams had agreements with organizations in the minor leagues whereby the parent team could stash players, protected as they were, from the other teams. The accompanying contract between the Maple Leafs and Providence Reds of the AHL lays out $2,000 for the rights to have six players on the Reds' roster. The named player is Dean McBride, who only ever got as far as the Leafs training camp and never played in the NHL. But Danny Lewicki was a different story, and he became a successful NHLer for the Leafs, Rangers, and Black Hawks. Lewicki understands how he ended up in Providence—his coach in Fort William, Ontario, Leo Barbini, was a scout for the Reds, but he has often wondered what went down to get him to Toronto. "He and [Leafs scout] Squib Walker must have gotten together somehow and I'm almost certain that he must have gotten paid by Squib. I belonged to Providence as far as the rights were concerned, and then they, in turn, traded me to Toronto." That transaction saw Jackie Hamilton go to Rhode Island with cash, completing the Lewicki deal on October 27, 1948. Getting sent to the minors was normal for the time, where authority was to be respected. Lewicki got sent to Pittsburgh just after he got married and rented a home in Toronto. Conn Smythe told him, "You're not playing well. You're laying in fertile valley too much." When Lewicki returned to the big club, Smythe offered him a home in town as a guarantee that he was in Toronto to stay. "He said, 'Now, can you live on $70 a week?'" recalled Lewicki. "I said, 'I beg your pardon?' He said, 'Well, I bought the house for you. Now you've got to pay me back.'"

Fleming Mackell, Danny Lewicki, and Ray Timgren.

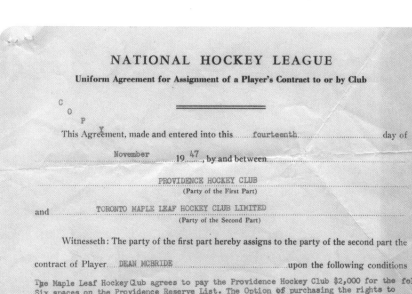

TEL. MARQUETTE 3438

NATIONAL HOCKEY LEAGUE

603 SUN LIFE BUILDING
MONTREAL

PRESIDENT'S OFFICE

June 12th, 1948.

Mr. Vesy note

RECEIVED
JUN 16 1948

Mr. Conn Smythe,
President,
Maple Leaf Gardens Ltd.,
Toronto 2, Ont.

Re: Dan Lewicki - File L-102

Dear Mr. Smythe:

I have your letter of June 10th, with which you enclose copy of the Agreement of November 14th, 1947 made between the Providence Hockey Club and your organization.

I note particularly that one of the considerations expressed in this Agreement is -

"The Option of purchasing the rights to service of Dan Lewicki from the Providence Hockey Club, at a price to be agreed upon by Mr. Pieri and Mr. Smythe."

I have given considerable thought to this matter and, in my opinion, it is not one in which this office could properly intervene.

It is clear that the price shall be mutually agreed upon, and I presume that Mr. Pieri would prefer to do business with your organization but naturally is loath to commit himself prematurely in case Lewicki should turn out to be a star. I cannot see anything in the Option which requires an immediate decision on his part, nor is there any reason why he should not offer Lewicki to other clubs for the purpose of determining a value upon which to place further negotiations with him.

There is nothing in the nature of the transaction which prevents other clubs making a bid for his services, and I think it would be unwise to try to prevent them from doing so.

- 2 -

Mr. Conn Smythe   June 12th, 1948.

As a matter of good faith Pieri will undoubtedly be obliged to give you final opportunity to bid for him, but I think that is the limit of his obligation, and I would not pursue the suggestion made in the final paragraph of your letter.

Yours very truly,

NATIONAL HOCKEY LEAGUE

President

CSC/PK

Barilko: Discovery, Victory, Tragedy

Scout Ernie Orlando first alerted the Leafs to Bill Barilko and his elder brother Alex, who were playing for the Porcupine Combines junior team in northern Ontario. They were "both husky lads," according to Orlando in his July 27, 1945 letter. He said that he encouraged the brothers to consider the Leafs' invitation to go to Tulsa rather than Pittsburgh of the International-American Hockey League. While Alex never made the NHL, getting only to senior-level hockey, he did become an AHL referee. As for Bashin' Bill, he became a key defenceman on the Leafs. "On the eve of his fifth NHL year, the 187-pound six footer could hardly be called a leading scorer—having amassed only 50 points in four years of regular play—but many have been timely slap-shot goals," previewed the *Toronto Star* of the 1950–51 season. Barilko had spent the off-season running his small appliance store in Toronto and hunting and fishing. "Barilko has appointed Turk Broda as his agent to collect television fees among the Leafs. For $1.50 per head, which pays cartage, installation charges, etc., Barilko has agreed to bring over a set from his Toronto store so the players can sit in on some big league ball games," wrote Milt Dunnell. In his final game on April 21, 1951, Barilko scored a "timely" goal on Gerry McNeil of the Montreal Canadiens that won the Leafs the Stanley Cup—his fourth. For his last contract, Barilko made $9,000, with unmet bonuses of $500 for the Second All-Star team and $1,000 for the First. He disappeared that summer, lost in a plane crash in Northern Ontario. His number 5 is one of only two Leafs numbers that have been retired. (The other is number 6 for "Ace" Bailey.)

A team meeting at the Barilko Bros. appliance store in Toronto with Sid Smith, Harry Watson, Bill Barilko, Turk Broda, Jim Thomson, Ray Timgren, and Fleming Mackell.

Toronto, Ontario
August 8th, 1950.

I hereby agree to sign, in duplicate, 1950-51
National Hockey League contract, when available, at
the terms set out in attached 1949-50 form, which I
have today signed.

William Barilko
Bill Barilko

M. McD.
Witness

IMPORTANT NOTICE TO PLAYER

Before signing this contract you should carefully examine it to be sure that all terms and conditions agreed upon have been incorporated herein, and if any has been omitted, you should insist upon having it inserted in the contract before you sign.

NATIONAL HOCKEY LEAGUE
STANDARD PLAYER'S CONTRACT

This Agreement

BETWEEN:

MAPLE LEAF GARDENS LIMITED
hereinafter called the "Club",
a member of the National Hockey League, hereinafter called the "League",

—AND—

WILLIAM BARILKO
hereinafter called the "Player",

Witnesseth:

of TIMMINS in [Province] of ONTARIO

agree as follows:— That in consideration of the respective obligations herein and hereby assumed, the parties to this contract severally

1. The Club hereby employs the Player as a skilled Hockey Player and agrees to pay the Player for the season of 1950-51 "season" meaning the period commencing the date on which the Player reports to the Club at its training camp or other place designated by the Club, and ending on the completion of the Club's games in the National Hockey League Championship Schedule, Play-off and Stanley Cup Series) a salary of

--Nine Thousand Dollars-- Dollars ($9000.00).

If the player B. Barilko makes the Second All Star Team, will receive bonus of $500.00

If the player B. Barilko makes the First N. H. L. All Star team, he will receive a bonus of $1000.00

Payment of such salary shall be in semi-monthly instalments following the commencement of the regular League Championship Schedule of Games or following the date of reporting, whichever is later. Provided, however, that if the Player is not in the employ of the Club for this entire period, then he shall receive such proportion of the salary as the number of days of actual employment bears to the total number of days in the said period.

And it is further mutually agreed that if the contract and the rights to the services of the player are assigned, exchanged, loaned or otherwise transferred to a club in another league, the player shall only be paid at the rate of

---Four Thousand Dollars--- Dollars for the season in the Any Minor League;

or _____ Dollars for the season in the _____ League.

2. The Player agrees to give his services and to play hockey in all League Championship, Exhibition, Play-Off and Stanley Cup games to the best of his ability under the direction and control of the Club for the said season in accordance with the provisions hereof.

The Player further agrees:
(a) to report to the Club training camp at the time and place fixed by the Club, in good physical condition,
(b) to keep himself in good physical condition at all times during the season,
(c) to give his best services and loyalty to the Club and to play hockey only for the Club unless his contract is released, assigned, exchanged or loaned by the Club,
(d) to co-operate with the Club and participate in any and all promotional activities of the Club and the League which will in the opinion of the Club promote the welfare of the Club or professional hockey generally,
(e) to conduct himself on and off the rink according to the highest standards of honesty, morality, fair play and sportsmanship, and to refrain from conduct detrimental to the best interests of the Club, the League or professional hockey generally.

3. In order that the Player shall be fit and in proper condition for the performance of his duties as required by this contract the Player agrees to report to the Club for practice at such time and place as the Club may designate and participate in such exhibition games as may be arranged by the Club within thirty days prior to the first scheduled Championship game. The Club shall pay the travelling expenses and meals en route from the Player's home to the Club's training camp. In the event of failure of the player to so report and participate in exhibition games a fine not exceeding Five Hundred Dollars may be imposed by the Club and be deducted from the compensation stipulated herein.

4. The Club may from time to time during the continuance of this contract establish rules governing the conduct and condition of the Player, and such rules shall form part of this contract as fully as if herein written. For violation of any of such rules or for any conduct impairing the thorough and faithful discharge of the duties incumbent upon the Player, the Club may impose a reasonable fine upon the Player and deduct the amount thereof from any money due or to become due to the Player. The Club may also suspend the Player for violation of any such rules. When the Player is fined or suspended he shall be given notice in writing stating the amount of the fine and/or the duration of the suspension and the reason therefor.

19. The Player agrees that the Club shall have the right to sell, assign, exchange and transfer this contract, and to loan his services to any other professional hockey club, and the Player agrees to accept such assignment and to faithfully perform and carry out this contract with the same purpose and effect as if it had been entered into by the Player with such other Club.

20. The Player hereby authorizes and directs the Club to deduct and pay, and the Club hereby agrees to deduct and pay, to the National Hockey League Pension Society, out of the salary stipulated in Section 1 hereof on behalf of the Player the sum of Nine Hundred Dollars ($900.00) or such lesser proportion thereof as the number of days' service of the Player with the Club under this contract bears to the number of days of the League Championship Schedule of games, and to obtain from the National Hockey League Pension Society a proper receipt for such sum in the name of the Player.

21. It is severally and mutually agreed that the only contracts recognized by the President of the League are the Standard Player's Contracts which have been duly executed and filed in the League's office and approved by him, and that this Agreement contains the entire agreement between the Parties and there are no oral or written inducements, promises or agreements except as contained herein.

In Witness Whereof, the parties have signed this Eighth day

of August A.D. 19 50

WITNESSES:

M. McDonald

M. McDonald

MAPLE LEAF GARDENS LIMITED

By *Conn Smythe* .... President

William Barilko .... Player

63 Sixth Avenue, Timmins, Ontario
Home Address of Player

Giving Up on Barilko

After five years of wondering, the Toronto Maple Leafs gave up on Bill Barilko with a telegram to the NHL offices on December 21, 1956, asking that he be moved to the Voluntary Retired List. Barilko had been missing since August 1951, when he went on a weekend fishing trip with his dentist, Henry Hudson, on Hudson's Fairchild 24 floatplane, from Timmins, Ontario, to Seal River, Quebec. At the time, it was the costliest air search in Canadian history, as aircraft spent two months hunting for the downed plane; more than 150 airmen were involved at an estimated cost of $385,000. "The Long Search Ends—Find Barilko's Plane" trumpeted the *Toronto Star*'s front page of the night edition on June 7, 1962. The plane was only about 75 miles from home when it crashed, its wings sheared off. "The skeletons were strapped in seat belts in the plane, partly submerged in swampy water, and the two men apparently had been killed on impact," reads the story. The Barilko family had erected a tombstone in Timmins in 1960, the stone carved with a head-and-shoulders picture of Barilko in his Leafs uniform. The pilot who found the wreckage, Gary Fields, learned after the discovery that the $10,000 reward put out by Maple Leaf Gardens had expired at the end of 1951.

Bill Barilko is carried by his teammates after the Stanley Cup winning overtime goal on April 21, 1951.

EXCLUSIVE CONNECTION WITH WESTERN UNION CABLE SERVICE

Form 6102 (6-55)

CANADIAN NATIONAL TELEGRAPHS

Canadian National Telegraphs

J. R. WHITE, GENERAL MANAGER
TORONTO

CLASS OF SERVICE DESIRED

FULL RATE

DAY LETTER

NIGHT MESSAGE

NIGHT LETTER

PLACE X OPPOSITE
SERVICE DESIRED

| CHECK | RECEIVERS NO. | TIME FILED | CHARGE TO DEPT. OR ADDRESS |

Send the following message, subject to the terms on back hereof, which are hereby agreed to

Toronto December 21st, 1956.

Central Registry
NHL 603 Sun Life Bldg.
Montreal, Quebec.

Please removed following players from Toronto Voluntarily Retired List:

Apps, Boesch, Wilson, Psutka, Lockhart, Broda, Barilko

C H Day

mlg em8 1641

Teeder's Money Matters

The Teeder Kennedy file is unique, and not just because his 1942–43 rookie contract was the first piece in the Stitt Collection. Stitt also acquired some of Kennedy's tax records after his death at age 83 in 2009. Did you know he made $20 for his radio appearance to plug the Bee Hive hockey picture promotion in March 1943? At the other end of the spectrum, there is the advice from the Johnston, Sheard & Johnston law firm on how the Leafs best deal with the money owing to Teeder upon his planned retirement at the end of the 1955 season—he was originally going to retire in 1954 but came back and, after sitting out a year, he did return in 1956–57 for 30 games, for which he was paid $358.14 per game. "Maple Leaf Gardens agrees to employ Ted Kennedy, and Ted Kennedy agrees, at his own discretion in his spare time, to act as Goodwill Ambassador for Maple Leaf Gardens, for a period of five years commencing the 1955–56 season, at Two Thousand Five Hundred Dollars per year, for a total of $12,500.00," reads a July 20, 1954 contract.

Syl Apps, Ted Kennedy, and George Armstrong at Leafs training camp in St. Catharines, Ontario, in September 1953.

T. S. KENNEDY

	Salary M.L.G	Bonuses M.L.G	Bonuses N.H.L.	Playoff split	Total
from March 3/43	1,000.	1,000. signing	–	–	2,000.
	3,500.	750.	–	633.33	4,883.33
	4,500.	1,750.	–	1,700.	7,950.
	5,000.	–	–	–	5,000.
	6,000.	–	–	2,500.	8,500.
	7,000.	1,000. Asst. Cap 2,000. spec.	–	3,000.	13,000.
	8,000.	1,000. Capt.	–	2,150.	11,150.
	10,000.	2,000. Capt. 1,000. spec	500.	850.	14,350.
	12,000.	500. 2nd All Star 1,500. spec.	250.	2,500.	16,750.
	14,000.	1,000. signing	–	850.	15,850.
	14,000.	–	–	–	14,000.
	15,000.	1,000. signing	500.	850.	17,350.
	100,000.	14500.	1250.	15,033.33	130,783.33

T. S. KENNEDY

Season	Salary M.L.G	Bonuses M.L.G	Bonuses N.H.L.
1942-43 from March 3/43	1,000.	1,000. signing	–
1943-44	3,500.	750.	–
1944-45	4,500.	1,750.	–
1945-46	5,000.	–	–
1946-47	6,000.	–	–
1947-48	7,000.	1,000. Asst. Cap 2,000. spec.	–
1948-49	8,000.	1,000. Capt.	–
1949-50	10,000.	2,000. Capt. 1,000. spec	500.
1950-51	12,000.	500. 2nd All Star 1,500. spec.	250.
1951-52	14,000.	1,000. signing	–
1952-53	14,000.	–	–
1953-54	15,000.	1,000. signing	500.
	100,000.	14500.	1250.

NHL President Clarence Campbell and the guest of honour on Ted Kennedy Night on October 8, 1955, at Maple Leaf Gardens.

Teeder Kennedy's Long Goodbye

When Teeder Kennedy retired, GM Hap Day turned on the charm in attempt to get him to come back: *Come on, Teeder!* King Clancy followed up with Teeder at Day's behest, and a secretary recorded the reply on June 8, 1955: "Mr. Clancy called this morning. He asked me to tell you that 'he talked to Kennedy as you requested, and Kennedy stated definitely that he was finished and that he positively would not give it another try.'" In August 1957, Kennedy returned his application to the Voluntary Retired list—his final retirement. Details of his pension with the National Hockey League are spelled out, as well as the lump-sum cheque of $7,632.32 in March 2006 ($11,224.00 before taxes) that came about as a result of Carl Brewer's lawsuit with the National Hockey League Pension Society. After hockey, Kennedy coached the juniors in Peterborough briefly, worked for a trucking company, had a stable in St. Mary's, Ontario for thoroughbred horses, and was director of security at the Fort Erie racetrack. His #9 hangs in the Air Canada Centre alongside *his* hero's #10. "To share that honour with Syl Apps, a superb player and perfect gentleman, was a great moment," Kennedy told the *Toronto Star*'s Frank Orr. "When I replaced him as captain in '48, it was the proudest moment of my life."

```
                                              June 8/55. 9:50 a.m.

Mr. Day:

        Mr. Clancy called this morning.  He asked me to tell you that
"he talked to Kennedy as you requested, and Kennedy stated definitely that
he was finished and that he positively would not give it another try".

        Mr. Clancy said he would be back in Toronto in the near future
and would be in touch with you, or will drop you a note.

                                              dl
```

March 31st, 1955.

Mr. Ted Kennedy,
R. R. #2,
Westhill, Ontario.

Dear Teeder:

As you know, I am not a very demonstrative individual. However, I do feel impelled to write you and try to express my unbounded admiration and appreciation for the wonderful service you have always given the Leafs.

My indoctrination as a Leaf now extends 28 years and I am very proud of those years. In that time, Teeder, there has been no one who has given to our team, beyond the call of duty, like you have. I am sorry and regret more than I can say, that I could not have made your retirement a more significant and successful one by giving you the type of players to captain who could have won the Cup for you, as you have done for us so many times.

When I look back at all the effort you have given me and the team, I feel most conscienceless in the part I played in extracting the last drop of blood. I can only say that with me too, the team always came first.

For everything you have done on behalf of the team and me, I can only say a most sincere thank you. Your exploits are among my most prized memories, and in my book, have put you at the top of the Honour Roll of all great Leafs.

Thanks again and believe me to be most grateful and,

Sincerely yours,

C. H. Day.

CHD/dl

July 20, 1954.

MEMORANDUM OF AGREEMENT between

TED KENNEDY

and

MAPLE LEAF GARDENS LIMITED

Maple Leaf Gardens agrees to employ Ted Kennedy, and Ted Kennedy agrees, at his own discretion in his spare time, to act as Goodwill Ambassador for Maple Leaf Gardens, for a period of five years commencing the 1955-56 season, at Two Thousand Five Hundred Dollars per year, for a total of $12,500.00

MAPLE LEAF GARDENS, LIMITED.

_____

Theodore Kennedy
Ted Kennedy.

Bob Nevin and Dick Duff
after the 1962 Stanley Cup
win in Chicago.

Dick Duff's First Payday

Dick Duff's rookie contract, from 1956–57, came *after* he made his NHL debut with the Leafs. According to the rules of the time, a player could get into three games without losing his amateur status. Duff was skating with the St. Michael's Majors when he got the call at the end of the 1955–56 season. "Before I signed pro, I played three games in the NHL in Montreal, New York, and Detroit," recalled Duff, a Hall of Fame left winger. "They were in the process of trying to get me to sign. Then they asked me to stay, but I couldn't play in the playoffs because I wasn't signed." Instead, he hung around the club, which lost in the semi-final against Detroit, and signed on for the next season. Duff was retroactively paid $100 per game from the previous year. That initial contract was signed with GM Hap Day, who asked Duff if he wanted to seek out his father's thoughts on the deal. "I said, 'No. I don't know very much about it, but my father's not very informed about what you people do.' That's the advantage that they had; it was their business and their business to present the contract however they wanted to do it," said Duff. "They had the upper hand, so all the conversation didn't really matter, did it? Because it's going to end up being what they want it to be. Simple as that. We had an alternative—we could say, 'We're not playing anymore.'"

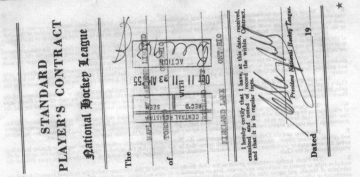

STANDARD PLAYER'S CONTRACT

National Hockey League

The ....

MAPLE LEAF GARDENS LIMITED

of ....

KIRKLAND LAKE, ONT. H.O.

RECD .... WITH .... Oct 11 '33 AM 55 .... SEEN

CENTRAL REGISTRY

ACTION

I hereby certify that I have, at this date, received, examined and noted of record the within Contract, and that it is in regular form.

.... President National Hockey League.

Dated .... 19 ....

<u>IMPORTANT NOTICE TO PLAYER</u>

Before signing this contract you should carefully examine it to be sure that all terms and conditions agreed upon have been incorporated herein, and if any has been omitted, you should insist upon having it inserted in the contract before you sign.

NATIONAL HOCKEY LEAGUE

STANDARD PLAYER'S CONTRACT

This Agreement

BETWEEN: MAPLE LEAF GARDENS LIMITED

hereinafter called the "Club".

a member of the National Hockey League, hereinafter called the "League".

— AND —

RICHARD DUFF

hereinafter called the "Player".

of   KIRKLAND LAKE   in (Province) of   ONTARIO (State)

Witnesseth:

That in consideration of the respective obligations herein and hereby assumed, the parties to this contract severally agree as follows:—

1. The Club hereby employs the Player as a skilled Hockey Player for the term of one two year commencing October 1st, 19 55 and agrees, subject to the terms and conditions hereof, to pay the Player a salary of

Seven Thousand Dollars=== .... Dollars (\$ 7000.00)

-1955-55 ===Seven Thousand Dollars===

- 1956-57--- Seven Thousand Dollars ---(\$7000.00) or \$8000.00 if recommended by Coach King Clancy.

Player Dick Duff has received the sum of Four Thousand Dollars (\$4000.00) for signing this contract.

1954-55 Season - Player Duff to receive One Hundred Dollars (\$100.00) for each game played.

Payment of such salary shall be in consecutive semi-monthly instalments following the commencement of the regular League Championship Schedule of games or following the date of reporting, whichever is later; provided, however, that if the Player is not in the employ of the Club for the whole period of the Club's games in the National Hockey League Championship Schedule, then he shall receive only part of the said salary in the ratio of the number of days of actual employment to the number of days of the League Championship Schedule of games.

And it is further mutually agreed that if the Contract and rights to the services of the Player are assigned, exchanged, loaned or otherwise transferred to a Club in another League, the Player shall only be paid at the rate of

.... Dollars in the .... League.

or.................................... Dollars in the .... League.

or.................................... Dollars in the .... League.

2. The Player agrees to give his services and to play hockey in all League Championship, Exhibition, Play-Off and Stanley Cup games to the best of his ability under the direction and control of the Club for the said season in accordance with the provisions hereof.

The Player further agrees:

(a) to report to the Club training camp at the time and place fixed by the Club, in good physical condition,

(b) to keep himself in good physical condition at all times during the season,

(c) to give his best services and loyalty to the Club and to play hockey only for the Club unless his contract is released, assigned, exchanged or loaned by the Club,

(d) to co-operate with the Club and participate in any and all promotional activities of the Club and the League which will in the opinion of the Club promote the welfare of the Club or professional hockey generally,

(e) to conduct himself on and off the rink according to the highest standards of honesty, morality, fair play and sportsmanship, and to refrain from conduct detrimental to the best interests of the Club, the League or professional hockey generally.

3. In order that the Player shall be fit and in proper condition for the performance of his duties as required by this contract the Player agrees to report for practice at such time and place as the Club may designate and participate in such exhibition games as may be arranged by the Club within thirty days prior to the first scheduled Championship game. The Club shall pay the travelling expenses and meals en route from the Player's home to the Club's training camp. In the event of failure of the player to so report and participate in exhibition games a fine not exceeding Five Hundred Dollars may be imposed by the Club and be deducted from the compensation stipulated herein.

4. The Club may from time to time during the continuance of this contract establish rules governing the conduct and conditioning of the Player, and such rules shall form part of this contract as fully as if herein written. For violation of any of such rules or for any conduct impairing the thorough and faithful discharge of the duties incumbent upon the Player, the Club may impose a reasonable fine upon the Player and deduct the amount thereof from any money due or to become due to the Player. The Club may also suspend the Player for violation of any such rules. When the Player is fined or suspended he shall be given notice in writing stating the amount of the fine and/or the duration of the suspension and the reason therefor.

21. It is severally and mutually agreed that the only contracts recognized by the President of the League are the Standard Player's Contracts which have been duly executed and filed in the League's office and approved by him, and that this Agreement contains the entire agreement between the Parties and there are no oral or written inducements, promises or agreements except as contained herein.

In Witness Whereof, the parties have signed this .... Twelfth .... day

of .... March .... A.D. 19 55

WITNESSES:

MAPLE LEAF GARDENS LIMITED

....   Club

........Sheslew........   By for C A Hay

President

Richard Terrance Duff

Player

........Sheslew........   124 Taylor Avenue, Kirkland Lake, Ont.

Home Address of Player

St. Michael's Majors Pat
Hannigan, Frank Howarth,
and Frank Mahovlich.

Mahovlich's Demands

The Frank Mahovlich file clearly shows he's in a different category than many others. His father, Pete, was heavily involved in negotiations, and his uncle, Mike Butcher, acted as his agent in Toronto. From the get-go, when Frank agreed to leave Timmins, Ontario, to attend St. Michael's College, he was specific in his demands: $10 a week for spending money; $10 a week to the bank; and $10 a week to his father. The family requested that Frank's education be guaranteed in case of injury. His pro contract, signed February 18, 1956, called for $6,000 if he stayed with the big league squad; notable is a rider where Butcher received $1,000 for scouting as well. By the time the deals for the 1957–58 season were being signed, the Mahovlichs were asking for much more—but would settle for $10,000 in each of the following two seasons, and a $2,000 signing bonus. Things weren't all that different for Mahovlich in Detroit. In his 1969–70 and 1970–71 contracts, he got $45,000 a season, and a slew of bonuses were spelled out, including "$150 for each goal scored from 26 to 35; $2,000.00 if the player scores 36 goals; $200.00 per goal from 37 to 41; $2,500.00 if the player scores 42 goals; $250.00 for each goal from 42 to 50 and $5,000.00 for 50 goals; $300.00 for each goal scored over 50." (He would net 38 with Detroit the first year of the deal, and 14 and 17 split between Detroit and Montreal the following season.)

OPTION AGREEMENT "C"

(Form "C")

DATE....February 18th, 1956.

**MEMORANDUM
OF AGREEMENT
BETWEEN:**

FRANK MAHOVLICH

hereinafter called the "Player"

—and—

MAPLE LEAF GARDENS LIMITED

hereinafter called the "Club"

In consideration of the sum of................One Hundred Dollars................Dollars ($100.00) which the Player acknowledges he has received from the Club, the Player covenants and agrees with the Club that he will, upon request of the Club made within one year from the date hereof, sign a contract with the Club to serve the Club as a hockey player for a period of .... year(s), subject to the terms and conditions set out in the Standard Player's Contract (a copy of which has been shown to and examined by the Player), and for the following remuneration payable to the Player by the Club:

One Thousand Dollars................Dollars ($1000.00)

payable forthwith upon the signing of a
Standard Player's Contract,

—and— Thirty-five Hundred Dollars................Dollars ($3500.00)

per hockey season if the player is assigned
by the Club to play for a club in the
~~Pacific Coast Hockey League,~~ Quebec Hockey League

—or— Thirty-five Hundred Dollars................Dollars ($3500.00)

per hockey season if the player is assigned
by the Club to play for a club in the
~~United States Hockey League,~~ Western Hockey League

—or— Four Thousand Dollars................Dollars ($4000.00)

per hockey season if the player is assigned
by the Club to play for a club in the
American Hockey League,

—or— Six Thousand Dollars................Dollars ($6000.00)

per hockey season if the player is assigned
by the Club to play for a club in the
National Hockey League.

ALL such payments, excepting the................One Thousand Dollars................ payable for signing the contract, shall be pro rated according to the proportion of the hockey season for which the Player is employed in each of such Leagues.

The Player further agrees that he will present himself at the Club's training camp at the Club's expense (hotel, meals and railway fare) whenever requested to do so by the Club during the currency of this Agreement, or extension thereof, for the purpose of demonstrating his skill and ability as a hockey player.

During the currency of this Agreement or extension thereof, the Player covenants and agrees that he will play hockey only for such hockey team as may be designated by the Club.

(TURN OVER)

OPTION AGREEMENT "C" (continued)

...all have the right to sell, exchange, assign or other-
...ights to the Player's services to any professional
...accept and be bound by such sale, exchange, assign-
...rform and carry out the terms of the Agreement
...d been entered into by the Player and the assignee

...further periods of one year each upon payment to
...Player by the Club before the expiration of this Agreement or any extension thereof
the sum of....One Hundred Dollars....Dollars ($100.00) for each such
extension.

DATED AT....Toronto, Ontario....this....18th....day of....February....19 56

WITNESS: _M. Britker_

PLAYER: _Frank Mahovlich_

32 A Forth Ave
ADDRESS

Schumacher, Ontario
CITY   PROVINCE OR STATE

WITNESS: _R. E. Davidson_

CLUB: Maple Leaf Gardens, Limited.

PER _C H Day_

FOR PLAYER ONLY

NAME IN FULL....._Frank Mahovlich_

PLACE OF BIRTH....._Timmins_

DAY _10_ MONTH _Jan._ YEAR _1938_

HEIGHT _6 ft_ WEIGHT _195 lb_

POSITION...._left wing_ SHOOTS _L_
(R or L)

FORM "C"

Stanley-Morrison Trade Leads to Four Stanley Cups

When Allan Stanley died in October 2013, Jim Morrison found himself reminiscing. The two defencemen were traded for each other in October 1958, with Stanley going to Toronto and Morrison to Boston. "I was the guy involved in him coming to Toronto, and he ended up winning all those Cups. So he did all right," said Morrison, comparing Stanley's four Cups to his own zero. Stanley is in the Hockey Hall of Fame—and Morrison in the AHL Hockey Hall of Fame. Punch Imlach wrote in his book, *Hockey Is a Battle*, that the Leafs also got $7,500, and he praised Stanley as "as honest and dependable a hockey player as a coach could hope for—half of one of the best defence pairs in the years when we were going big: Stanley and Horton." The trade was one of Imlach's first roster moves as GM. "I knew that when Imlach came to the Leafs that I was in trouble because we had a history of conflicts back a few years earlier," said Morrison. Imlach had tried to sign Morrison to the Quebec Aces in the Quebec Senior Hockey League. "We had quite a few meetings and he offered me a pretty good deal, but I just decided that I didn't want to play there. Long story short, he always held that against me, plus a couple of other things that happened along the way." The deal would begin Morrison's second tour of duty in Boston, the team that originally signed him to an NHL deal; he had ended up in Toronto in a trade for Fleming Mackell.

Jim Morrison.

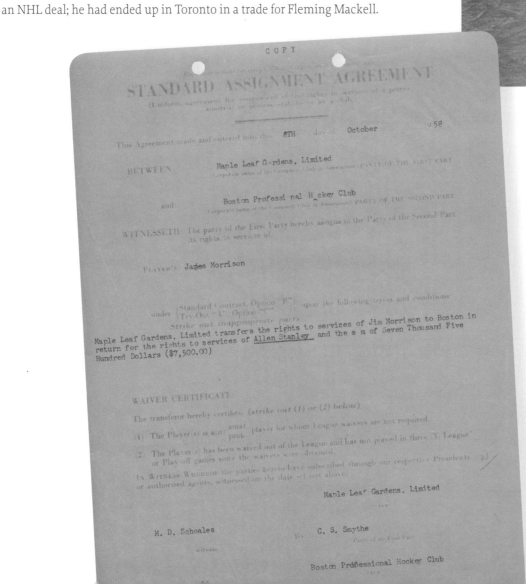

1958 - 1959

STANDARD PLAYER'S CONTRACT

National Hockey League

The .... Maple Leaf Gardens, Limited .... of .... Toronto, Ontario, ... WITH .... Allen Stanley .... Timmins, Ontario.

I hereby certify that I have, at this date, received, examined and noted of record the within Contract, and that it is in regular form.

....
President National Hockey League.

Dated .... 19......

Amended Form – June 1958

IMPORTANT NOTICE TO PLAYER

Before signing this contract you should carefully examine it to be sure that all terms and conditions agreed upon have been incorporated herein, and if any has been omitted, you should insist upon having it inserted in the contract before you sign.

NATIONAL HOCKEY LEAGUE
STANDARD PLAYER'S CONTRACT

This Agreement

BETWEEN: .... Maple Leaf Gardens, Limited ....
hereinafter called the "Club",
a member of the National Hockey League, hereinafter called the "League".

—AND— .... Allen Stanley ....
hereinafter called the "Player".

of .... Timmins .... in {Province/State} of .... Ontario

Witnesseth:

That in consideration of the respective obligations herein and hereby assumed, the parties to this contract severally agree as follows:—

1.   The Club hereby employs the Player as a skilled Hockey Player for the term of one year commencing October 1st, 19 58 and agrees, subject to the terms and conditions hereof, to pay the Player a salary of

– – – – Ten Thousand Dollars – 00/100 Dollars ($ 10,000.00)

Should the player finish the season with Toronto Maple Leafs, he will be paid following bonuses:

1. $1,000. if the Club finishes 1st, 2nd or 3rd in final standing, provided we are within 5 points of second place.
2. $500.00 if Club in finals of Stanley Cup play-offs
3. $1,000. if Club wins Stanley Cup.

Payment of such salary shall be in consecutive semi-monthly instalments following the commencement of the regular League Championship Schedule of games or following the date of reporting, whichever is later; provided, however, that if the Player is not in the employ of the Club for the whole period of the Club's games in the National Hockey League Championship Schedule, then he shall receive only part of the salary in the ratio of the number of days of actual employment to the number of days of the League Championship Schedule of games.

And it is further mutually agreed that if the Contract and rights to the services of the Player are assigned, exchanged, loaned or otherwise transferred to a Club in another League, the Player shall only be paid at the rate of

– Eight Thousand Five Hundred Dollars – ($8,500.00) – – .... Dollars in the .... American .... League.
or .... Dollars in the .... League.
or .... Dollars in the .... League.

2.   The Player agrees to give his services and to play hockey in all League Championship, Exhibition, Play-Off and Stanley Cup games to the best of his ability under the direction and control of the Club for the said season in accordance with the provisions hereof.
The Player further agrees,
    (a) to report to the Club training camp at the time and place fixed by the Club,
    (b) to keep himself in good physical condition at all times during the season, in good physical condition,
    (c) to give his best services and loyalty to the Club and to play hockey only for the Club unless his contract is released, assigned, exchanged or loaned by the Club,
    (d) to co-operate with the Club and participate in any and all promotional activities of the Club or professional hockey generally,
    (e) to conduct himself on and off the rink according to the highest standards of honesty, morality, fair play and sportsmanship, the opinion of the Club promote the welfare of the Club and the League which will in and to refrain from conduct detrimental to the best interests of the Club, the League or professional hockey generally.
The Club agrees that in exhibition games played after the start of the regular schedule (except where the proceeds are to go to charity, or where the player has agreed otherwise) the player shall receive his pro rata share of the gate receipts after deduction of legitimate expenses of such game.

3.   In order that the Player shall be fit and in proper condition for the performance of his duties as required by this contract the Player agrees to report for practice at such time and place as the Club may designate and participate in such exhibition games as may be arranged by the Club within thirty days prior to the first scheduled Championship game. The Club shall pay the travelling expenses and meals en route from the Player's home to the Club's training camp. In the event of failure of the player to so report and participate in exhibition games a fine not exceeding Five Hundred Dollars may be imposed by the Club and be deducted from the compensation stipulated herein. At the conclusion of the season the Club shall provide transportation direct to the Player's home.

4.   The Club may from time to time during the continuance of this contract establish rules governing the conduct and conditioning of the Player, and such rules shall form part of this contract as fully as if herein written. For violation of any such rules or for any conduct impairing the thorough and faithful discharge of the duties incumbent upon the Player, the Club may impose a reasonable fine upon the Player and deduct the amount thereof from any money due or to become due to the Player. The Club may also suspend the Player for violation of any such rules. When the Player is fined or suspended he shall be given notice in writing stating the amount of the fine and/or the duration of the suspension and the reason therefor.

In Witness Whereof, the parties have signed this .... day
of .... October .... A.D. 19 58

WITNESSES:

....   Maple Leaf Gardens, Limited
                                                           Club

....   By .... for MLG .... President

                                              Allan Stanley .... Player

231 Toke St., Timmins, Ontario.
Home Address of Player

An Exhibition Lineup

Need to jot down some salary figures? Grab a piece of scrap paper. On the back of some notes that Punch Imlach made before Ron Stewart signed his 1959–60 contract ($12,500, plus three different bonus clauses amounting to $750), there's a mock lineup dated September 23, 1959, with notations in Punch Imlach's handwriting. It's fun to consider the thought process that may or may not have gone into preseason tilt in Peterborough, Ontario, against the AHL's Cleveland Barons. Larry Regan, who arrived partway through the previous season from Boston, gets an okay. Pat Hannigan, a left winger, was scratched and replaced by Ted Hampson, a centre; and Marc Reaume got into the game on defence at the expense of Noel Price, who would be shipped to the New York Rangers on October 3. And Price's name is listed right above Dr. Murray—is that why he sat out? Though the Leafs won 5–3, Imlach snarled afterward, "They played like minor leaguers and should get paid like minor leaguers."

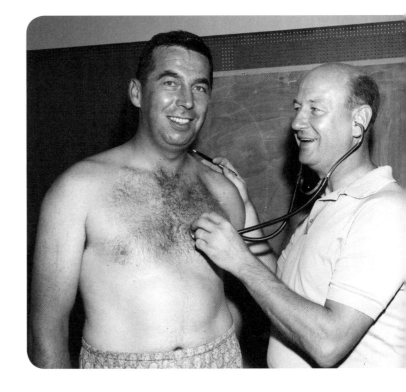

Punch Imlach plays doctor and examines Ron Stewart.

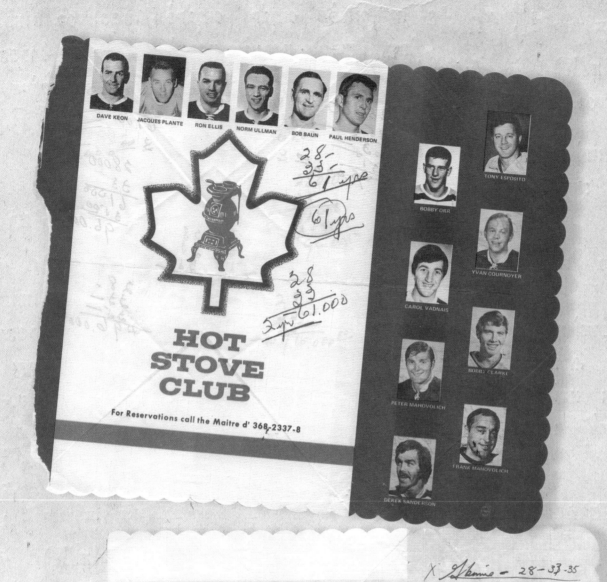

HOT
STOVE
CLUB

For Reservations call the Maitre d' 368-2337-8

DAVE KEON   JACQUES PLANTE   RON ELLIS   NORM ULLMAN   BOB BAUN   PAUL HENDERSON

BOBBY ORR   TONY ESPOSITO

CAROL VADNAIS   YVAN COURNOYER

PETER MAHOVOLICH   BOBBY CLARKE

DEREK SANDERSON   FRANK MAHOVOLICH

28 -
33 -
61 yrs

61 yrs

28
33
2 yr 61.000

X Stemie — 28 - 33 - 35
Siller — 28 plus 2
Polyk — 28 500
X Ellis — 100 - 2 yr
X Henderson — 110 2 yr
X Ullman — 75⁰⁰ 2y 100
X McKenny — 37⁵⁰ 42⁵
             37 - 45

Teg 5.500
Cheap. 31.000⁰⁰

f. 20000
28000

CHAPTER 4

THE 1960s

Frank Mahovlich
and Punch Imlach.

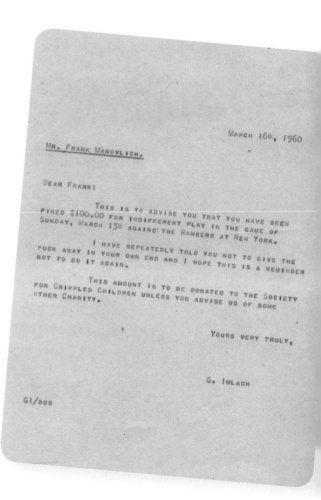

Mahovlich Gets Punched

Coach Punch Imlach fined Frank Mahovlich for an error during a game on Sunday, March 13, 1960, a 2–2 tie with the last-place Rangers, in which Mahovlich had scored the team's opening marker. According to Al Nickelson of the *Globe and Mail*, the Leafs "were guilty of a lack of finish, erratic shooting, and poor passing. They lacked cohesion and at least a couple appeared short on try." It was the second game in two nights between the Leafs and Rangers, following a 4–1 NY win at Maple Leaf Gardens. Mahlovich was fined $100 for "indifferent play." The tie guaranteed the Leafs second place in the NHL playoffs, and they downed the Red Wings in six games. However, in the finals the Leafs were swept in four by the Montreal Canadiens, who claimed the last of five-straight Cups. In *Hockey Is a Battle*, Imlach explained his attempts at motivating The Big M: "Very seldom would I go into a dressing room and tell off one player, once or twice a year at the most. Only twice can I remember really blasting Mahovlich in front of everybody. Once was later, in the spring of 1967, and another time was in Detroit in the playoffs in 1964, when he'd given away the puck for Detroit's winning goal. I used to talk team effort. Maybe I'd swear like hell at all of them, but there wasn't one who hadn't been told at one time or another that swearing was just my way of saying what I had to say. I told them: 'If I swear at you, if I call you a stupid son-of-a-bitch some time, take it as a term of endearment. That's the way it's meant to be taken.'"

Coach Punch Imlach directs his players from the bench.

115

Imlach Defends Horton

On January 18, 1961, the New York Rangers came to Maple Leaf Gardens for a game and ended up in a war. A fight broke out between Bert Olmstead and Lou Fontinato, and Horton left the bench to help his teammate, leading to a bench-clearing brawl. In a letter dated January 25, 1961, President Campbell threatened Horton with a suspension over and above the fine. While GM Imlach may have been a tough cookie in negotiations, he believed in team spirit and stood up for Horton—and the Leafs paid the $25 fine. Campbell responded to Imlach's letter on February 8, 1961: "I have no intentions of interfering with your efforts as the person responsible to instil spirit into your players and certainly do not consider that disciplinary action for obvious violation of the playing rules constitutes any such interference." At the end of the season, Imlach okayed a $100 bonus for Horton "for play above and beyond the call of duty."

Tim Horton gets some advice from King Clancy.

FEBRUARY 1, 1961

Mr. C.S. Campbell,
National Hockey League,
601 Sun Life Bldg.,
Montreal, Quebec.

Dear Mr. Campbell:

   I received a copy of the letter that you have addressed to Tim Horton. I am indeed surprised that you have even entertained the idea that further action should be taken against this player. I would like to know what you would expect him to do.

   I am trying to instill spirit, both team and competitive, in our players and you are apparently trying to work in the opposite direction. I do not mind you fining me but I certainly am not in harmony with the idea of any action against my players.

   I also object to the fact that you state that Horton is responsible for all the other players leaving the bench and entering the altercation. My players are not sheep and they certainly do not follow one another around. They have minds of their own and I try to develop this individuality so that in any given circumstance they can think for themselves. If you feel that Horton was responsible for the fracas, why should the rest of the players be fined at all?

   I think this instance has been blown up out of all proportion. After all it is one of the many things that happens in, and is part of a hockey game.

   Hoping that after you receive Horton's reply, no further action will be taken.

                    Yours very truly,

                                   George Imlach.

cc: Carl Voss.

GI/BDS

FEB 10 1961 RECD

NATIONAL HOCKEY LEAGUE

601 SUN LIFE BUILDING
MONTREAL 2

PRESIDENT'S OFFICE

February 8, 1961.

Horton fine of $25.00
take off pay

Mr. George Imlach,
Maple Leaf Gardens Limited,
Toronto 2, Ontario.

Re: Game - New York Rangers vs.
Toronto Maple Leafs at
Toronto, January 18th
_____

Dear Mr. Imlach:

I have for acknowledgment your letter of February
1st commenting on the contents of my letter to Horton, reference
the above incident, and I have noted your observations concerning
our respective responsibilities.

I have no intention of interfering with your
efforts as the person responsible to instill spirit into your players
and certainly I do not consider that disciplinary action for obvious
violation of the playing rules constitutes any such interference.
It is my responsibility to see that the provisions of the playing
rules are enforced and I have been fixed with that responsibility
specifically in cases of this kind and to my mind the provisions
of Rule 66(b) are designed to take care of cases of this precise
character.

I do not want to quibble either about the use of
the word "responsible" and I would be the last to suggest that
your players are "sheep" or anything of a kindred nature. In
stating that Horton's conduct was, in this case, "largely
responsible for the incidents which subsequently transpired," I
was simply referring to a chain of causation.

Horton was the first person who violated the
rule on that occasion and for quite a substantial period of time
he was the only person who violated it and he was quite
extensively involved in it. Apart from his intervention, the
teams were at even strength on the ice and, having chosen to
intervene in this fashion, he thereby subjects himself to the
full penalties provided in the Section.

- 2 -

February 8, 1961.

I enclose herewith a copy of my letter to Horton
imposing a fine of $25 in which I have advised him of the
authorization to deduct it from his salary. I will appreciate
your usual compliance.

Yours very truly,

NATIONAL HOCKEY LEAGUE

President

CSC:t

Encl.

The Education of Al Arbour

By October 1962, Sudbury, Ontario's Alger Arbour had played hockey for minor-league teams in Detroit, Windsor, Washington, Edmonton, Sherbrooke, and Quebec City, as well as in the NHL in Detroit, Chicago, and Toronto. The transfer to the AHL's Rochester Americans, though, marked both a new destination and a new league for the bespectacled defenceman. "It was a very good league at that time," Arbour said of the AHL. On a two-way contract, he spent a lot of time in Rochester from 1962 to 1967, with only sporadic duty with the Leafs. Some of his bonuses in Rochester for 1965–66 and1966–67: $1,500 assistant coach, playoffs $500, first place $500, semi-finals $500, win Calder Cup $1,000. The Amerks won the Calder Cup as AHL champs in both 1965 and 1966. For Arbour, who was team captain, a four-time All-Star, and named the AHL's best defenceman in 1965, the time apprenticing under coach Joe Crozier was invaluable. It also helped propel him on his way to the Hockey Hall of Fame in the Builder category and earned him four Stanley Cups coaching the New York Islanders. "I learned a lot from Joe Crozier, how to handle the players, and everything else," said Arbour. "I spent a lot of time in Rochester."

Al Arbour in Rochester.

LOAN AGREEMENT
Uniform Agreement for Loan of Players' Services to or by Club

This agreement, made and entered into this ....6th......

day of ....October...............1962....

BETWEEN :

..................MAPLE LEAF GARDENS, LIMITED..................
Party of the First Part
— and —
..................ROCHESTER AMERICANS HOCKEY CLUB..................
Party of the Second Part.

Witnesseth : The Party of the First Part hereby loans to the Party of the Second Part the services of Player ....ALGER ARBOUR...............
upon the following conditions : —
   (a) Subject to immediate recall;
   (b) For a period of .... days from the date hereof;
   (c) Special terms (salary, etc.) :

(STRIKE OUT INAPPROPRIATE CLAUSES)

In witness whereof the parties hereto have, by their duly authorized agents, subscribed hereunder

WITNESS :

..................MAPLE LEAF GARDENS, LIMITED..................
CLUB   (Party of the First Part)
By.......................................
(Signature)

..................ROCHESTER AMERICANS HOCKEY CLUB.................
CLUB   (Party of the Second Part)
By.......................................
(Signature)

The Corporate name of the Company, Club or Association of each party should be written in the first paragraph and should be signed by an authorized officer of each Party at the bottom.

NEW AGREEMENT SHOULD BE MADE FOR EACH LOAN PERIOD

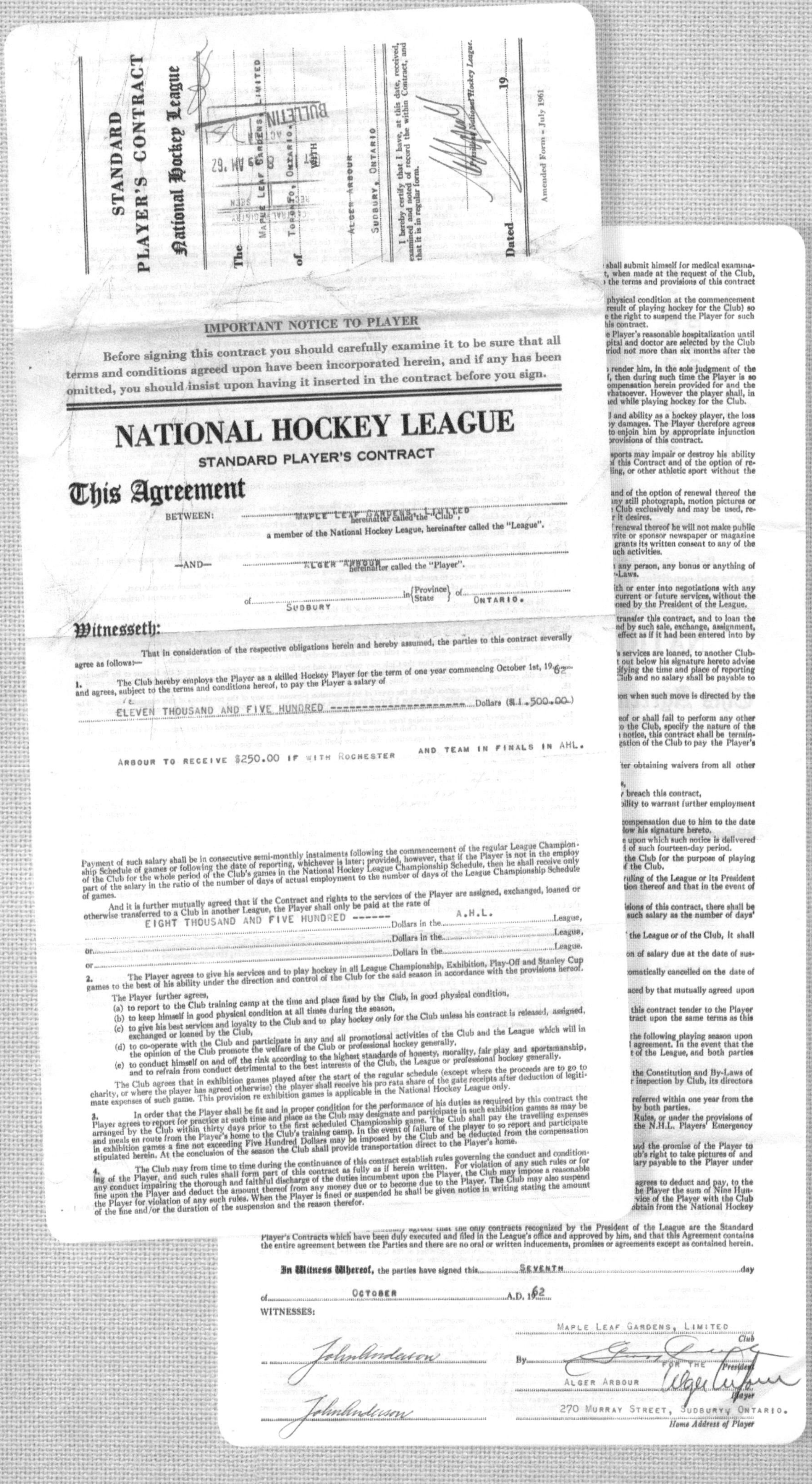

IMPORTANT NOTICE TO PLAYER

Before signing this contract you should carefully examine it to be sure that all terms and conditions agreed upon have been incorporated herein, and if any has been omitted, you should insist upon having it inserted in the contract before you sign.

NATIONAL HOCKEY LEAGUE
STANDARD PLAYER'S CONTRACT

This Agreement

BETWEEN: .... MAPLE LEAF GARDENS, LIMITED ....
hereinafter called the "Club",

a member of the National Hockey League, hereinafter called the "League".

—AND— .... ALGER ARBOUR ....
hereinafter called the "Player".

of .... SUDBURY .... in (Province) (State) of .... ONTARIO. ....

Witnesseth:

That in consideration of the respective obligations herein and hereby assumed, the parties to this contract severally agree as follows:—

1.   The Club hereby employs the Player as a skilled Hockey Player for the term of one year commencing October 1st, 19 62 and agrees, subject to the terms and conditions hereof, to pay the Player a salary of

ELEVEN THOUSAND AND FIVE HUNDRED .... Dollars ($ 11,500.00)

ARBOUR TO RECEIVE $250.00 IF WITH ROCHESTER AND TEAM IN FINALS IN AHL.

Payment of such salary shall be in consecutive semi-monthly instalments following the commencement of the regular League Championship Schedule of games or following the date of reporting, whichever is later; provided, however, that if the Player is not in the employ of the Club for the whole period of the Club's games in the National Hockey League Championship Schedule, then he shall receive only part of the salary in the ratio of the number of days of actual employment to the number of days of the League Championship Schedule of games.

And it is further mutually agreed that if the Contract and rights to the services of the Player are assigned, exchanged, loaned or otherwise transferred to a Club in another League, the Player shall only be paid at the rate of   A.H.L.

EIGHT THOUSAND AND FIVE HUNDRED .... Dollars in the .... League,

.... Dollars in the .... League,

or .... Dollars in the .... League.

or

2.   The Player agrees to give his services and to play hockey in all League Championship, Exhibition, Play-Off and Stanley Cup games to the best of his ability under the direction and control of the Club for the said season in accordance with the provisions hereof.

The Player further agrees,

(a) to report to the Club training camp at the time and place fixed by the Club, in good physical condition,

(b) to keep himself in good physical condition at all times during the season,

(c) to give his best services and loyalty to the Club and to play hockey only for the Club unless his contract is released, assigned, exchanged or loaned by the Club,

(d) to co-operate with the Club and participate in any and all promotional activities of the Club and the League which will in the opinion of the Club promote the welfare of the Club or professional hockey generally,

(e) to conduct himself on and off the rink according to the highest standards of honesty, morality, fair play and sportsmanship, and to refrain from conduct detrimental to the best interests of the Club, the League or professional hockey generally.

The Club agrees that in exhibition games played after the start of the regular schedule (except where the proceeds are to go to charity, or where the player has agreed otherwise) the player shall receive his pro rata share of the gate receipts after deduction of legitimate expenses of such game. This provision re exhibition games is applicable in the National Hockey League only.

3.   In order that the Player shall be fit and in proper condition for the performance of his duties as required by this contract the Player agrees to report for practice at such time and place as the Club may designate and participate in such exhibition games as may be arranged by the Club within thirty days prior to the first scheduled Championship game. The Club shall pay the travelling expenses and meals en route from the Player's home to the Club's training camp. In the event of failure of the player to so report and participate in exhibition games a fine not exceeding Five Hundred Dollars may be imposed by the Club and be deducted from the compensation stipulated herein. At the conclusion of the season the Club shall provide transportation direct to the Player's home.

4.   The Club may from time to time during the continuance of this contract establish rules governing the conduct and condition of the Player, and such rules shall form part of this contract as fully as if herein written. For violation of any such rules or for any conduct impairing the thorough and faithful discharge of the duties incumbent upon the Player, the Club may impose a reasonable fine upon the Player and deduct the amount thereof from any money due or to become due to the Player. The Club may also suspend the Player for violation of any such rules. When the Player is fined or suspended he shall be given notice in writing stating the amount of the fine and/or the duration of the suspension and the reason therefor.

[right column partially visible]

shall submit himself for medical examina-
t, when made at the request of the Club
the terms and provisions of this contract

physical condition at the commencement
result of playing hockey for the Club) so
the right to suspend the Player for such
his contract.

Player's reasonable hospitalization until
pital and doctor are selected by the Club
riod not more than six months after the

render him, in the sole judgment of the
f, then during such time the Player is so
compensation herein provided for and the
whatsoever. However the player shall, in
ed while playing hockey for the Club.

l and ability as a hockey player, the loss
y damages. The Player therefore agrees
to enjoin him by appropriate injunction
provisions of this contract.

sports may impair or destroy his ability
this Contract and of the option of re-
ling, or other athletic sport without the

nd of the option of renewal thereof the
ny still photograph, motion pictures or
Club exclusively and may be used, re-
r it desires.

renewal thereof he will not make public
rite or sponsor newspaper or magazine
grants its written consent to any of the
such activities.

any person, any bonus or anything of
-Laws.

th or enter into negotiations with any
current or future services, without the
osed by the President of the League.

transfer this contract, and to loan the
nd by such sale, exchange, assignment,
effect as if it had been entered into by

s services are loaned, to another Club
t out below his signature hereto advise
fying the time and place of reporting
lub and no salary shall be payable to

on when such move is directed by the

eof or shall fail to perform any other
to the Club, specify the nature of the
notice, this contract shall be termination of the Club to pay the Player's

ter obtaining waivers from all other

y breach this contract,

bility to warrant further employment

compensation due to him to the date
low his signature hereto.

e upon which such notice is delivered
d of such fourteen-day period.

the Club for the purpose of playing
f the Club.

ruling of the League or its President
tion thereof and that in the event of

isions of this contract, there shall be
such salary as the number of days'

the League or of the Club, it shall

on of salary due at the date of sus-

omatically cancelled on the date of

aced by that mutually agreed upon

this contract tender to the Player
tract upon the same terms as this

the following playing season upon
l agreement. In the event that the
t of the League, and both parties

the Constitution and By-Laws of
r inspection by Club, its directors

referred within one year from the
by both parties.

Rules, or under the provisions of
e N.H.L. Players' Emergency

and the promise of the Player to
lub's right to take pictures of and
ary payable to the Player under

agrees to deduct and pay, to the
 e sum of Nine Hun-
vice of the Player with the Club
obtain from the National Hockey

mutually agreed that the only contracts recognized by the President of the League are the Standard Player's Contracts which have been duly executed and filed in the League's office and approved by him, and that this Agreement contains the entire agreement between the Parties and there are no oral or written inducements, promises or agreements except as contained herein.

In Witness Whereof, the parties have signed this .... SEVENTH .... day

of .... OCTOBER .... A.D. 19 62

WITNESSES:

MAPLE LEAF GARDENS, LIMITED

John Anderson   By ....
                                                    [signature]
                                   FOR THE   President

                                   ALGER ARBOUR   *[signature]*
                                                          Player

John Anderson   270 MURRAY STREET, SUDBURY, ONTARIO.
                                        Home Address of Player

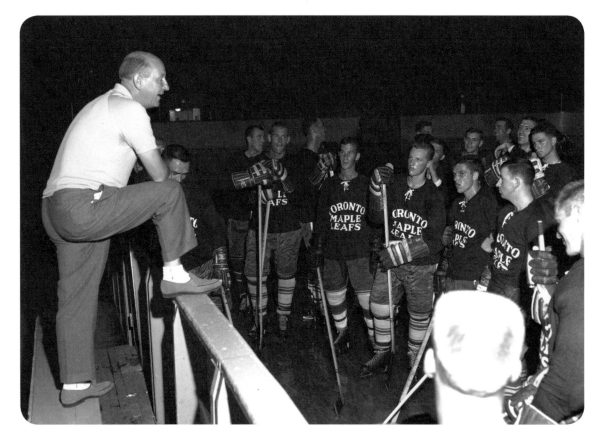

Punch Imlach addresses Leaf training camp.

Punch's Training Camp

Training camp has changed a lot over the years. Today's players stay in tip-top shape over the summer, and newspaper copy often refers to added muscle and new diets. But back in the day, training camp was meant to give the players a chance to get *back* in shape. This 1964 letter, sent to Ron Ellis, shares Punch Imlach's expectations for his team, including push-ups, sit-ups, knee bends—and *golf*. "It was standard for the day, and there's good reason for that, I think. Most of us had jobs in the summer, so we weren't training like they are today," said Ellis, a Leaf from 1964 until 1981. "We were making, in my estimation, fair money, but it certainly wasn't the way it is today—the guys today have to train because everybody is training and you can't give anybody an edge." Murray Oliver, who played with the Leafs from 1967 to 1970, said that Imlach was a taskmaster. "He was tough, but I was probably in my best shape ever under him. He worked us hard and I enjoyed it," said Oliver. Both Ellis and Oliver got a little misty-eyed over the golf. "We played almost every day," said Oliver. "It's camaraderie. You get out there together, relax, and have some fun." It was a great way to pass an afternoon after a tough morning practice, said Ellis. "He made us walk; we couldn't take golf carts. But you're certainly not going to get in shape for the game of hockey while walking the golf course. I think it was more an opportunity to mix up the foursomes, get to know different people, spend some time with them, do some team building."

MAPLE LEAF GARDENS
LIMITED

TORONTO 2, ONTARIO, CANADA

CORNER OF CARLTON AND CHURCH STREETS
TELEPHONE 368-1641

July, 1964.

We will start our training camp on Friday, September 4th at Peterboro, Ontario.

All players are to report to the Empress Hotel by 9:00 a.m. Friday morning September 4th. Physical examinations will start at 9:00 a.m. through to noon. Dinner will be at 1:00 p.m. After dinner all players will report at the arena at 2:30 p.m. and draw their equipment and go for a skate.

Golf will be a must in the training camp schedule. Be sure to bring along your golfing equipment. Arrangements have been completed for the use of The Kwartha Golf Club during training camp.

In view of the fact that nearly all players have cars, I am assuming that you will not need transportation. However, if you do wish transportation, kindly let us know as soon as possible, but we would prefer that you arrange your own transportation and you will be reimbursed at camp.

We hope that you have enjoyed the summer. We feel that this is a crucial year because of our third place finish and we expect you to be in fair shape when you come to camp. That is not more than seven pounds over your playing weight, with a minimum of being able to do:

> 25 Push Ups
> 25 Sit Ups
> 30 Knee Bends

The competition for jobs on the Club should make training camp very interesting this year, so let's be ready for the competition and not sorry.

See you in September and let us make this another profitable year with a big playoff split.

Yours sincerely,

G. Imlach,
General Manager.

Trying to Keep Cheevers

By his own admission, Punch Imlach did his darnedest to keep future Hockey Hall of Fame goaltender Gerry Cheevers in the Leafs system. "At the annual meetings in June of 1965 I'd tried every trick in the book to hang on to Gerry Cheevers," wrote Imlach in *Hockey Is a Battle*. But Cheevers had Johnny Bower and Terry Sawchuk ahead of him in the Leafs net. "Actually, I tried to keep him as an ordinary player, listing him with the forwards and defencemen. But the league ruled against that." Imlach didn't stop there. When the Bruins missed the 10-day deadline for paying for the transfer, he protested, comparing how teams lost players for not paying "C" forms promptly. Campbell assured Imlach that the matter was settled, and a letter from Weston W. Adams, president of the Bruins, put the matter to rest: "When our claim to Cheevers was made, he became our property and Toronto's only interest from then on was for the money due them. Due to a change in general managers and the delay in receiving the assignments, Boston's check to the Central Registry may not have been received within the time specified." Adams also mentioned that Detroit owed the Bruins $60,000 for player transactions and offered to pay Toronto the interest on the $30,000 from the delay.

Gerry Cheevers and Billy Harris.

June 30th, 1965.

Mr. C.S.Campbell,
President,
NHL 922 Sun Life Building,
Montreal, Quebec.

Dear Mr. Campbell:

According to our treasurer Mr. L.C.Heath Maple Leaf Gardens has not received payment for one Jerry Cheevers drafted on June 9th by the Boston Bruins Hockey Club.

It is also my understanding that the payment has not been received by Central Registry.

Under the terms of the draft, 16 A.6, I quote: " A Standard Assignment giving effect to each claim made shall be completed and filed with the President within ten days of the making of the claim and shall be accompanied by the payment for the claimed player."

As the conditions have not been fulfilled I would appreciate it if you would transfer Jerry Cheevers back to our Reserve List.

See. Paragraph 3. 8A.

Yours sincerely,

G. Imlach
General Manager.

GI/JA.

NATIONAL HOCKEY LEAGUE

922 SUN LIFE BUILDING · MONTREAL 2, P.Q. · 866-3755 · AREA CODE 514

PRESIDENT'S OFFICE

July 2, 1965

Mr. G. M. Imlach,
Maple Leaf Gardens Ltd.,
60 Carlton Street,
Toronto 2, Ontario

Re: Jerry Cheevers - C-344

Dear Mr. Imlach:

I have for acknowledgment your letter of June 30th reference the settlement of the above player claim.

We have in the interval received the Boston cheque for the total amount of all their outstanding purchases including Cheevers and this money will be forwarded to you as soon as Mr. Ellis returns to the office to make the necessary distribution.

It has been the practice of this office to try to avoid the necessity of clubs purchasing U.S. funds for payments when they are actually creditors of other clubs and in the end this has worked out very satisfactorily. I am sure that it will work out satisfactorily in this case also.

Yours very truly,

CENTRAL REGISTRY

C. S. Campbell

CSC/r

Lash, Johnston, Sheard & Pringle

BARRISTERS & SOLICITORS

R. W. S. JOHNSTON, Q.C.　　TERENCE SHEARD, Q.C.　　D. M. PRINGLE, Q.C.
IAN S. JOHNSTON, Q.C.　　H. R. DOUGLAS, Q.C.　　J. B. CLEMENTS, Q.C.
G. I. PRINGLE　　J. H. MORLOCK, Q.C.　　RODNEY HULL
I. G. MILNE　　T. G. DEACON　　D. R. CAMERON
W. L. HOOEY　　J. W. WINCH　　T. G. JAMIESON

TELEPHONE: 362-2311
AREA CODE 416
CABLE ADDRESS "JOHNLAW"

NATIONAL TRUST BUILDING
21 KING STREET EAST
TORONTO 1
CANADA

6th August, 1965.

G.M. Imlach, Esq.,
Maple Leaf Gardens Limited,
Carlton and Church Streets,
TORONTO 2,
Ontario.

Dear Punch,

Re: Jerry Cheevers. — File

I have a copy of Mr. Campbell's letter to you of 19th July and Mr. Bassett's letter of 4th August.

In a Court of Law our chances would be slim. There is clearly a technical breach of contract by Boston. Time, however, is not the essence of the matter and I have no doubt that a Court would exercise its equitable jurisdiction and would relieve against forfeiture. A Court would allow us damages, but in this case it would be purely nominal.

On the other hand, I have advised Stafford that the proper procedure would be either an Appeal to the Governors under the By-laws, or Arbitration under the Constitution, Arbitration being the preferable course. In arbitration proceedings the Chairman would probably not be trained in law and he might decide in our favour.

Yours very truly,

Ian Johnston

ISJ:MG
cc: Mr. John Bassett.
　　Mr. Stafford Smythe.
　　Mr. Harold Ballard.

July 5, 1965

Mr. C. S. Campbell
President
National Hockey League
922 Sun Life Building
MONTREAL, Quebec

Dear Mr. Campbell:

I have for acknowledgement your letter of July 2nd. I do not feel that your letter is satisfactory with regards to the disposition of Gerry Cheevers. I find no answer to my specific charges that the Boston Bruins were in error in not filing their cheque with Central Registry. You feel that you are prepared to overlook this condition of the by-law. If we cannot go by the by-laws we might as well throw the book away.

I would like to quote from a letter over your signature dated June 23, 1958, and I quote, "that they should pay to 'Central Registry' the draft price within 10 days of the receipt by Central Registry of the duly completed assignment."

The assignment transferring Gerry Cheevers was stamped by Central Registry at 8.16 a.m. on either June 17th or 18th. Our treasurer was advised when he called ten days later that no payment had been received as of June 29th, by Central Registry.

I feel that you are handling this claim in a very relaxed manner. If you don't pay a "C" form on time you lose your player. I feel that your interpretation of the ruling in 1958 should be the same in 1965. I feel that as General Manager of the Toronto Maple Leafs our claim is a legitimate one and I am passing it on to our owners.

Yours very truly,

George Imlach
General Manager

GI/jp

cc: John Bassett
　　Stafford Smythe
　　Harold Ballard
　　Brig. Ian Johnston

Brian Conacher's Letter to Punch

The summer of 1965 was a turning point for Brian Conacher. He was on the campus of the University of British Columbia, helping to run a hockey school, and sought the counsel of Father David Bauer, the famed steward of Canada's Olympic and World Championship hockey teams. "We had long discussions, because he wanted me to continue to play with the Olympic team," recalled Conacher, whose father was the legendary Lionel Conacher. "I was at this crossroads." He'd been invited to the Toronto Maple Leaf training camps since his days in junior hockey with the Toronto Marlboros, but never felt he had what it took to make the team, especially given Punch Imlach's love of seasoned players over rookies. "When the Leafs didn't win the Stanley Cup that spring, I thought there might be a chance—there was an opportunity to make the Leafs where I hadn't thought there was one before." Having bulked up and experienced the international game, he made his pitch. While he only got into two Leafs games in 1965–66, over the next two years, he played centre and was a part of the memorable 1967 Stanley Cup squad. "I don't think I would have made the Leafs if I hadn't played for Father Bauer, because I think he developed me into a more complete hockey player." Later, Conacher would return to the Olympics, manage teams and arenas, and offer up his expertise as a colour commentator on the 1972 Summit Series.

Brian Conacher in action as the Leafs faced Harry Howell and the NHL All-Stars.

Aug. 14/65.

Dear Mr. Imlach,

I am writing in respect to the coming hockey season of 1965-6. I have just completed my second year of university leaving me with but 5 courses to get for my degree. I think that I should first try to clear up our previous misunderstandings. I have always had the desire to play hockey, and if I could with the best players, that is the N.H.L. However, after my Junior hockey was over and the Toronto Maple Leafs had just won there first of three successive Stanley Cups I felt that as opposed to doing my apprenticeship in the Minor Leagues that I would be smarter if I got some of my university behind me. Anyone I had ever discussed hockey with advised me that it was a good profession as long as you had an education behind you. With the emphases being put on schooling today, I'm not saying I like it, but I felt that this was how it was to be. The year I took off school after my first year to play under Father Bauer has been my most valuable to date. He taught me a tremendous amount about the game and gave me the discipline to do my job as a left winger. It was after the Olympics that I for the first time felt that I had the ability to give the N.H.L. a good try. However, last that year you won the Stanley Cup again and I felt that I might as well get another year of school behind me, because I realized that you don't start tinkering with winning teams.

Well this brings us up to last year. After finishing out of the money, and the trades that your team

has made this spring that there are opportunities for some young players to make the team. I did not play a lot of hockey last winter but have played everyday for the past seven weeks. I am working in Vancouver at a Hockey School here at the University of British Columbia. I have worked out on points of my game which are weak all summer. I have also lifted weights and added 7 pounds to my arms and shoulders. I feel a lot stronger now at 195 and 6'2" than I ever have before. Up till now this has probably been idle chatter to you so I will get to the point.

I am very serious about trying to make the Toronto Maple Leafs this fall. I feel confident that I can do my job as a left winger where your team was weak last year. I know that you have a lot of young prospects trying for the open positions and I'm prepared to fight for my spot. However, as I said way back in Junior, if I can't make it I want to get out, as I feel I have other opportunities as well. I have no intention of playing one opportunity against the other except to say that I will do the one that is made worth my while. I want to make it as a player not a sitter. One job that does interest me is a penta penalty killing role as I have done a lot of work in the past while at this. If I am to play hockey this winter for you I would take one course by correspondence in school and then go to summer school next year. I should be able to complete my degree easily in two summers in this manner.

A lot of water has gone under the bridge in the past few years and as far as I'm concerned I would just as soon let it be. I did what I felt I had to do

and now that it is done I would like to do what I want to do. I have written this letter without knowing even whether you still have an interest in me as a hockey player. I should arrive in Toronto no later that Aug. 31 from Vancouver and if you are interested I would like to come and see you. If not the matter can lay in this letter and I will return to Western and complete my degree this fall. Thank you for your time.

Yours sincerely,

Brian Conacher.

TORONTO
ADDRESS:

BRIAN CONACHER,
55 TEDDINGTON PK.,
TORONTO 12, ONT.

Referee Bill Friday
metes out penalties
to Leafs Bob Baun and
Larry Hillman and Bill
Hay and Bobby Hull
of the Hawks.

Friday's Mistake

Referee Bill Friday called thousands of games over his career. Asking him about a specific incident from a game decades ago would normally be pointless. But in the case of a game from Saturday, November 27, 1965, with the Maple Leafs losing to the Boston Bruins 2–1 at home, it took only a couple of lines from a newspaper story to bring back the memory of goaltender Terry Sawchuk drawing a misconduct. Reggie Fleming scored the winner on a power play while Sawchuk was tied up by Forbes Kennedy in the goal crease. "Oh, somebody was behind him when they scored a goal!" Friday recalled. "He was in behind him . . . I didn't see him, because he wasn't that big." (For the record, Kennedy was 5-foot-8, three inches shorter than Sawchuk.) "I saw a replay later, and I was wrong," confessed Friday, who is a key figure in the history of refereeing. A native of Hamilton, Ontario, he gave up firefighting for a sales job so that he could referee Ontario Hockey Association games from 1955 to 1959. He actually took a pay cut to $5,000 to become a referee in the NHL in 1960. In 1969, Friday was a founder and the first president of the NHL Officials Association. In 1972, the World Hockey Association was founded, and Friday jumped ship, helping to raise referee salaries in all leagues. "I did the first game there and the last game there," he said proudly. Friday was appointed the WHA referee-in-chief in 1976 and is a member of the WHA Hall of Fame. Unlike the players, Friday was *persona non grata* with the NHL after the merger in 1979. "I was never offered a chance to come back. They never asked me, and I wasn't going to ask them."

NATIONAL HOCKEY LEAGUE

922 SUN LIFE BUILDING · MONTREAL 2, P.Q. · 866-3755 · AREA CODE 514

PRESIDENT'S OFFICE   December 21, 1965.

Mr. George Imlach,
Maple Leaf Gardens Limited,
Toronto 2, Ontario.

                    Re: Sawchuk - Game November 27th

Dear Mr. Imlach:

        The official penalty record of the above game shows
that the above-named player received a misconduct penalty.

        Under Rule 29(b) this calls for an automatic fine of
$25 which, by Clause 18 of the Player's Contract, you are
authorized to deduct from his salary.

        Will you please advise him of this fine and remit
same to this office, charging it to this player's account?

                        Yours very truly,

                    NATIONAL HOCKEY LEAGUE

                            President

CSC:t

(In duplicate)

The Many Transgressions of Eddie Shack

Eddie Shack and Punch Imlach had a special relationship, as the tongue-in-cheek invitation to training camp attests. "Eddie the Entertainer was one of my favourite people. Even when he made me mad, I couldn't help laughing at him," wrote Imlach in *Heaven and Hell in the NHL*. "He liked me," explained Shack. "When he went to Buffalo, he got me." As Leafs GM Imlach also "got" Shack in 1963 with a fine of $50 for violating "paragraph 4 of your contract"—out after curfew—on December 25! "That's terrible, isn't it?" says Shack of the Grinch-like fine. Another note dated September 26, 1965, addresses Shack being suspended under section 2D (players required to "participate in any and all promotional activities of the club and league") *and* section 3 ("player must participate in such exhibition games arranged by the club"); the latter clause also brought a $500 fine. While the memo is vague, the incident was on the front page of the sports section the next day. Shack ended up suspended for just one day, for refusing to play with the Rochester Americans against the Leafs in a charity game in Peterborough, Ontario. "Actually, it was a lot of fuss over nothing," said Imlach at the time. Shack didn't remember that specific incident: "I got fined quite a bit."

Eddie Shack and Punch Imlach.

December 27th, 1963.

Mr. Ed Shack,
Maple Leaf Gardens, Limited,
Toronto, Ontario.

Dear Mr. Shack:

This is to notify you that you have been fined the sum of $50.00 under paragraph 4 of your contract.

This fine was imposed because you were out after curfew December 25th in Boston. This is also to let you know that should you break curfew again the fine will be $100.00.

The sum of $50.00 will be deducted from your pay on January 15th.

Yours very truly,

G. Imlach
General Manager.

GI/JA

cc: Mr. L.C. Heath.

MAPLE LEAF GARDENS
LIMITED
TORONTO 2, ONTARIO, CANADA

CORNER OF CARLTON AND CHURCH STREETS
TELEPHONE 368-1641

August 4, 1966.

Mr. Edward Shack,
56 Avremore Crescent,
Toronto.

Dear, dear Eddie:

     If it is not too much trouble, or too great an inconvenience for you, I would deem it a great pleasure if you could honour us with your presence at training camp anytime between September 15th and September 30th. Hope you can fit this in to your schedule.

     Kindly let me know what times you would be available to practice.

                Yours sincerely,

                George Imlach,
                General Manager.

GI/br

R.S.V.P.

Allan Stanley Gets Back on the Ice

Puzzled by a charge from the hospital following off-season surgery on his right knee, Allan Stanley wrote to Punch Imlach to try to establish just what the $5.25 per day fee was for. Of more interest to Imlach, however, was the note that Stanley was expected back on the ice. The Leafs defenceman had turned 40 in March, but his wonky knee kept him out of the final 11 games of the 1965–66 season, and he saw only spot duty in the first couple of semifinal matches with the Canadiens before calling it a year. Stanley was going to test out his knee at Frank Stukus' Byrnell Manor hockey school in Fenelon Falls, Ontario, where fellow trainers that summer included Milt Schmidt and Ed Chadwick. A couple of days after sending Imlach the letter, the Leafs announced that Stanley was the recipient of the J.P. Bickell Memorial Trophy (named for a former Toronto executive), awarded to the most valuable Leaf the previous season. Stanley received a $600 model of the $10,000 gold trophy. "Sam"—as he was known by teammates—also got a new contract. Red Burnett of the *Toronto Star* asked King Clancy if it was a conditional contract based on the status of Stanley's knee. "There's no condition at all. It's just a regular NHL contract and I'm sure Sam will have another fine season for us. He's one of the great ones," said Clancy. "I'm very happy with my contract and sure that I have another season or two left," said Stanley. He made good on his promise, with two more campaigns in Toronto and one in Philadelphia.

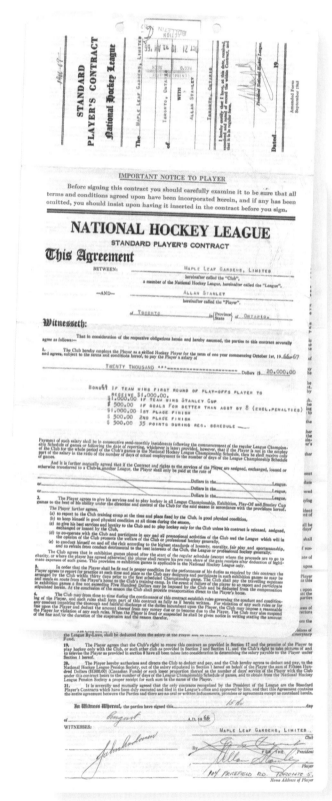

Allan Stanley and Ken Schinkel battle behind the net.

A. Stanley,
Bunnelt Manor,
Fenelon Falls, Ont.,
June 25, 1966.

Mr. George Imlach
Maple Leaf Gardens,
Toronto, Ont..

Dear Punch:

I received this bill from the hospital and don't know what the 5²⁵ per day charge is for. I thought you would want to check on it before it was paid.

Our camp started to-day but we skate for the first time to-morrow.

Best regards to Mrs. Imlach from Barbara & me.

Sincerely,
Allan Stanley.

A Real Gamble

So Bruce Gamble was chastised for shooting a puck into the stands? Maybe he was frustrated about not getting his break. Consider that during his time in the Rangers system, he was stuck behind Gump Worsley and an ascendant Ed Giacomin; claimed by the Bruins, he got a shot in 1961–62 and led the league in losses, with 33; the following season Don Head was the primary starter in Head's only NHL campaign. "We always rent furnished," Gamble once said. The Bruins banished him to the Springfield Indians, where Eddie Shore was dictator; Gamble balked, spending time with the EPHL's Kingston squad for 1962–63 and walked out on the Indians during the 1963–64 season rather than be tied up in net during practices. Suspended for not honouring his assignment, Gamble went home to Port Arthur, Ontario, and Punch Imlach rescued him from working in a grain elevator. The Leafs needed him to spell off Johnny Bower and Terry Sawchuk on multiple occasions, while playing regularly in the minors the rest of the time. With NHL expansion came a regular gig in the Toronto nets. "Gamble often is described as a streak goalie. That means he has hot stretches, then will cool off for a while," wrote the *Toronto Star*'s Jim Proudfoot in 1970. Traded to Philadelphia, in the Bernie Parent deal, Gamble suffered a heart attack during a game in Vancouver in February 1972, ending his career. He died a decade later of another heart attack.

Bruce Gamble.

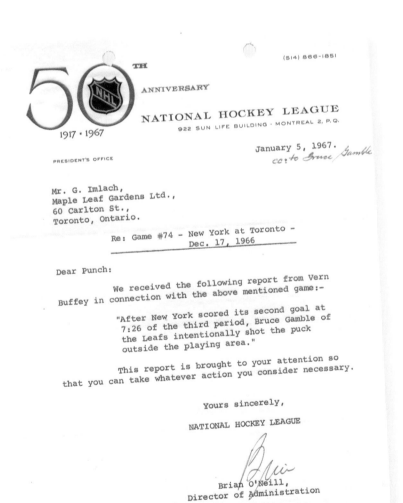

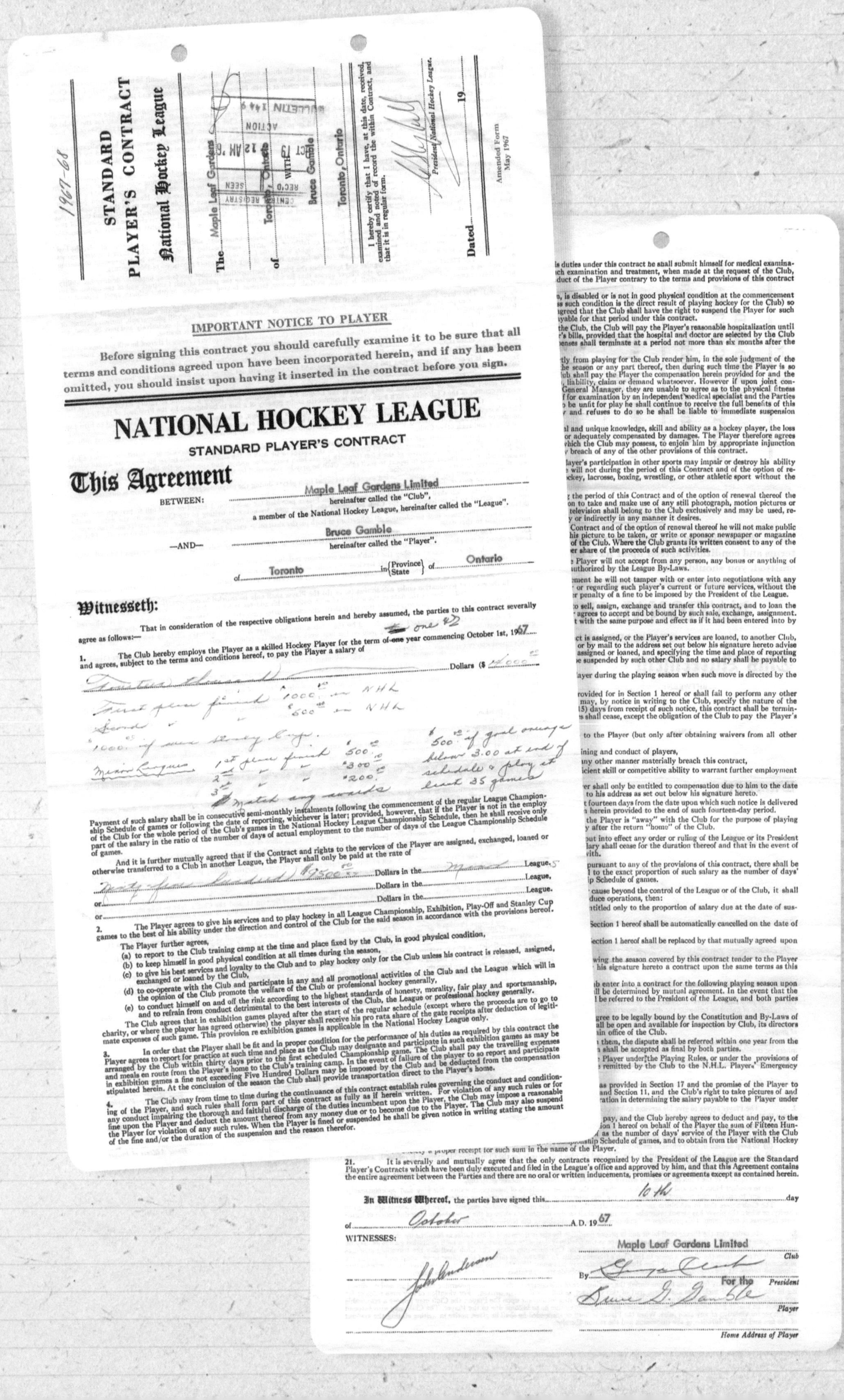

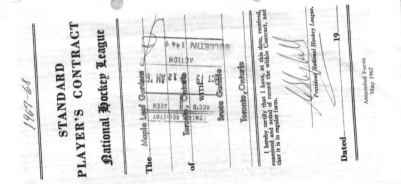

1967-68

STANDARD
PLAYER'S CONTRACT
National Hockey League

The Maple Leaf Gardens
of
Toronto, Ontario
WITH
Bruce Gamble
Dated

19

(rotated stamp/notation) BULLETIN 144½ ACTION SEEN RECD OCT 19 12 AM '67 CENTRAL REGISTRY Toronto, Ontario

I hereby certify that I have, at this date, received, examined and noted of record the within Contract, and that it is in regular form.

President National Hockey League.

Amended Form
May 1967

IMPORTANT NOTICE TO PLAYER

Before signing this contract you should carefully examine it to be sure that all terms and conditions agreed upon have been incorporated herein, and if any has been omitted, you should insist upon having it inserted in the contract before you sign.

NATIONAL HOCKEY LEAGUE
STANDARD PLAYER'S CONTRACT

This Agreement

BETWEEN: Maple Leaf Gardens Limited
hereinafter called the "Club",
a member of the National Hockey League, hereinafter called the "League".

—AND—

Bruce Gamble
hereinafter called the "Player".

of Toronto in { Province State } of Ontario

Witnesseth:

That in consideration of the respective obligations herein and hereby assumed, the parties to this contract severally agree as follows:

1. The Club hereby employs the Player as a skilled Hockey Player for the term of one year commencing October 1st, 1967 and agrees, subject to the terms and conditions hereof, to pay the Player a salary of

_____ Dollars ($14,000⁰⁰)

Fourteen thousand

First place finish $1000⁰⁰ in NHL
Second " " $500⁰⁰ in NHL

$1000⁰⁰ if won Stanley Cup.

Minor Leagues   1st place finish $500⁰⁰ $500⁰⁰ if goal average
                2nd " " $300⁰⁰   below 3.00 at end of
                3rd " " $200⁰⁰   schedule + play at
                                      least 35 games

match any awards

Payment of such salary shall be in consecutive semi-monthly instalments following the commencement of the regular League Championship Schedule of games or following the date of reporting, whichever is later; provided, however, that if the Player is not in the employ of the Club for the whole period of the Club's games in the National Hockey League Championship Schedule, then he shall receive only part of the salary in the ratio of the number of days of actual employment to the number of days of the League Championship Schedule of games.

And it is further mutually agreed that if the Contract and rights to the services of the Player are assigned, exchanged, loaned or otherwise transferred to a Club in another League, the Player shall only be paid at the rate of

Twenty four hundred $9500⁰⁰ Dollars in the _____ League.
or _____ Dollars in the _____ League.
or _____ Dollars in the _____ League.

2. The Player agrees to give his services and to play hockey in all League Championship, Exhibition, Play-Off and Stanley Cup games to the best of his ability under the direction and control of the Club for the said season in accordance with the provisions hereof.

The Player further agrees,
(a) to report to the Club training camp at the time and place fixed by the Club, in good physical condition,
(b) to keep himself in good physical condition at all times during the season,
(c) to give his best services and loyalty to the Club and to play hockey only for the Club unless his contract is released, assigned, exchanged or loaned by the Club,
(d) to co-operate with the Club and participate in any and all promotional activities of the Club and the League which will in the opinion of the Club promote the welfare of the Club or professional hockey generally,
(e) to conduct himself on and off the rink according to the highest standards of honesty, morality, fair play and sportsmanship, and to refrain from conduct detrimental to the best interests of the Club, the League or professional hockey generally.

The Club agrees that in exhibition games played after the start of the regular schedule (except where the proceeds are to go to charity, or where the player has agreed otherwise) the player shall receive his pro rata share of the gate receipts after deduction of legitimate expenses of such game. This provision re exhibition games is applicable in the National Hockey League only.

3. In order that the Player shall be fit and in proper condition for the performance of his duties as required by this contract the Player agrees to report for practice at such time and place as the Club may designate and participate in exhibition games as may be arranged by the Club within thirty days prior to the first scheduled Championship game. The Club shall pay the travelling expenses of the Player to report and participate in exhibition games a fine not exceeding Five Hundred Dollars may be imposed by the Club and be deducted from the compensation stipulated herein. At the conclusion of the season the Club shall provide transportation direct to the Player's home.

4. The Club may from time to time during the continuance of this contract establish rules governing the conduct and condition-ing of the Player, and such rules shall form part of this contract as fully as if herein written. For violation of any such rules or for any conduct impairing the thorough and faithful discharge of the duties incumbent upon the Player, the Club may impose a reasonable fine upon the Player and deduct the amount thereof from any money due or to become due to the Player. The Club may also suspend the Player for violation of any such rules. When the Player is fined or suspended he shall be given notice in writing stating the amount of the fine and/or the duration of the suspension and the reason therefor.

(right page fragments)

his duties under this contract he shall submit himself for medical examina-
...ch examination and treatment, when made at the request of the Club,
...duct of the Player contrary to the terms and provisions of this contract

...is disabled or is not in good physical condition at the commencement
...ss such condition is the direct result of playing hockey for the Club) so
...eed that the Club shall have the right to suspend the Player for such
...yable for that period under this contract.
...the Club, the Club will pay the Player's reasonable hospitalization until
...r's bills, provided that the hospital and doctor are selected by the Club
...enses shall terminate at a period not more than six months after the

...ly from playing for the Club render him, in the sole judgment of the
...he season or any part thereof, then during such time the Player is so
...ub shall pay the Player the compensation herein provided for and at the
...liability, claim or demand whatsoever. However if upon joint con-
...General Manager, they are unable to agree as to the physical fitness
...f for examination by an independent medical specialist and the Parties
...be unfit for play he shall continue to receive the full benefits of this
...y and refuses to do so he shall be liable to immediate suspension

...al and unique knowledge, skill and ability as a hockey player, the loss
...or adequately compensated by damages. The Player therefore agrees
...which the Club may possess, to enjoin him by appropriate injunction
...y breach of any of the other provisions of this contract.

...layer's participation in other sports may impair or destroy his ability
...will not during the period of this Contract and of the option of re-
...hockey, lacrosse, boxing, wrestling, or other athletic sport without

...g the period of this Contract and of the option of renewal thereof the
...on to take and make use of any still photograph, motion pictures or
...television shall belong to the Club exclusively and may be used, re-
...y or indirectly in any manner it desires.

...Contract and of the option of renewal thereof he will not make public
...his picture to be taken, or write or sponsor newspaper or magazine
...of the Club. Where the Club grants its written consent to any of the
...er share of the proceeds of such activities.

...e Player will not accept from any person, any bonus or anything of
...authorized by the League By-Laws.

...ment he will not tamper with or enter into negotiations with any
...or regarding such player's current or future services, without the
...r penalty of a fine to be imposed by the President of the League.

...to sell, assign, exchange and transfer this contract, and to loan the
...agrees to accept and be bound by such sale, exchange, assignment,
...t with the same purpose and effect as if it had been entered into by

...ct is assigned, or the Player's services are loaned, to another Club,
...or by mail to the address set out below his signature hereto advise
...assigned or loaned, and specifying the time and place of reporting
...e suspended by such other Club and no salary shall be payable to

...layer during the playing season when such move is directed by the

...provided for in Section 1 hereof or shall fail to perform any other
...may, by notice in writing to the Club, specify the nature of the
...15) days from receipt of such notice, this contract shall be termin-
...shall cease, except the obligation of the Club to pay the Player's

...to the Player (but only after obtaining waivers from all other

...raining and conduct of players,
...any other manner materially breach this contract,
...ficient skill or competitive ability to warrant further employment

...er shall only be entitled to compensation due to him to the date
...to his address as set out below his signature hereto.
...t fourteen days from the date upon which such notice is delivered
...n herein provided to the end of such fourteen-day period.
...the Player is "away" with the Club for the purpose of playing
...y after the return "home" of the Club.

...ut into effect any order or ruling of the League or its President
...ary shall cease for the duration thereof and that in the event of
...with.

...pursuant to any of the provisions of this contract, there shall be
...d to the exact proportion of such salary as the number of days'
...ip Schedule of games.

...cause beyond the control of the League or of the Club, it shall
...duce operations, then:
...entitled only to the proportion of salary due at the date of sus-

...Section 1 hereof shall be automatically cancelled on the date of

...ection 1 hereof shall be replaced by that mutually agreed upon

...wing the season covered by this contract tender to the Player
...his signature hereto a contract upon the same terms as this

...b enter into a contract for the following playing season upon
...ll be determined by mutual agreement. In the event that the
...l be referred to the President of the League, and both parties

...agree to be legally bound by the Constitution and By-Laws of
...ll be open and available for inspection by Club, its directors
...in office of the Club.

...them, the dispute shall be referred within one year from the
...shall be accepted as final by both parties.

...Player under the Playing Rules, or under the provisions of
...remitted by the Club to the N.H.L. Player's Emergency

...as provided in Section 17 and the promise of the Player to
...and Section 11, and the Club's right to take pictures of and
...ation in determining the salary payable to the Player under

...pay, and the Club hereby agrees to deduct and pay, to the
...on 1 hereof on behalf of the Player the sum of Fifteen Hun-
...ed as the number of days' service of the Player with the Club
...Championship Schedule of games, and to obtain from the National Hockey
...a proper receipt for such sum in the name of the Player.

21. It is severally and mutually agree that the only contracts recognized by the President of the League are the Standard Player's Contracts which have been duly executed and filed in the League's office and approved by him, and that this Agreement contains the entire agreement between the Parties and there are no oral or written inducements, promises or agreements except as contained herein.

In Witness Whereof, the parties have signed this 16th day
of October A.D. 19 67

WITNESSES: Maple Leaf Gardens Limited

John Anderson   By _____ Club
                                                                          President
                                                  Bruce G. Gamble
                                                                          for the Player

                                                  _____ Home Address of Player

J.P. Parise's Day in Blue and White

J.P. Parise played only a single game for the Toronto Maple Leafs, and when the accounting department got around to the paperwork, they realized his social security number wasn't on file, so they wrote to the Minnesota North Stars, his new home, for the information. Parise got an assist on a Mike Walton goal against the Bruins on November 15, 1967. The dressing room was welcoming. "Those guys made me feel like I belonged and had been there for 10 years. It was unbelievable," he recalled. That he ended up in a Toronto game at all is a bit of a whirlwind. He'd played 21 games for Boston in the previous two seasons and was chosen by the Oakland Seals in the expansion draft. He was one of the leading scorers in training camp in London, Ontario, but got on the wrong side of the coach. "I had an argument with Bert Olmstead and it didn't go very well because I told him where to go," admitted Parise. He was immediately traded to Rochester in the AHL, which had a relationship with Toronto, and he was called up when Frank Mahovlich and Dave Keon were both out of the lineup. After the Leafs game, Americans coach Joe Crozier drove Parise back to Rochester. Crozier was a believer. "He says, 'If you get out of the frickin' funk that you're in, I'll have you back in the National Hockey League by Christmas.'" Playing with Bronco Horvath, Parise shone in Rochester and went to the Minnesota North Stars just before the holiday. "I remained in the National Hockey League for 12 years."

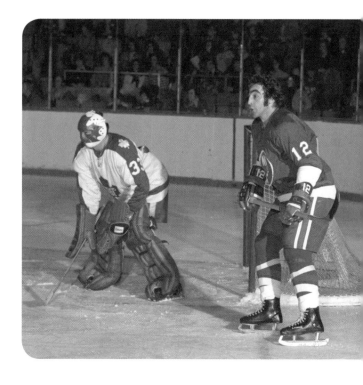

J.P. Parise only played one game *for* the Leafs, but lots *against* them.

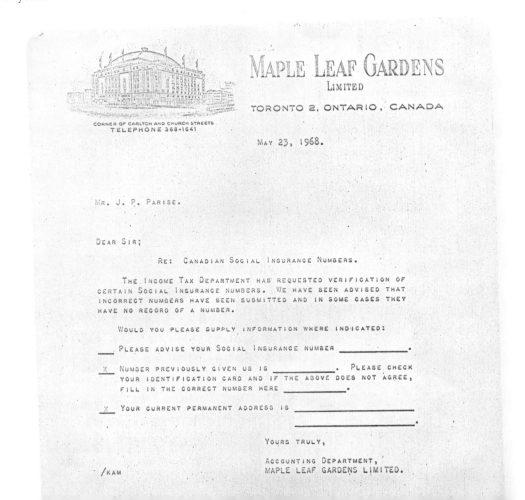

MAPLE LEAF GARDENS
LIMITED

TORONTO 2, ONTARIO, CANADA

CORNER OF CARLTON AND CHURCH STREETS
TELEPHONE 368-1641

MAY 23, 1968.

MR. J. P. PARISE.

DEAR SIR;

RE: CANADIAN SOCIAL INSURANCE NUMBERS.

THE INCOME TAX DEPARTMENT HAS REQUESTED VERIFICATION OF CERTAIN SOCIAL INSURANCE NUMBERS. WE HAVE BEEN ADVISED THAT INCORRECT NUMBERS HAVE BEEN SUBMITTED AND IN SOME CASES THEY HAVE NO RECORD OF A NUMBER.

WOULD YOU PLEASE SUPPLY INFORMATION WHERE INDICATED:

____ PLEASE ADVISE YOUR SOCIAL INSURANCE NUMBER _____.

X NUMBER PREVIOUSLY GIVEN US IS _____. PLEASE CHECK YOUR IDENTIFICATION CARD AND IF THE ABOVE DOES NOT AGREE, FILL IN THE CORRECT NUMBER HERE _____.

X YOUR CURRENT PERMANENT ADDRESS IS _____

_____

YOURS TRULY,

ACCOUNTING DEPARTMENT,
MAPLE LEAF GARDENS LIMITED.

/KAM

IMPORTANT NOTICE TO PLAYER

Before signing this contract you should carefully examine it to be sure that all terms and conditions agreed upon have been incorporated herein, and if any has been omitted, you should insist upon having it inserted in the contract before you sign.

NATIONAL HOCKEY LEAGUE
STANDARD PLAYER'S CONTRACT

This Agreement

BETWEEN: THE HOCKEY CLUB OF MINNESOTA INC.
hereinafter called the "Club",
a member of the National Hockey League, hereinafter called the "League".

—AND—

JEAN PAUL PARISE
hereinafter called the "Player".

of Smooth Rock Falls in {Province/State} of Ontario

Witnesseth:

That in consideration of the respective obligations herein and hereby assumed, the parties to this contract severally agree as follows:

1. The Club hereby employs the Player as a skilled Hockey Player for the term of one year commencing October 1st, 19.... and agrees, subject to the terms and conditions hereof, to pay the Player a salary of

Dollars ($15,000.00)

Fifteen Thousand NO/100

For Minor league contract, see American Hockey League contract previously signed.

Payment of such salary shall be in consecutive semi-monthly instalments following the commencement of the regular League Championship Schedule of games or following the date of reporting, whichever is later; provided, however, that if the Player is not in the employ of the Club for the whole period of the Club's games in the National Hockey League Championship Schedule, then he shall receive only part of the salary in the ratio of the number of days of actual employment to the number of days of the League Championship Schedule of games.

And it is further mutually agreed that if the Contract and rights to the services of the Player are assigned, exchanged, loaned or otherwise transferred to a Club in another League, the Player shall only be paid at the rate of

_____ Dollars in the _____ League.

or _____ Dollars in the _____ League.

or _____ Dollars in the _____ League.

2. The Player agrees to give his services and to play hockey in all League Championship, Exhibition, Play-Off and Stanley Cup games to the best of his ability under the direction and control of the Club for the said season in accordance with the provisions hereof.

The Player further agrees,

(a) to report to the Club training camp at the time and place fixed by the Club, in good physical condition,

(b) to keep himself in good physical condition at all times during the season,

(c) to give his best services and loyalty to the Club and to play hockey only for the Club unless his contract is released, assigned, exchanged or loaned by the Club,

(d) to co-operate with the Club and participate in any and all promotional activities of the Club and the League which will in the opinion of the Club promote the welfare of the Club or professional hockey generally,

(e) to conduct himself on and off the rink according to the highest standards of honesty, morality, fair play and sportsmanship, and to refrain from conduct detrimental to the best interests of the Club, the League or professional hockey generally.

The Club agrees that in exhibition games played after the start of the regular schedule (except where the proceeds are to go to charity, or where the player has agreed otherwise) the player shall receive his pro rata share of the gate receipts after deduction of legitimate expenses of such game. This provision re exhibition games is applicable in the National Hockey League only.

3. In order that the Player shall be fit and in proper condition for the performance of his duties as required by this contract the Player agrees to report for practice at such time and place as the Club may designate and participate in such exhibition games as may be arranged by the Club within thirty days prior to the first scheduled Championship game. The Club shall pay the travelling expenses in exhibition games a fine not exceeding Five Hundred Dollars may be imposed by the Club and be deducted from the Player's home. At the conclusion of the season the Club shall provide transportation direct to the Player's home.

4. The Club may from time to time during the continuance of this contract establish rules governing the conduct and condition-ing of the Player, and such rules shall form part of the duties incumbent upon the Player. For violation of any such rules or for any conduct impairing the thorough and faithful discharge of the duties incumbent upon the Player. The Club may also suspend fine upon the Player and deduct the amount thereof from any money due or to become due to the Player. When the Player is fined or suspended he shall be given notice in writing stating the amount of the fine and/or the duration of the suspension and the reason therefor.

_____ December 27th A.D. 19 67 _____ day

WITNESSES:

THE HOCKEY CLUB OF MINNESOTA INC.
_____ Club

Wren a Blair

By Walter L. Bush, Jr.
Walter L. Bush, Jr.
_____ President

Wren a Blair

Jean Paul Parise
Jean Paul Parise
_____ Player

Smooth Rock Falls Ont Box 257
_____ Home Address of Player

Dorey Needs a Ride

In the winter of 1968, Jim Dorey was an NHL rookie, having survived three minor leagues—WHL, AHL, and Central Professional Hockey League—in his first year as a pro after graduating from the OHA's London Nationals. The 23rd overall choice in the 1964 amateur draft, the defenceman entered the NHL with a bang—a then-record eight penalties for 48 minutes in an October 16 game against Pittsburgh. But in December, he ran into a different problem: he missed practice because his ride, Norm Ullman, forgot to pick him up. GM/coach Punch Imlach fined Dorey, but Dorey protested in a letter. The other handwriting is Imlach's, forgiving the fine. Dorey said that Punch wasn't as bad as some people say: "He'd give and take; that's what he would do. He'd fine you, then buy you a meal maybe two weeks later, or give you some extra spending cash on the road. Actually, he was pretty fair." Dorey would outlast Imlach in Toronto, and compared the outgoing GM to his protégé, Jim Gregory. "Jim was old-school. Punch had brought him along. Christ, they were inseparable in some ways," said Dorey. "[Gregory] was a better negotiator than Punch." Injuries played a role in Dorey's career—shoulder surgery, spinal surgery—but the defenceman still played 12 years in the NHL and WHA, including an Avco Cup win with the 1973 New England Whalers.

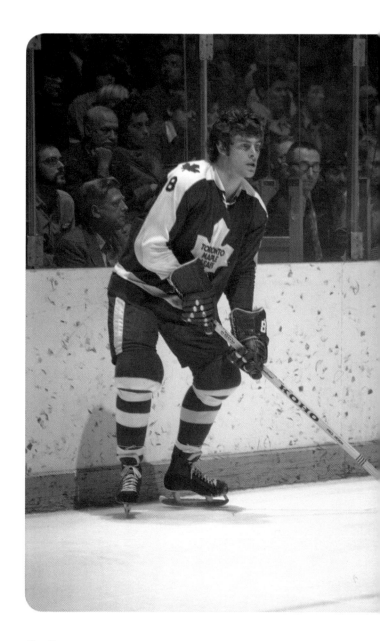

Jim Dorey.

File
Jim Dorey

Dec 31, 1968

Mr. G. Imlach:

Dear Sir

I would appreciate it very much if you would forgive me for being late on Monday, Dec. 30.

Arrangements had been made with Mr. M. Ulman for transportation to the Gardens. Either through error or lack of knowledge of my residence I wasn't picked up.

I would like to point out that I made the trip to the Gardens on Saturday morning through the snow and hazardous driving. Appreciation of this matter should be looked into.

No blame should be put on Mr. Ulman though.

Thank you very much.

Jim Dorey

Fine cancelled
Won game against
NY 5-3
GI

Brian Spencer.

An Early Glimpse into Spinner's Mind

Seeking to better understand their new player, taken 55th overall in the 1969 draft, the Toronto Maple Leafs sent Brian Spencer a questionnaire. His responses, dated October 14, 1969, perhaps give a glimpse into the tragedy to come, or at least his propensity to exaggerate. He detailed his summer job as a heavy-duty truck operator and his hobbies, which included karate, badminton (he was in the provincial finals in high school), and working with old cars (he once had a 1927 Chevrolet). "Do much hunting, fishing, used to trap furs when I was young for pocket money, have shot moose, bear, beaver, etc.," he details, describing his upbringing in Fort St. James, B.C. "Was on a man hunt 2 yrs ago for some criminals in North B.C." (A claim debunked in *Gross Misconduct*, the book on his life.) Nicknamed "Spinner" for his skating style, he carved out a 10-year NHL career that included time in Toronto; Long Island, after he was taken in the expansion draft ("It was with a great amount of apprehension that our Organization decided to leave you unprotected," wrote Leafs GM Jim Gregory); Buffalo; and Pittsburgh. Post-hockey, he drifted, ran into trouble for drunk driving, and was arrested in January 1987 for a murder that had taken place five years earlier on an isolated dirt road in West Palm Beach, Florida. He was acquitted of the crime in a high-profile trial. His life came to a sudden, tragic end on June 2, 1988, when he was shot in a robbery attempt in Riviera Beach, Florida, while trying to buy cocaine.

QUESTIONNAIRE FOR PLAYERS
Please PRINT

Date OCT 14 19 69

NAME IN FULL BRIAN ROY SPENCER

Nick Name SPINNER

HOME ADDRESS

Number and Street Box 67 R

City FORT ST JAMES

Province or State B.C.

BIRTHPLACE

City FORT ST JAMES Province or State B.C.

Day 3 Month 9 Year 49

Playing Weight 179 Height 5-11½

What Position do you Play? LEFT WING, RIGHT WING

Do you Handle Stick Right or Left? LEFT

Have you Ever Been Selected for a Professional All-Star Team? — NO

What Year or Years? NO

By Whom? NO

Are you Married or Single? SINGLE

Children? — (Boys) — (Girls)

What is your Summer Occupation? HEAVY DUTY OPERATOR CAT TRUCK, SKIDDER

What are Your Hobbies? AUTO MECHANIC, KARATE

GENERAL REMARKS

FIND much enjoyment in working with cars, had a 1927 chev original, then a 1955 chev convertable 327 customized 275 horse

* Do much hunting fishing used to trap furs when I was young for pocket money, have shot moose, bear, beaver etc. (OVER)

* Was on a manhunt 2 yrs ago for some criminals in North B.C.

PLEASE LIST OFF SEASON AMATEUR CLUBS PLAYED WITH AND AMATEUR AWARDS RECEIVED INCLUDING ALL-STAR SELECTIONS.

1967 Calgary Centenials
1968 Estevan Bruins

PLEASE GIVE DETAILED HISTORY OF CLUBS PLAYED WITH AS A PROFESSIONAL.

Date of turning professional? SEPT - OCT 1969

With what Club? TULSA OILERS

Other professional clubs (Give name and year)

PLEASE GIVE DETAILED HISTORY OF SPORTS YOU HAVE TAKEN PART IN OTHER THAN HOCKEY.

KARATE 3 years general practice then was taking soccer instruction in Calgary but a hockey trade moved FOOT BALL me to a different town, I only got to a white belt formally ½ BADMINTON

② Badminton - was on the northern B.C. champion team to participate in the provincial finals in high school.

③ Enjoy playing rough sports, have played football in high school

④ Soccer - high school soccer

Tiptoeing with Tiny Tim

Preseason hockey doesn't mean much, especially the traditional Blue and White games, with the Leafs splitting the squads for an exhibition match. For the game in October 1969, Brian McFarlane, then working as the public relations man for the team, came up with the idea of bringing in a celebrity to help goose ticket sales. Singer Tiny Tim ("Tiptoe Through the Tulips") was in the news, as he was about to get married to 17-year-old Vicki Budinger on *The Tonight Show*. And he was a Leafs fan, often cheering on the team at Madison Square Garden. In an interview, Tiny Tim said he chose the Leafs because their name "struck me as being close to nature, you know, leafs and maple. Rhythmic too, and very sensual." McFarlane got the "very strange man" to and from Maple Leaf Gardens. "He took a shot on goal," said McFarlane, the Hockey Hall of Fame broadcaster. "He tried to put one in the empty net and missed. He was kind of an attraction, but they didn't have too many fans at the game." Tiny Tim (real name Herbert Khaury) wore Eddie Shack's #23 sweater and skates, and the *Globe and Mail* reported that he "wobbled across the ice on legs like tapioca pudding, supported by two big strong Leaf players." After his moment, he told reporter Melinda McCracken of the *Globe and Mail*, "Just being on the ice was great," and that he never learned to skate because "I was always athletic spiritually, not physically."

Tiny Tim cheers on the Leafs at Madison Square Garden in New York City.

BLUE AND WHITE GAME

October 7, 1969

6:45 p.m.	-	Turnstiles open
6:45 - 7:00	-	Usherettes (6) distribute 1,000 Bic Pens
7:00 - 7:20	-	Leafs on ice for photos and autographs. Side glass removed.
7:20 - 7:30	-	Leafs back in room. Glass replaced.
7:30 - 7:45	-	Leafs in warmup.
7:45 - 7:55	-	Resurface ice
7:55 - 8:00	-	Leafs return. B. McFarlane at centre ice (carpet down) Welcome. Introduces Bobby Hull. Introduces Tiny Tim. Meets Big Tim (Horton). Tim expresses desire to take shot on Bower. Does so..SCORES! Tim promises to sing during intermission. Tim drops puck for official faceoff.
8:00 p.m.		Game.

First Intermission: Ice resurfaced
                     Carpet down
                     Five fans (selected by ticket number during
                       first period of play) try to shoot and score.
                       Hull takes part. Winners get two NHL tickets.
                     Tiny Tim tries shot as finale. Then sings song.
                     Picks winning ticket on ukelele draw.
                     Also picks winning tickets on ten Kodak Cameras.
                     Winners to report during second intermission.

                     Second period begins.

Second Intermission: Ice resurfaced
                      Carpet down.
                      Tiny Tim hands out 10 cameras to lucky winners.
                      Tim then gives away ukelele.
                      Five fans (selected by ticket number during second
                      period play) try to shoot and score.
                      McFarlane reminds youngsters re sportswiters' contest.

                      Third period begins.

CHAPTER 5

THE 1970s

Henderson Is Busted

Punch Imlach was always big on fines. When he started coaching, there was a $5 charge for giving away the puck. That fee was gone by the time the Leafs obtained Paul Henderson from Detroit in 1968 as a part of the Frank Mahovlich deal. But there were other fines, including this pair for violating curfew. "I don't know if it was in the contract, it was just stipulated with Imlach. It was automatic, if you missed curfew, it was a $100 fine," said Henderson. The rules were never formally laid out. "It's just one of those things we accepted. I have no problem with it at all. There needs to be some guidelines on that sort of stuff. The one I really struggled with was the hundred dollars for not wearing a tie to practice. That was one that made no sense, but that was a different time, a different era. And you knew [what the rules] were there, so you tried to respect them. You knew the consequences." Imlach explained in *Heaven and Hell in the NHL* where the money went: "All the little fines I levied for various things during the season went into a pot that paid for a players' party when it was all over." Henderson chuckled, confirming Imlach's collection: "Imlach would keep the money and give it to us at the end of the year for our team party. We usually had a few dollars!"

The colourful Harold Ballard in his Maple Leaf Gardens office.

Paul Henderson.

PAUL HENDERSON

8 April, 1970.

J.M. GREGORY

This is to advise that you have been fined the amount of $75.00 for your violation of curfew in St. Louis on January 15th, 1970 ($50.00) and in Oakland on January 23rd, 1970 ($25.00).

This amount will be deducted from your personal bonus cheque.

JMG/sb

J.M. GREGORY,
General Manager

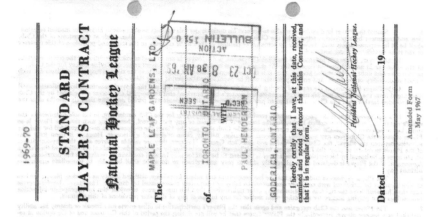

1969-70

STANDARD
PLAYER'S CONTRACT

National Hockey League

Amended Form
May 1967

The........MAPLE LEAF GARDENS, LTD.........

of........TORONTO, ONTARIO.........

GODERICH, ONTARIO
PAUL HENDERSON

I hereby certify that I have, at this date, received, examined and noted of record the within Contract, and that it is in regular form.

........President National Hockey League.

Dated........19........

IMPORTANT NOTICE TO PLAYER

Before signing this contract you should carefully examine it to be sure that all terms and conditions agreed upon have been incorporated herein, and if any has been omitted, you should insist upon having it inserted in the contract before you sign.

NATIONAL HOCKEY LEAGUE

STANDARD PLAYER'S CONTRACT

This Agreement

BETWEEN: MAPLE LEAF GARDENS, LTD

hereinafter called the "Club",

a member of the National Hockey League, hereinafter called the "League".

—AND—   PAUL HENDERSON

hereinafter called the "Player".

of   GODERICH   in {Province/State} of   ONTARIO

Witnesseth:

That in consideration of the respective obligations herein and hereby assumed, the parties to this contract severally agree as follows:—

1.   The Club hereby employs the Player as a skilled Hockey Player for the term of one year commencing October 1st, 19__69__ and agrees, subject to the terms and conditions hereof, to pay the Player a salary of

THIRTY-TWO THOUSAND--Dollars ($ 32,000.00

BONUSES: IF LEAFS MAKE PLAYOFFS.....................$3,000.00
20 GOALS DURING REGULAR SH SCHEDULE.......$1,000.00
PER GOAL AFTER 20 IN REGULAR SCHEDULE.......$ 100.00
35 GOALS DURING REGULAR SCHEDULE...........$1,000.00

Payment of such salary shall be in consecutive semi-monthly instalments following the commencement of the regular League Championship Schedule of games or following the date of reporting, whichever is later; provided, however, that if the Player is not in the employ of the Club for the whole period of the Club's games in the National Hockey League Championship Schedule, then he shall receive only part of the salary in the ratio of the number of days of actual employment to the number of days of the League Championship Schedule of games.

And it is further mutually agreed that if the Contract and rights to the services of the Player are assigned, exchanged, loaned or otherwise transferred to a Club in another League, the Player shall only be paid at the rate of

_____Dollars in the_____League.

or_____Dollars in the_____League,

or_____Dollars in the_____League.

2.   The Player agrees to give his services and to play hockey in all League Championship, Exhibition, Play-Off and Stanley Cup games to the best of his ability under the direction and control of the Club for the said season in accordance with the provisions hereof.

The Player further agrees,
(a) to report to the Club training camp at the time and place fixed by the Club, in good physical condition,
(b) to keep himself in good physical condition at all times during the season,
(c) to give his best services and loyalty to the Club and to play hockey only for the Club unless his contract is released, assigned, exchanged or loaned by the Club,
(d) to co-operate with the Club and participate in any and all promotional activities of the Club and the League which will in the opinion of the Club promote the welfare of the Club or professional hockey generally,
(e) to conduct himself on and off the rink according to the highest standards of honesty, morality, fair play and sportsmanship, and to refrain from conduct detrimental to the best interests of the Club, the League or professional hockey generally.

The Club agrees that in exhibition games played after the start of the regular schedule (except where the proceeds are to go to charity, or where the player has agreed otherwise) the player shall receive his pro rata share of the gate receipts after deduction of legitimate expenses of such game. This provision re exhibition games is applicable in the National Hockey League only.

3.   In order that the Player shall be fit and in proper condition for the performance of his duties as required by this contract the Player agrees to report for practice at such time and place as the Club may designate and participate in such exhibition games as may be arranged by the Club within thirty days prior to the first scheduled Championship game. The Club shall pay the travelling expenses and meals en route from the Player's home to the Club's training camp. In the event of failure of the player to so report and participate in exhibition games a fine not exceeding Five Hundred Dollars may be imposed by the Club and be deducted from the compensation stipulated herein. At the conclusion of the season the Club shall provide transportation direct to the Player's home.

4.   The Club may from time to time during the continuance of this contract establish rules governing the conduct and conditioning of the Player, and such rules shall form part of this contract as fully as if herein written. For violation of any such rules or for any conduct impairing the thorough and faithful discharge of the duties incumbent upon the Player, the Club may impose a reasonable fine upon the Player and deduct the amount thereof from any money due or to become due to the Player. The Club may also suspend the Player for violation of any such rules. When the Player is fined or suspended he shall be given notice in writing stating the amount of the fine and/or the duration of the suspension and the reason therefor.

5. Should the Player be disabled or unable to perform his duties under this contract he shall submit himself for medical examination and treatment by a physician selected by the Club, and such examination and treatment, when made at the request of the Club, shall be at its expense unless made necessary by some act or conduct of the Player contrary to the terms and provisions of this contract or the rules established under Section 4.

If the Player, in the sole judgment of the Club's physician, is disabled or is not in good physical condition at the commencement of the season or at any subsequent time during the season (unless such condition is the direct result of playing hockey for the Club) so as to render him unfit to play skilled hockey, then it is mutually agreed that the Club shall have the right to suspend the Player for such period of disability or unfitness, and no compensation shall be payable for that period under this contract.

If the Player is injured as the result of playing hockey for the Club, the Club will pay the Player's reasonable hospitalization until discharged from the hospital, and his medical expenses and doctor's bills, provided that the hospital and doctor are selected by the Club and provided further that the Club's obligation to pay such expenses shall terminate at a period not more than six months after the injury.

It is also agreed that if the Player's injuries resulting directly from playing for the Club render him, in the sole judgment of the Club's physician, unfit to play skilled hockey for the balance of the season or any part thereof, then during such time the Player is so unfit, but in no event beyond the end of the current season, the Club shall pay the Player the compensation herein provided for and the Player releases the Club from any and every additional obligation, liability, claim or demand whatsoever. However if upon joint consultation between the Player, the Club's physician and the Club General Manager, they are unable to agree as to the physical fitness of the Player to return to play, the Player agrees to submit himself for examination by an independent medical specialist and the Parties hereto agree to be bound by his decision. If the Player is declared to be unfit for play he shall continue to receive the full benefits of this Agreement. If the Player is declared to be physically able to play and refuses to do so he shall be liable to immediate suspension without pay

6. The Player represents and agrees that he has exceptional and unique knowledge, skill and ability as a hockey player, the loss of which cannot be estimated with certainty and cannot be fairly or adequately compensated by damages. The Player therefore agrees that the Club shall have the right, in addition to any other rights which the Club may possess, to enjoin him by appropriate injunction proceedings from playing hockey for any other team and/or for any breach of any of the other provisions of this contract.

7. The Player and the Club recognize and agree that the Player's participation in other sports may impair or destroy his ability and skill as a hockey player. Accordingly the Player agrees that he will not during the period of this Contract and of the option of renewal thereof engage or participate in football, baseball, softball, hockey, lacrosse, boxing, wrestling, or other athletic sport without the written consent of the Club.

8. (a) The Player hereby irrevocably grants to the Club during the period of this Contract and of the option of renewal thereof the exclusive right to permit or authorize any person, firm or corporation to take and make use of any still photograph, motion pictures or television of himself, and agrees that all rights in such pictures and television shall belong to the Club exclusively and may be used, reproduced, distributed or otherwise disseminated by the Club directly or indirectly in any manner it desires.

(b) The Player further agrees that during the period of this Contract and of the option of renewal thereof he will not make public appearances, participate in radio or television programs, or permit his picture to be taken, or write or sponsor newspaper or magazine articles, or sponsor commercial products without the written consent of the Club. Where the Club grants its written consent to any of the activities recited in this sub-section the Player shall receive his proper share of the proceeds of such activities.

9. It is mutually agreed that the Club will not pay, and the Player will not accept from any person, any bonus or anything of value for winning any particular game or series of games except as authorized by the League By-Laws.

10. The Player agrees that during the currency of this agreement he will not tamper with or enter into negotiations with any player under contract or reservation to any Club of the League for or regarding such player's current or future services, without the written consent of the Club with which such player is connected under penalty of a fine to be imposed by the President of the League.

11. It is mutually agreed that the Club shall have the right to sell, assign, exchange and transfer this contract, and to loan the Player's services to any other professional hockey club, and the Player agrees to accept and be bound by such sale, exchange, assignment. transfer or loan, and will faithfully perform and carry out this contract with the same purpose and effect as if it had been entered into by the Player and such other Club.

It is further mutually agreed that in the event that this contract is assigned, or the Player's services are loaned, to another Club, the Club shall, by notice in writing delivered personally to the Player or by mail to the address set out below his signature hereto advise the Player of the name and address of the Club to which he has been assigned or loaned, and specifying the time and place of reporting to such club. If the Player fails to report to such other Club he may be suspended by such other Club and no salary shall be payable to him during the period of such suspension.

The Club shall pay the actual moving expenses incurred by a player during the playing season when such move is directed by the Club and is not part of disciplinary action.

12. If the Club shall default in the payments to the Player provided for in Section 1 hereof or shall fail to perform any other obligation agreed to be performed by the Club hereunder, the Player may, by notice in writing to the Club, specify the nature of the default, and if the Club shall fail to remedy the default within fifteen (15) days from receipt of such notice, this contract shall be terminated, and upon the date of such termination all obligations of both parties shall cease, except the obligation of the Club to pay the Player's compensation to that date.

13. The Club may terminate this contract upon written notice to the Player (but only after obtaining waivers from all other League clubs) if the player shall at any time:

(a) fail, refuse or neglect to obey the Club's rules governing training and conduct of players,

(b) fail, refuse or neglect to render his services hereunder or in any other manner materially breach this contract,

(c) fail, in the opinion of the Club's management, to exhibit sufficient skill or competitive ability to warrant further employment as a member of the Club's team.

In the event of termination under sub-section (a) or (b) the Player shall only be entitled to compensation due to him to the date such notice is delivered to him or the date of the mailing of such notice to his address as set out below his signature hereto.

In the event of termination under sub-section (c) it shall take effect fourteen days from the date upon which such notice is delivered to the Player, and the Player shall only be entitled to the compensation herein provided to the end of such fourteen-day period.

In the event that this contract is terminated by the Club while the Player is "away" with the Club for the purpose of playing games the instalment then falling due shall be paid on the first week-day after the return "home" of the Club.

14. The Player further agrees that the Club may carry out and put into effect any order or ruling of the League or its President for his suspension or expulsion and that in the event of suspension his salary shall cease for the duration thereof and that in the event of expulsion this contract, at the option of the Club, shall terminate forthwith.

15. The Player further agrees that in the event of his suspension pursuant to any of the provisions of this contract, there shall be deducted from the salary stipulated in Section 1 hereof an amount equal to the exact proportion of such salary as the number of days' suspension bears to the total number of days of the League Championship Schedule of games.

16. If because of any condition arising from a state of war or other cause beyond the control of the League or of the Club, it shall be deemed advisable by the League or the Club to suspend or cease or reduce operations, then:

(a) in the event of suspension of operations, the Player shall be entitled only to the proportion of salary due at the date of suspension,

(b) in the event of cessation of operations, the salary stipulated in Section 1 hereof shall be automatically cancelled on the date of cessation, and

(c) in the event of reduction of operations, the salary stipulated in Section 1 hereof shall be replaced by that mutually agreed upon between the Club and the Player.

17. The Club agrees that it will on or before September 1st next following the season covered by this contract tender to the Player personally or by mail directed to the Player at his address set out below his signature hereto a contract upon the same terms as this contract save as to salary.

The Player hereby undertakes that he will at the request of the Club enter into a contract for the following playing season upon the same terms and conditions as this contract save as to salary which shall be determined by mutual agreement. In the event that the Player and the Club do not agree upon the salary to be paid the matter shall be referred to the President of the League, and both parties agree to accept his decision as final.

18. The Club and the Player severally and mutually promise and agree to be legally bound by the Constitution and By-Laws of the League and by all the terms and provisions thereof, a copy of which shall be open and available for inspection by Club, its directors and officers, and the Player, at the main office of the League and at the main office of the Club.

The Club and the Player further agree that in case of dispute between them, the dispute shall be referred within one year from the date it arose to the President of the League as an arbitrator and his decision shall be accepted as final by both parties.

The Club and the Player further agree that al lfines imposed upon the Player under the Playing Rules, or under the provisions of the League By-Laws, shall be deducted from the salary of the Player and be remitted by the Club to the N.H.L. Players' Emergency Fund.

19. The Player agrees that the Club's right to renew this contract as provided in Section 17 and the promise of the Player to play hockey only with the Club, or such other club as provided in Section 2 and Section 11, and the Club's right to take pictures of and to televise the Player as provided in section 8 have all been taken into consideration in determining the salary payable to the Player under Section 1 hereof.

20. The Player hereby authorizes and directs the Club to deduct and pay, and the Club hereby agrees to deduct and pay, to the National Hockey League Pension Society, out of the salary stipulated in Section 1 hereof on behalf of the Player the sum of Fifteen Hundred Dollars ($1500.00) (Canadian Funds) or such lesser proportion thereof as the number of days' service of the Player with the Club under this contract bears to the number of days of the League Championship Schedule of games, and to obtain from the National Hockey League Pension Society a proper receipt for such sum in the name of the Player.

21. It is severally and mutually agree that the only contracts recognized by the President of the League are the Standard Player's Contracts which have been duly executed and filed in the League's office and approved by him, and that this Agreement contains the entire agreement between the Parties and there are no oral or written inducements, promises or agreements except as contained herein.

In Witness Whereof, the parties have signed this 20th day

of October A.D. 1969

WITNESSES:

MAPLE LEAF GARDENS LTD.
Club

Howard Starkman

By .... FOR THE President

Paul Henderson
Player

118 Blake St W Goderich
Home Address of Player

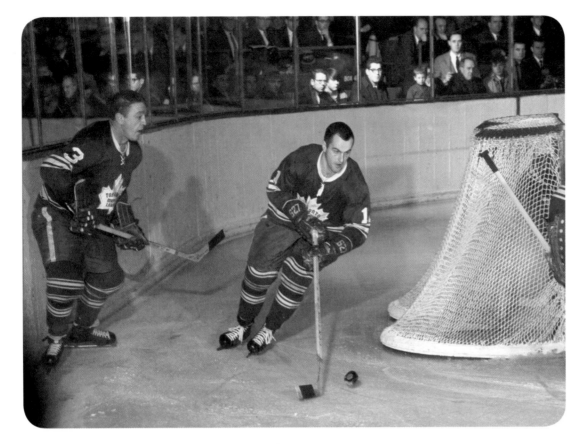

Marcel Pronovost and Murray Oliver.

Murray Oliver Moves to Minnesota

Getting traded from the Maple Leafs to the Minnesota North Stars wan't a surprise for Murray Oliver. After all, he had said his piece about the mismanagement of the team: a management that had just dumped Punch Imlach as general manager and coach. "I spoke up and said that I was sorry that Punch got fired," recalled Oliver, stressing that he was okay with the new GM, but not the powers that be. "It wasn't Jim [Gregory], it was Ballard and the owners." After nine years playing in Detroit (and its farm team in Edmonton) and Boston, Oliver loved being in Toronto. "I was from Hamilton. It was home. I was going to end my career in Toronto, but I ended up living here in Minnesota." The deal, made on May 22, 1970, but announced four days later, as the Leafs had to hunt Oliver down on a fishing trip, saw Terry O'Malley (who never made the NHL, but played for three Canadian Olympic teams), the rights to Brian Conacher, and cash go back to Toronto (though the newspapers reported it as "future considerations"). "We carried on quite a little bidding war until we finally won out," said North Stars GM Wren Blair at the time. Earlier, the Leafs had dangled Oliver to the St. Louis Blues in exchange for goaltender Jacques Plante, but the Blues were centre-heavy; and when the Black Hawks asked for Oliver and Bob Pulford in exchange for Jim Pappin, they were turned away. So Murray ended up in Minnesota.

STANDARD ASSIGNMENT AGREEMENT

(Uniform agreement for assignment of the rights to services of a player, amateur or professional, to or by a club.)

This Agreement made and entered into this **22** day of **MAY** 19**70**,

BETWEEN :   **MAPLE LEAF GARDENS, LTD.**

(Corporate name of the Company, Club or Association) PARTY OF THE FIRST PART

and :   **THE HOCKEY CLUB OF MINNESOTA, INC.**

(Corporate name of the Company, Club or Association) PARTY OF THE SECOND PART

WITNESSETH : The party of the First Part hereby assigns to the Party of the Second Part its rights to services of

PLAYER(S)   **MURRAY OLIVER**

under {Standard Contract ~~Option "B"~~} upon the following terms and conditions
       {~~Try Out "A" Option "C"~~}
Strike out inappropriate parts

"IN EXCHANGE FOR CASH AND PLAYERS TO BE NAMED LATER"

WAIVER CERTIFICATE :

The transferor hereby certifies : *(strike out (1) or (2) below)*

(1) The Player(s) is a (n) amat. / prof. player for whom League waivers are not required.

(2) The Player(s) has been waived out of the League and has not played in six (6) League or Play-off games since the waivers were obtained.

IN WITNESS WHEREOF the parties hereto have subscribed through our respective Presidents or authorized agents, witnessed on the date set out above.

MAPLE LEAF GARDENS, LTD.
CLUB

Howard Starkman
WITNESS   By *J. M. Gregory* (Party of the First Part)

THE HOCKEY CLUB OF MINNESOTA, INC.
CLUB

Marilyn A. Vaughan
WITNESS   By *Wren A Blair* (Party of the Second Part)

Joe Sgro was the 1972
Summit Series trainer.

Bad Goalie, Good Trainer

The name Joe Sgro might not be familiar to all Leafs fans, but he was a key figure with the team in the 1970s as the trainer. There aren't a lot of memos about him, like this one detailing players who switched teams during the 1970 off-season. "Not a lot of paperwork," explained Sgro. "Whatever I had to do, I did." Sgro was a goaltender and baseball player in South Porcupine, Ontario. Veteran minor-league centre John McLellan was from the same town and invited Sgro to help him out in his initial coaching gig with the Eastern Hockey League's Nashville Dixie Flyers. Like many trainers during the era, Sgro was pressed into action as a keeper here and there. "I tried to be a goal-tender, and I wasn't very good at goaltending, eh?" confessed Sgro. Ray Miron knew Sgro in the EHL and took the trainer with him when he moved to Tulsa, Oklahoma, to run the Leafs' farm club in the CHL. When the Leafs' trainer, Bob Haggert, left the team, Punch Imlach hired Sgro. "Punch called me one night at home. He said, 'If you want to be the trainer of the Toronto Maple Leafs, meet you at 10:00 in the morning at Maple Leaf Gardens.'" Sgro worked with the Leafs for nine years before leaving to deal with family issues. He served as the trainer for Team Canada into the 1980s, including for the Summit Series in 1972. As an aside, the Stitt Collection includes the stick that Ian Turnbull used to score five goals in one game, personally autographed to Joe Sgro.

MAPLE LEAF GARDENS, LIMITED

Memo to: JOE SGRO   26 June, 1970.

from: J.M. GREGORY

Subject: <u>SKATES AND SPECIAL EQUIPMENT</u>

The following players have either been traded, sold or picked-up by other teams in the NHL Draft.

I would appreciate if you would forward to the respective Clubs any skates and special equipment that we might have belonging to these players.

1. Murray Oliver   Minnesota
2. Pat Quinn   Vancouver
3. Dan Johnson   Vancouver
4. Ron Ward   Vancouver
5. Serge Aubry   Vancouver
6. Tom Martin   Detroit
7. Chris Evans   Buffalo

JMG/sb

J.M. GREGORY,
General Manager

cc: Bud Poile
       Sid Abel
       George Imlach
       R. Miron
       B. Whitlow
       W. Blair

COPY FOR

MAPLE LEAF GARDENS LIMITED

60 CARLTON STREET, TORONTO, ONTARIO • (416)368-1641

26 June, 1970.

Mr. Wren Blair,
General Manager,
Minnesota North Stars Hockey Club,
Metropolitan Sports Center,
7901 Cedar Ave. S.,
BLOOMINGTON, Minn. 55420,
U.S.A.

Dear Wren,

Enclosed please find a copy of player MURRAY OLIVER's Standard Player's Contract and a copy of a memorandum sent to our Trainer, JOE SGRO, advising that he forward skates and any special equipment belonging to OLIVER.

Yours very truly,

J.M. GREGORY,
General Manager

JMG/sb

encls.

Plante's Apartment

Hockey fans rarely give thought to the complications of life for their heroes away from the rink. Veteran goaltender Jacques Plante arrived in Toronto with more than a thousand NHL games under his belt. For 1970–71, he earned $39,800. The Leafs helped out with little things, like taxes. But not listed in the contract is the apartment that the Leafs rented for Plante from Mrs. Madeleine McDonald (a long-time Maple Leaf Gardens secretary)—4000 Yonge Street, just south of the 401, in the north end of the city. From October to February, it was $200 per month, plus $15 for phone and hydro, and for the next three months, $225 per; the Leafs paid in advance and again in the 1971–72 season. "Jacques was more than pleased in these lovely surroundings and was very happy to hear that they would be available to him again next year," GM Jim Gregory wrote to McDonald in March 1971, asking whether "Jake the Snake" could leave some things there over the summer. Mrs. McDonald okayed the storage, and Gregory let Jacques know: "She informs me that it will be quite in order for you to leave anything in her apartment during the summer and these items can be left in the cupboards and storage space in the apartment." When McDonald pressed Gregory about the 1972–73 season, he revealed, "Although I have not issued a public announcement in regards to Jacques Plante, I have signed him for next season and he will be playing for the Maple Leafs Hockey Club." He did rent the apartment again and play in Toronto, but only until March 3, 1973, when he was dealt to Boston.

Jacques Plante.

DEC 1 REC'D

MAPLE LEAF GARDENS, LIMITED

Memo to: J.M. Gregory   December 1st, 1970

from: R.E. Giroux

Subject: Jacques Plante - Annuity for 1970-71 Season

I have calculated the tax Jacques Plante would have to pay if we paid him $30,000 in 1970 and $30,000 in 1971. The tax would be $10,100.00 in each year. This results in net after tax income of $19,900 to Plante in each year.

Following our discussions last week, we will have to provide Plante with annuities with a present value of $39,800.00. Plante has already signed an application for an annuity with a present value of $20,500.00 If we bought that annuity and an additional one during the first week of January 1971 in the amount of $19,300, $20,500 is taxable in Plante's hands in 1970 and $19,300 in 1971.

If this is agreeable with you and Jacques, we can proceed in this manner.

REG/mk

455 Worth Avenue Apt 406,
Palm Beach, Fla. 33480
March 27, 1972

Dear Mr. Gregory: Ap# 523, 4000 Yonge St.

        Just a note to let you know that I have
contacted the Manager of 4000 Yonge St., and have
arranged for a further one-year lease on Apt 523,
June 1/72 to May 31/73 - with permission to sub-
let.

        You may, therefore, have this apartment
for Mr. Plante for another hockey season, on the
same terms as we had last year, ie, M.L.G. to
pay the rental for the full year and I will be free
to make use of the Apartment myself during the
months of,approximately, May,June,July,August,Sept
depending on when your training starts in the Fall,
and how far you go in the play-offs this spring.
I think Mr. Plante was there briefly in May last
year, and also a good part of September. Anthing
inthat order o.k. with me as I very seldom go into
Toronto in the summer any more. However, it is nice
to know I have a spot to land in the City when I do
have to come in to Doctors, Dentists, etc.

        The only change will be (what else) the rent!
There has been a small rise in the rent and, also, I
intend to spend some money on a professional house clean
of the apartment and furniture and rugs, both to preserve
same and make it right for Mr. Plante also.   I would
like a rental of $230.00 per month - $2,760.00 for the
year.

        I will be glad to have your confirmation of
this arrangement, as I have told the Management of the
4000,that I will enter into the year's lease with them -
assuming that you will be able to absorb an increase of
$10.00 per month, as I did not have time,before the Mch.
31st deadline to be sure of the mails and contact you, on
                                           this point.

                Yours very truly,

* I will continue
to pay hydro +   Madeleine McDonald
telephone (except   (Mrs)Madeleine McDonald.
    long distance calls)
        McD.

Mike Walton.

Who Pays Shakey?

Getting traded is one thing; being traded twice on the same day is another. It happened to Mike "Shakey" Walton on February 1, 1971. Toronto shipped him with Bruce Gamble and Toronto's first-round choice in that year's draft to Philadelphia for goalie Bernie Parent and the Flyers' second-round pick. The Flyers turned around and sent him to Boston for Danny Schock and Rick MacLeish. Complicating things was a clause in Walton's contract that called for a bonus if his team made the playoffs. Well, both the Leafs and Bruins made the playoffs, and, after much back and forth between Walton's agent, Alan Eagleson, Leafs GM Jim Gregory, and Bruins GM Milt Schmidt, the NHL President, Clarence Campbell, made his ruling—that the money owing be shared between the teams. "In those days, remember, clubs were not making much money. The Leafs made a bit, Montreal made a bit," said Eagleson. "What people don't understand is that many of the clubs in the 1970s didn't have a pot to piss in. If they could stall and get the other club to pay it, that's what they did."

NOV 26 1971

NATIONAL HOCKEY LEAGUE

922 SUN LIFE BUILDING · MONTREAL 110, P.Q. · (514) 866-1851 · TWX 610-421-3260

PRESIDENT'S OFFICE

November 25, 1971.

Mr. J.M. Gregory
Maple Leaf Gardens Limited
60 Carlton Street
Toronto 200, Ontario

Re: Mike Walton 1970 Bonus
     for Making the Play-offs

Dear Jim:

Your letter of November 23rd received and contents noted which puts a completely new complexion on the subject.

Toronto signed Walton to the 1970-71 contract which provided for a bonus of $2,500 "for making the play-offs." Before the play-off positions were determined, Walton was traded to Boston via Philadelphia.

Both Boston and Toronto made the play-offs and Walton was credited with 28 of the 78 games Boston played to achieve that result. While Walton only played 23 games of Toronto's 78 games, he was officially awarded 50 games as a member of the Toronto Club.

Walton is clearly entitled to collect $2,500 under his contract. Boston has already contributed 28/78ths of that amount. In my judgment the equitable solution would be for the Toronto Club to pay its pro rata share - the balance of the $2,500.

This is my best advice in the circumstances.

Yours very truly,

NATIONAL HOCKEY LEAGUE

President

CSC:t

Walton file

BLANEY, PASTERNAK, SMELA, EAGLESON & WATSON

BARRISTERS AND SOLICITORS

J. W. BLANEY, Q.C.	I. W. PASTERNAK, Q.C.	J. A. BRULÉ, Q.C
R. H. SMELA, Q.C.	R. A. EAGLESON	R. J. WATSON
J. D. CADSBY	W. M. BOWEN	J. S UBLANSKY
J. FREYSENG	J. H. CLARKE Q C	J. L. BOWLES
S. H. AARONS	W. A. PEARCE	D. C. CHAMPAGNE
A. J. MESBUR	L. DUSO	I. W. ANGUS
P. DROZDOSKI	R. J. SHAW	G. MAITLAND-CARTER

TELEPHONE 364-9421
CABLE ADDRESS "BLANLAW" TORONTO

365 BAY STREET
TORONTO 105, CANADA

COUNSEL

R. S. MACKAY, Q C., LL.M.   WM. R. McMURTRY

PLEASE REFER TO:

December 14, 1971

Mr. J.M. Gregory
General Manager
Toronto Maple Leafs
60 Carlton Street
Toronto, Ontario

Dear Jim: Re: Mike Walton

I have received a copy of a letter addressed to your
attention from Mr. Campbell, dated November 25, 1971.

Would you be kind enough to draft a cheque, in the
amount of $1,602.56, which constitutes 50/78 of the
$2,500.00 amount involved. This will confirm that
the Boston Bruins Hockey Club has already paid the
28/78 amount involved.

If you wish to send this cheque directly to Mike
Walton at the Boston Gardens, please do so by
registered mail and please be kind enough to send
me a copy of the letter you address to his attention.
If this matter has already been looked after, would
you please ignore this correspondence.

Sincerely yours,

BLANEY, PASTERNAK, SMELA, EAGLESON
& WATSON

R. Alan Eagleson

RAE/df

Give Glennie Credit

Brian Glennie.

Somewhere along the way, it was suggested to Brian Glennie, the thumping Leafs defenceman, that he incorporate. His 1973–74 contract is made out to Brian Glennie Enterprises Limited. His next deal, for 1976–78, is done with Briglex Corporation, Limited. The first one is easy to understand, but what the heck is Briglex? "I wanted it to sound like Chargex," chuckled Glennie, referring to the credit card now known as Visa. A Toronto native, Glennie played his junior hockey with the Marlies and was the captain when the team won the 1967 Memorial Cup. Glennie also suited up for Canada at the 1968 Olympics, and he was along for the ride too at the 1972 Summit Series, a backup blueliner who never saw action against the Russians. Despite not playing, he considers it a career highlight and is a part of Canada's Sports Hall of Fame because of his involvement with "The Team of the Century." Back with the Leafs, Glennie's 1976 contract includes bonuses for plus/minus, but he doesn't remember how he did. "Maybe they owe me money."

NATIONAL HOCKEY LEAGUE
STANDARD PLAYER'S CONTRACT
(1974 FORM)

This Agreement

BETWEEN: MAPLE LEAF GARDENS LTD.,
hereinafter called the "Club",
a member of the National Hockey League, hereinafter called the "League"

— AND —

BRIGLEX CORPORATION, LIMITED
hereinafter called the "Player"

of TORONTO in {Province} of ONTARIO
{State}

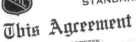

BULLETIN 1684

SEP 27 10 45 AM '76

Witnesseth:

That in consideration of the respective obligations herein and hereby assumed, the parties to this contract severally
agree as follows :—

1. The Club hereby employs the Player as a skilled Hockey Player for the term of 1 year(s) commencing October 1st, 19 76
and agrees, subject to the terms and conditions hereof, to pay the Player a salary of

1976-77 EIGHTY THOUSAND AND NO................................... Dollars ($ 80,000.00)

BONUSES:

1st Place - $5,000.00 (in our division)
2nd Place - $2,500.00 (in our division)

Each plus to 10   - $ 50.00   For plus 20 - $500.00
For plus 10   - $250.00
For each plus 11 and up - $100.00
For plus 15   - $250.00

Payment of such salary shall be in consecutive semi-monthly instalments following the commencement of the regular League Championship Schedule of games or following the date of reporting, whichever is later, provided, however, that if the Player is not in the employ
of the Club for the whole period of the Club's games in the National Hockey League Championship Schedule, then he shall receive only
part of the salary in the ratio of the number of days of actual employment to the number of days of the League Championship Schedule
of games.

And it is further mutually agreed that if the Contract and rights to the services of the Player are assigned, exchanged, loaned or
otherwise transferred to a Club in another League, the Player shall only be paid at the rate of

.... Dollars in the .... League.

.... Dollars in the .... League.

or .... Dollars in the .... League.

or

2. The Player agrees to give his services and to play hockey in all League Championship, Exhibition, Play-Off and Stanley Cup
games to the best of his ability under the direction and control of the Club for the said season in accordance with the provisions hereof.

The Player further agrees,

(a) to report to the Club training camp at the time and place fixed by the Club, in good physical condition,
(b) to keep himself in good physical condition at all times during the season,
(c) to give his best services and loyalty to the Club and to play hockey only for the Club unless his contract is released, assigned,
exchanged or loaned by the Club,
(d) to co-operate with the Club and participate in any and all promotional activities of the Club and the League which will in
the opinion of the Club promote the welfare of the Club or professional hockey generally, and to conduct himself on and off the rink according to the highest standards of honesty, morality, fair play and sportsmanship,
(e) to conduct himself on and off the rink according to the highest standards of honesty, morality, fair play and sportsmanship,
and to refrain from conduct detrimental to the best interests of the Club, the League or professional hockey generally.

The Club agrees that in exhibition games played after the start of the regular schedule (except where the proceeds are to go to
charity, or where the player has agreed otherwise) the player shall receive his pro rata share of the gate receipts after deduction of legitimate
expenses of such game. This provision re exhibition games is applicable in the National Hockey League only.

3. In order that the Player shall be fit in proper condition for the performance of his duties as required by this contract the
Player agrees to report for practice at such time and place as the Club may designate and participate in such exhibition games as may be
arranged by the Club within thirty days prior to the first scheduled Championship game. The Club shall pay the travelling expenses
of the Player to report to the Club's training camp. In the event of failure of the player to so report and participate
in exhibition games a fine not exceeding Five Hundred Dollars may be imposed by the Club and be deducted from the compensation
and meals en route from the Player's home to the Club's training camp. In the event of failure of the player to so report and participate
stipulated herein. At the conclusion of the season the Club shall provide transportation direct to the Player's home.

4. The Club may from time to time during the continuance of this contract establish reasonable rules governing the conduct and conditioning of the Player, and such rules shall form part of the duties incumbent upon the Player, the Club may impose a reasonable
fine upon the Player and deduct the amount thereof from any money due or to become due to the Player. When the Player is fined or suspended he shall be given notice in writing stating the amount
the Player for violation of any such rules. When the Player is fined or suspended he shall be given notice in writing stating the amount
of the fine and/or the duration of the suspension and the reason therefor.

5. Should the Player be disabled or unable to perform his duties under this contract he shall submit himself for medical examination and treatment by a physician selected by the Club, and such examination and treatment, when made at the request of the Club,
shall be at its expense unless made necessary by some act or conduct of the Player contrary to the terms and provisions of this contract
or the rules established under Section 4.

If the Player, in the sole judgment of the Club's physician, is disabled or is not in good physical condition at the commencement
of the season or at any subsequent time during the season (unless such condition is the direct result of playing hockey for the Club) so
as to render him unfit to play skilled hockey, then it is mutually agreed that the Club shall have the right to suspend the Player for such
period of disability or unfitness, and no compensation shall be payable for that period under this contract.

If the Player is injured as the result of playing hockey for the Club, the Club will pay the hospital and doctor are selected by the Club
and provided further that the hospital, and his medical expenses and doctor's bills, provided that the hospital and doctor are selected by the Club
discharged from the hospital, and his medical expenses and doctor's bills shall terminate at a period not more than six months after the
injury.

It is also agreed that if the Player's injuries resulting directly from playing for the Club render him, in the sole judgment of the
Club's physician, unfit to play skilled hockey for the balance of the season or any part thereof, then during such time the Player is so
unfit, but in no event beyond the end of the current season, the Club shall pay the Player the compensation herein provided for and the
Player releases the Club from any and every additional obligation, liability, claim or demand whatsoever. However if upon joint consultation between the Player, the Club's physician and the Club General Manager, they are unable to agree as to the physical fitness
of the Player to return to play, the Player agrees to submit himself for examination by an independent medical specialist and the Parties
hereto agree to be bound by his decision. If the Player is declared to be unfit for play he shall continue to receive the full benefits of this
of the Player to return to play, the Player is declared to be unfit for play he shall continue to receive the full benefits of this

In Witness Whereof, the parties have signed this 29th day

of June A.D. 1976.

WITNESSES :

John McFell   Toronto Maple Leaf Hockey Club
                                 Club
John McFell   60 Carlton Street, Toronto, Ont.
                                 Address of Club

By _Jim Gregory_
                                 President

BRIGLEX CORPORATION LIMITED for
Brian Glennie
Brian Glennie
15 Beach Avenue, Toronto, Ont.
                                 Player
                                 Home Address of Player

I hereby certify that I have, at this date, received, examined and noted of record the within Contract, and that it is in regular form.

Dated Oct 13th 19 76   _____
                                        NATIONAL HOCKEY LEAGUE

Ullman Chooses Security

Norm Ullman's 1972 contract kept the centreman from Provost, Alberta, in the NHL for another three years. (His career started in 1955 with the Detroit Red Wings.) "I was about 37 years old when I signed that contract with the Leafs. You have to keep that in mind too," said Ullman. "You get a pretty good raise, plus three-year no-trade. I probably could have signed one year for more, but the three years was a little more security at my age. If I had been 30, it would have been a different story." Back when Ullman was 30, he led the league with 42 goals. He arrived in Toronto in March 1968, in a huge trade, with Frank Mahovlich, Pete Stemkowski, Garry Unger, and the rights to Carl Brewer going to Motown for Ullman, Floyd Smith, Paul Henderson, and Doug Barrie. In 1970–71, Ullman set the Toronto record for points, with 85. But the arrival of the WHA, in 1972, decimated and demoralized the team. Bernie Parent, Rick Ley, and Brad Selwood left for greener pastures. "They lost a bunch of guys just over $20,000, $30,000. It was crazy," said Ullman. "Ballard, he wouldn't pay anybody any more than what he wanted to pay them." Ullman himself went to the WHA in September 1975 and played two seasons there. His 87-point season in 1975–76 (31 goals and 56 assists) was an Oilers record—until some kid named Gretzky came along.

Norm Ullman.

IMPORTANT NOTICE TO PLAYER

Before signing this contract you should carefully examine it to be sure that all terms and conditions agreed upon have been incorporated herein, and if any has been omitted, you should insist upon having it inserted in the contract before you sign.

NATIONAL HOCKEY LEAGUE
STANDARD PLAYER'S CONTRACT

This Agreement

BETWEEN: **MAPLE LEAF GARDENS, LTD.**

hereinafter called the "Club",

a member of the National Hockey League, hereinafter called the "League"

—AND—

NORM ULLMAN

hereinafter called the "Player"

of .... TORONTO .... in {Province}{State} of .... ONTARIO

Witnesseth:

That in consideration of the respective obligations herein and hereby assumed, the parties to this contract severally agree as follows:—

1. The Club hereby employs the Player as a skilled Hockey Player for the term of **THREE** years commencing October 1st, 19**72** and agrees, subject to the terms and conditions hereof, to pay the Player a salary of

1972-73 EIGHTY-FIVE THOUSAND AND NO..$85,000.00

1973-74 EIGHTY-FIVE THOUSAND AND NO.............................Dollars ($ 85,000.00

1974-75 EIGHTY-FIVE THOUSAND AND NO...$85,000.00

BONUSES: IF LEAFS FINISH 1ST OR 2ND IN OWN DIVISION.......$2,000.00

35 GOALS or 75 POINTS DURING............$3,500.00

THIS IS A THREE YEAR NO CUT NO TRADE CONTRACT. HOWEVER MAPLE LEAF GARDENS, LTD. RESERVES THE RIGHT, AT ITS DICRETION, THE DECISION OF WHETHER OR NOT TO PROTECT SAID PLAYER NORMAN ULLMAN AT THE NHL DRAFTS.

Payment of such salary shall be in consecutive semi-monthly instalments following the commencement of the regular League Championship Schedule of games or following the date of reporting, whichever is later; provided, however, that if the Player is not in the employ of the Club for the whole period of the Club's games in the National Hockey League Championship Schedule, then he shall receive only part of the salary in the ratio of the number of days of actual employment to the number of days of the League Championship Schedule of games.

And it is further mutually agreed that if the Contract and rights to the services of the Player are assigned, exchanged, loaned or otherwise transferred to a Club in another League, the Player shall only be paid at the rate of

or .... Dollars in the .... League.

.... Dollars in the .... League.

or .... Dollars in the .... League.

.... Dollars in the .... League.

2. The Player agrees to give his services and to play hockey in all League Championship, Exhibition, Play-Off and Stanley Cup games to the best of his ability under the direction and control of the Club for the said season in accordance with the provisions hereof.

The Player further agrees,

(a) to report to the Club training camp at the time and place fixed by the Club, in good physical condition,

(b) to keep himself in good physical condition at all times during the season,

(c) to give his best services and loyalty to the Club and to play hockey only for the Club unless his contract is released, assigned, exchanged or loaned by the Club,

(d) to co-operate with the Club and participate in any and all promotional activities of the Club and the League which will in the opinion of the Club promote the welfare of the Club or professional hockey generally,

(e) to conduct himself on and off the rink according to the highest standards of honesty, morality, fair play and sportsmanship, and to refrain from conduct detrimental to the best interests of the Club, the League or professional hockey generally.

The Club agrees that in exhibition games played after the start of the regular schedule (except where the proceeds are to go to charity, or where the player has agreed otherwise) the player shall receive his pro rata share of the gate receipts after deduction of legitimate expenses of such game. This provision re exhibition games is applicable in the National Hockey League only.

3. In order that the Player shall be fit in proper condition for the performance of his duties as required by this contract the Player agrees to report for practice at such time and place as the Club may designate and participate in such exhibition games as may be arranged by the Club within thirty days prior to the first scheduled Championship game. The Club shall pay the travelling expenses and meals en route from the Player's home to the Club's training camp. In the event of failure of the player to so report and participate in exhibition games a fine not exceeding Five Hundred Dollars may be imposed by the Club and be deducted from the compensation stipulated herein. At the conclusion of the season the Club shall provide transportation direct to the Player's home.

4. The Club may from time to time during the continuance of this contract establish rules governing the conduct and conditioning of the Player, and such rules shall form part of this contract as fully as if herein written. For violation of any such rules or condition, any conduct impairing the thorough and faithful discharge of the duties incumbent upon the Player, the Club may impose a reasonable fine upon the Player and deduct the amount thereof from any money due or to become due to the Player. The Club may also suspend the Player for violation of any such rules. When the Player is fined or suspended he shall be given notice in writing stating the amount of the fine and/or the duration of the suspension and the reason therefor.

23 RD .... day

of .... JUNE .... A.D. 19**72**.

WITNESSES: MAPLE LEAF GARDENS, LTD.
                                                                                                    Club

Howard Starkman   By *Jim Gregory*
                                                                                                    President

                                                       Norman Ullman
                                                                                                    Player

                                                       19 Overton Cr. Don Mills Ont.
                                                                                           Home Address of Player

T.V.R. © NATIONAL HOCKEY LEAGUE

Bernie Bolts

By the summer of 1972, it was pretty evident that Bernie Parent did not want to be the Leafs goalie. He had played in 47 games in the 1971–72 season, and four playoff games, but wanted out. The Leafs sent him two contracts: the first, sent in August and signed by Harold Ballard, was for three years, from 1972 to 1975, for a total of $167,500, plus bonuses; the second, from September and signed by Jim Gregory, was for $150,000 for the next five years. Neither deal was ever signed. "Many stories circulated after Bernie defected to the WHA, and it's difficult to know exactly what went on," Darryl Sittler wrote in his autobiography. "One theory had it that Harold Ballard interfered with Jim Gregory's efforts to negotiate with the Philadelphia lawyer, Howard Casper, who was operating as Parent's agent." Did Ballard really utter, "If he can get that kind of money, I won't stop him," giving Parent an out? The Leafs felt that Parent was "legally bound and permitted to play hockey only for the Toronto Maple Leafs" and fought for Parent, ultimately unsuccessfully. It wasn't the last time that Parent ended up in controversy. He signed for $750,000 over five years with the Miami Screaming Eagles, but that team never played a game, and he settled with the WHA's Philadelphia Blazers for $600,000. During the 1973 WHA playoffs, Parent walked out on the Blazers and rejoined the NHL's Philadelphia Flyers, with whom he'd win Stanley Cups in 1974 and 1975, and eventually carve out a Hall of Fame career.

Bernie Parent.

August 2, 1972.

Mr. Bernard Parent,
121 Sharrowvale Road,
Cherry Hills, N.J.

Dear Bernie:

I am enclosing for your signature four copies of an NHL
Standard Player's Contract between yourself and Maple Leaf
Gardens Limited. This contract covers the 2 year period
which commenced last October 1 and contains the terms including salary and bonuses that were agreed upon at the
meeting which you and your attorney, Mr. Howard Casper, had
with me in my office on September 17, 1971.

In our view you are legally obliged to sign this contract.
I am well aware, however, that a dispute exists between us
in this regard. Mr. Casper's view, apparently, is that you
never became bound to the terms which are set out in this
contract. As matters now stand, this dispute between us may
not be settled short of legal action. If a Court should
determine that you are not bound by the terms of this contract,
the present situation may be that the 3 year contract which
you signed with Philadelphia Hockey Club, Inc. and which was
assigned to Maple Leaf Gardens, Limited in February of 1971
continues effective until September 30, 1972. To protect the
position of our company in this eventuality and in accordance
with the terms of paragraph 17 of that contract, on behalf of
Maple Leaf Gardens, Limited I am hereby tendering on you four
copies of a contract for a period of 3 years from October 1,
1972 upon the same terms as that contract save as to salary.

As you are aware, failing mutual agreement between us as to
salary under this latter contract, it will be determined by
arbitration under the Arbitration Agreement between the League

- 2 -

I am sure you are aware that Maple Leaf Gardens, Limited
considers that you are legally bound and permitted to play
hockey only for the Toronto Maple Leafs. I must formally
advise you that Maple Leaf Gardens, Limited intends to enforce
its legal rights in this regard and intends to seek damages
against you and an injunction preventing you from playing for
any other hockey team if you do not fulfil your commitments in
this regard.

Yours very truly,

jmg/r   J. M. Gregory,
Encls.   General Manager.

Registered Mail

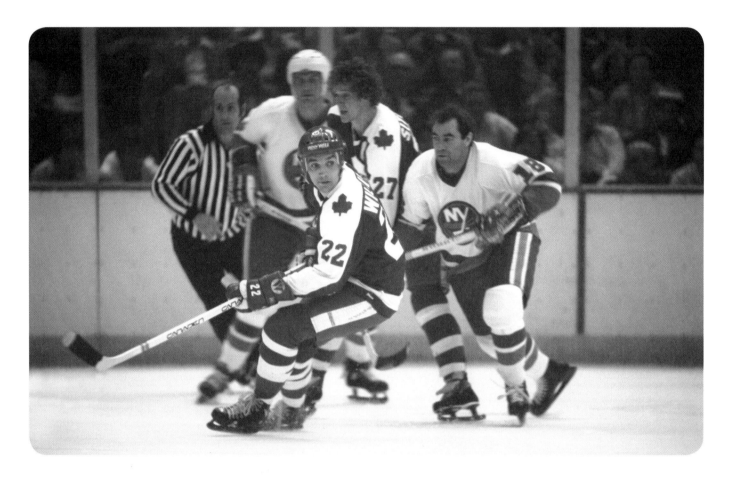

Tiger "an excellent team man"

Tiger Williams.

In August 1974, the Leafs trotted out four new signees for the media—three from the junior ranks in Canada and a 20-year-old Swede. One, a left winger from the Swift Current Broncos, was described by Dan Proudfoot of the *Globe and Mail*: "He's tough and he enjoys scoring—a description that couldn't easily be applied to the current left wingers." Sure enough, he'd etch his name in the record books as Dave "Tiger" Williams, with an NHL-record 3,966 penalty minutes in 962 games. "I'm going to come to camp figuring to play for the Leafs," Williams said at the press conference, standing alongside newcomers Mike Palmateer, a local goalie from the Marlboros, Jack Valiquette, who led the OHL with 63 goals and 135 points in Sault Ste. Marie, and Per-Arne Alexandersson from Leksand, Sweden. "The key to making the team is play-ing my style," Tiger said. "My aggressiveness put me here today and it'll keep me here with the team." During his 14-year NHL career, with Toronto, Vancouver, Detroit, Los Angeles, and Hartford, Williams counted a respectable 241 goals and 272 assists, including 35 goals for the Canucks in 1980–81. Leafs coach Red Kelly was eager to see Williams in action. "The thing we like about Dave," Kelly said, "I mean Tiger, I guess that's what they call him out west, is that he's an excellent team man. That's what really impressed us from our scouts' reports."

IMPORTANT NOTICE TO PLAYER

Before signing this contract you should carefully examine it to be sure that all terms and conditions
agreed upon have been incorporated herein, and if any has been omitted, you should insist upon having
it inserted in the contract before you sign.

NATIONAL HOCKEY LEAGUE
STANDARD PLAYER'S CONTRACT
(1974 FORM)

This Agreement

BETWEEN: MAPLE LEAF GARDENS, LTD.

hereinafter called the "Club",
a member of the National Hockey League, hereinafter called the "League"

—AND—

DAVE WILLIAMS

hereinafter called the "Player"

of SWIFT CURRENT in {Province} of SASK.
{State}

BULLETIN 1641

Witnesseth:

That in consideration of the respective obligations herein and hereby assumed, the parties to this contract severally
agree as follows: —

1.   The Club hereby employs the Player as a skilled Hockey Player for the term of THREE year(s) commencing October 1st, 19 74
and agrees, subject to the terms and conditions hereof, to pay the Player a salary of $60,000.00
1975-76 ONE HUNDRED THOUSAND AND NO 100,000.00
1976-77 ONE HUNDRED AND TEN THOUSAND .... Dollars ($110,000.00)
BONUSES: FOR SIGNING THIS CONTRACT..$30,000.00; FOR EVERY 10 GOALS OR 20
POINTS AFTER 20 GOALS OR 40 POINTS..$1,000.00; FOR EVERY GOAL OR 2 POINTS AFTER 20 GOALS
NHL BONUSES ONLY; FOR EVERY GOAL OR 2 POINTS AFTER..$500.00;
POINTS AFTER AN ADDITIONAL $1,000.00; FOR PLUS 10 AFTER..$500.00;
ON 40 POINTS..$100.00; FOR PLUS 10...$500.00; FOR EVERY PLUS 10 AFTER..$500.00;
FOR EACH PLUS OVER 10...$100.00.

Payment of such salary shall be in consecutive semi-monthly instalments following the commencement of the regular League Championship Schedule of games or following the date of reporting, whichever is later; provided, however, that if the Player is not in the employ
of the Club for the whole period of the Club's games in the National Hockey League Championship Schedule, then he shall receive only
part of the salary in the ratio of the number of days of actual employment to the number of days of the League Championship Schedule
of games.

And it is further mutually agreed that if the Contract and rights to the services of the Player are assigned, exchanged, loaned or
otherwise transferred to a Club in another League, the Player shall only be paid at the rate of .... MINORS .... League.
...FIFTY-FIVE THOUSAND AND NO .... Dollars in the MINORS. League.
or 1975-76 SIXTY-FIVE THOUSAND AND NO .... Dollars in the MINORS. League.
or 1976-77 SEVENTY-FIVE THOUSAND AND NO .... Dollars in the League.

2.   The Player agrees to give his services and to play hockey in all League Championship, Exhibition, Play-Off and Stanley Cup
games to the best of his ability under the direction and control of the Club for the said season in accordance with the provisions hereof.

The Player further agrees,

(a) to report to the Club training camp at the time and place fixed by the Club, in good physical condition,
(b) to keep himself in good physical condition at all times during the season,
(c) to give his best services and loyalty to the Club and to play hockey only for the Club unless his contract is released, assigned,
exchanged or loaned by the Club,
(d) to co-operate with the Club and participate in any and all promotional activities of the Club and the League which will in
the opinion of the Club promote the welfare of the Club or professional hockey generally,
(e) to conduct himself on and off the rink according to the highest standards of honesty, morality, fair play and sportsmanship,
and to refrain from conduct detrimental to the best interests of the Club, the League or professional hockey generally.

The Club agrees that in exhibition games played after the start of the regular schedule (except where the proceeds are to go to
charity, or where the player has agreed otherwise) the player shall receive his pro rata share of the gate receipts after deduction of legitimate
expenses of such game. This provision re exhibition games is applicable in the National Hockey League only.

3.   In order that the Player shall be fit in proper condition for the performance of his duties as required by this contract the
Player agrees to report for practice at such time and place as the Club may designate and participate in such exhibition games as may be
arranged by the Club within thirty days prior to the first scheduled Championship game. The Club shall pay the travelling expenses
and meals en route from the Player's home to the Club's training camp. In the event of failure of the player to so report and participate
in exhibition games a fine not exceeding Five Hundred Dollars may be imposed by the Club and be deducted from the compensation
stipulated herein. At the conclusion of the season the Club shall provide transportation direct to the Player's home.

4.   The Club may from time to time during the continuance of this contract establish rules governing the conduct and conditioning of the Player, and such rules shall form part of this contract as fully as if herein written. For violation of any such rules or for
any conduct impairing the thorough and faithful discharge of the duties incumbent upon the Player, the Club may impose a reasonable
fine upon the Player and deduct the amount thereof from any money due to or become due to the Player. The Club may also suspend
the Player for violation of any such rules. When the Player is fined or suspended he shall be given notice in writing stating the amount
of the fine and/or the duration of the suspension and the reason therefor.

5.   Should the Player be disabled or unable to perform his duties under this contract he shall submit himself for medical examination and treatment by a physician selected by the Club, and such examination and treatment, when made at the request of the Club,
shall be at its expense unless made necessary by some act or conduct of the Player contrary to the terms and provisions of this contract
or the rules established under Section 4.

If the Player, in the sole judgment of the Club's physician, is disabled or is not in good physical condition at the commencement
of the season or at any subsequent time during the season (unless such condition is the direct result of playing hockey for the Club) so
as to render him unfit to play skilled hockey, then it is mutually agreed that the Club shall have the right to suspend the Player for such
period of disability or unfitness, and no compensation shall be payable for that period under this contract.

If the Player is injured as the result of playing hockey for the Club, the Club will pay the Player's reasonable hospitalization until
discharged from the hospital, and his medical expenses and doctor's bills, provided that the hospital and doctor are selected by the Club
and provided further that the Club's obligation to pay such expenses shall terminate at a period not more than six months after the
injury.

It is also agreed that if the Player's injuries resulting directly from playing for the Club render him, in the sole judgment of the
Club's physician, unfit to play skilled hockey for the balance of the season or any part thereof, then during such time the Player is so
unfit, but in no event beyond the end of the current season, the Club shall pay the Player the compensation herein provided for and the
Player releases the Club from any and every additional obligation, liability, claim or demand whatsoever. However if upon joint consultation between the Player, the Club's physician and the Club General Manager, they are unable to agree as to the physical fitness
of the Player to return to play, the Player agrees to submit himself for examination by an independent medical specialist and the Parties
hereto agree to be bound by his decision. If the Player is declared to be unfit to play he shall continue to receive the full benefits of this
Agreement. If the Player is declared to be physically able to play and refuses to do so he shall be liable to immediate suspension without
pay.

If upon joint consultation between the Player, the Club's Physician and the Club General Manager, they are unable to agree
upon the physical fitness to return to play following an injury not resulting directly from playing for the Club, to be bound by his decision. If the
submit himself for examination by an independent medical specialist and the Parties hereto agree to be bound by his decision. It he is declared to be not
Player is declared to be fit for play, he shall be entitled to receive the full benefits of this agreement. If he is declared to be physically fit to play
physically able to play, he shall not be entitled to the benefits of this agreement until he has been declared to be physically fit to play
by the independent medical specialist.

6.   The Player represents and agrees that he has exceptional and unique knowledge, skill and ability as a hockey player, the loss
of which cannot be estimated with certainty and cannot be fairly or adequately compensated by damages. The Player therefore agrees
that the Club shall have the right, in addition to any other rights which the Club may possess, to enjoin him by appropriate injunction
proceedings from playing hockey for any other team and/or for any breach of any of the other provisions of this contract.

7.   The Player and the Club recognize that the Player's participation in other sports may impair or destroy his ability
and skill as a hockey player. Accordingly the Player agrees that he will not during the period of this Contract and during any period when
he is obligated under this contract to enter into a further contract with the Club engage or participate in football, baseball, softball, hockey,

---

(Second page / reverse side, partially visible)

... certainty and cannot be fairly or adequately compensated by damages. The Player therefore agrees
...addition to any other rights which the Club may possess, to enjoin him by appropriate injunction
...any other team and/or for any breach of any of the other provisions of this contract.

...recognize and agree that the Player's participation in other sports may impair or destroy his ability
...ly the Player agrees that he will not during the period of this Contract and during any period when
...er into a further contract with the Club engage or participate in football, baseball, softball, hockey,
...athletic sport without the written consent of the Club.

...ocably grants to the Club during the period of this Contract and during any period when he is
...into a further contract with the Club the exclusive right to permit or authorize any person, firm
...of any still photograph, motion pictures or television of himself, and agrees that all rights in such
...e Club exclusively and may be used, reproduced, distributed or otherwise disseminated by the
...ner it desires.

...that during the period of this Contract and during any period when he is obligated under this
...ct with the Club he will not make public appearances, participate in radio or television programs,
...or sponsor newspaper or magazine articles, or sponsor commercial products without the written
...not be withheld unreasonably. Where the Club grants its written consent to any of the activities
...all receive his proper share of the proceeds of such activities.

...the Club will not pay, and the Player will not accept from any person, any bonus or anything of
...or series of games except as authorized by the League By-Laws.

...ing the period of this contract and during any period when he is obligated under this contract to
...Club he will not tamper with or enter into negotiations with any player under contract or reserva-
...arding such player's current or future services, without the written consent of the Club with which
...of a fine to be imposed by the President of the League.

...the Club shall have the right to sell, assign, exchange and transfer this contract, and to loan the
...d hockey club, and the Player agrees to accept and be bound by such sale, exchange, assignment,
...and carry out this contract with the same purpose and effect as if it had been entered into by the

...in the event that this contract is assigned, or the Player's services are loaned, to another Club,
...red personally to the Player or by mail to the address set out below his signature hereto advise
...e Club to which he has been assigned or loaned, and specifying the time and place of reporting
...to such other Club he may be suspended by such other Club and no salary shall be payable to

...expenses incurred by a player during the playing season when such move is directed by the
...

...payments to the Player provided for in Section 1 hereof or shall fail to perform any other
...Club hereunder, the Player may, by notice in writing to the Club, specify the nature of such
...ly the default within fifteen (15) days from receipt of such notice, this contract shall be termin-
...all obligations of both parties shall cease, except the obligation of the Club to pay the Player's

...contract upon written notice to the Player (but only after obtaining waivers from all other
...time:
...Club's rules governing training and conduct of players,
...this services hereunder or in any other manner materially breach this contract.
...sub-section (a) or (b) the Player shall only be entitled to compensation due to him to the date
...f the mailing of such notice to his address as set out below his signature hereto.
...rminated by the Club while the Player is "away" with the Club for the purpose of playing
...be paid on the first week-day after the return "home" of the Club.

...the Club may carry out and put into effect any order or ruling of the League or its President
...e event of suspension his salary shall cease for the duration thereof and that in the event of
...Club, shall terminate forthwith.

...in the event of his suspension pursuant to any of the provisions of this contract, there shall be
...n 1 hereof an amount equal to the exact proportion of such salary as the number of days'
...of the League Championship Schedule of games.

...ng from a state of war or other cause beyond the control of the League or of the Club, it shall
...to suspend or cease or reduce operations, then:

...rations, the Player shall be entitled only to the proportion of salary due at the date of

...ions, the salary stipulated in Section 1 hereof shall be automatically cancelled on the date of

...ions, the salary stipulated in Section 1 hereof shall be replaced by that mutually agreed upon

...ust 10th of the final year of this contract, tender the Player a Player's Termination Contract
...ing said Player's Termination Contract and delivering it to the Club on or before September
...ditionally released from any further obligation to provide services under this contract and
...'s Termination Contract shall be on the same terms and conditions as this contract except
...t the Player's previous year's salary and shall provide for the Player's unconditional release
...under said Player's Termination Contract effective the following June 1st.

...tion permitted under subsection (a), it shall no later than September 1st of the final year
..."protected" player or played at least fifty NHL games in the preceding season), tender the
...e same terms and conditions (including this Section 17) as this Standard Player's Contract
...ts fixed term may be different.

...en by the Club under subsections (a) or (b), the Player may notify the Club no later than
...d that it wishes to sign a Player's Option Contract. If the Player gives such notice, the
...year tender the Player a Player's Option Contract, and the Player shall forthwith enter
...shall be on the same terms and conditions as this contract except that it shall be for only
...year's salary and shall provide that effective the following June 1st the Player will be a
...provide services under said Player's Option Contract, and as such shall have the right, as
...the text of which Section is printed on the reverse side hereof, to negotiate and contract
...Club.

...tion permitted under subsection (a) and the Player does not give notice to the Club in
...shall enter into a new Standard Player's Contract by mutual agreement or, failing
...w one-year Standard Player's Contract for the succeeding season upon the same terms and
...Standard Player's Contract, except as to salary, which shall be determined by neutral
...ning agreement providing a mechanism for such arbitration, provided, however,
...s then in effect, the Player's salary shall be the same as his salary for the previous year.
..."final year of this contract" means the final year of the term specified in Section 1
...contract a special option provision agreed to by the parties, in which case the phrase
...which any exercised special option adds to the fixed term specified in Section 1.

...igations under this Section 17 shall be deemed fulfilled if the Club delivers the required
...t to the Player in person on or before the applicable deadline date or mails same by
...deadline date to the Player at the address set forth below his signature hereto. The
...s Section 17 shall be deemed fulfilled if the Player hand delivers the required written
...the applicable deadline date or mails it by registered mail postmarked no later than
...orth below.

...mutually promise and agree to be legally bound by the Constitution and By-Laws of
...eof, a copy of which shall be open and available for inspection by Club, its directors
...he League and at the main office of the Club.
... case of dispute between them, except as to the compensation to be paid to the Player
...in one year from the date it arose to the President of the League as an arbitrator and
...es.
...fines imposed upon the Player under the Playing Rules, or under the provisions of
...salary of the Player and be remitted by the Club to the N.H.L. Players' Emergency

...led in Section 17 and in any Addendum hereto and the promise of the Player to
...b as provided in Section 2 and Section 11, and the Club's right to take pictures of
...ve all been taken into consideration in determining the salary payable to the Player

...be only contracts recognized by the President of the League are the Standard Player's
...'s Option Contracts which have been duly executed and filed in the League's office
...ins the entire agreement between the Parties and there are no oral or written induce-
...erein.

...as aforesaid, the parties have signed this 8TH day

of AUGUST A.D. 19 74

WITNESSES: MAPLE LEAF GARDENS, LTD.
60 CARLTON STREET, TORONTO, ONTARIO Club
Address of Club

Howard Starkman

By _Jim Gregory_ ..... President

_H.W. ____ Jr._

Dave Tiger Williams
Player

Home Address of Player

I hereby certify that I have, at this date, received, examined and noted of record the within Contract, and that it is in regular form.

Dated _Nov 27th_ 19 74

President NATIONAL HOCKEY LEAGUE

Mike Palmateer.

Palmateer Never Lacked Confidence

Mike Palmateer graduated from the OHA's Toronto Marlboros with the Memorial Cup and the Dave Pinkney Trophy as the league's top goalie on his résumé. He was drafted by the Cincinnati Stingers of the WHA (24th overall) and the Toronto Maple Leafs (85th overall, in the fifth round). He chose the NHL. Never lacking in confidence, the story goes that when he first walked into the Maple Leaf dressing room in 1976, after serving his apprenticeship in the minors, he announced, "Your troubles are over, I'm here." Darryl Sittler appreciated what Palmy brought to the team: "He had a little bit of arrogance and cockiness to him, but in a good way, not in a bad way. He really believed in himself." Represented by Alan Eagleson, Palmateer signed an initial three-year contract under Leafs GM Jim Gregory. By the time his second contract was signed, for 1977–79, an addendum was added: $10,000 for playing 50 games or more (at least 3,000 minutes), $5,000 for a GAA of 3.00 or less, an additional $5,000 for a GAA of 2.75 or less, an additional $5,000 for a GAA of 2.50 or less, and $250 "for each shutout or 1-goal game that we win or tie that he participates in." To qualify, though, he had to play at least 25 games. Not everyone could survive the media spotlight in Toronto, said Paul Harrison, his backup from 1978 to 1980. "I think it took a guy like Mike to thrive under that environment," said Harrison. "It's extremely difficult to play in the spotlight like that."

IMPORTANT NOTICE TO PLAYER

Before signing this contract you should carefully examine it to be sure that all terms and conditions
agreed upon have been incorporated herein, and if any has been omitted, you should insist upon having
it inserted in the contract before you sign.

NATIONAL HOCKEY LEAGUE
STANDARD PLAYER'S CONTRACT
(1974 FORM)

This Agreement

BULLETIN 1653

BETWEEN: MAPLE LEAF GARDENS, LTD.

hereinafter called the "Club",
a member of the National Hockey League, hereinafter called the "League"

—AND—

MIKE PALMATEER

hereinafter called the "Player"

of TORONTO in the [Province]/[State] of ONTARIO

Witnesseth:

That in consideration of the respective obligations herein and hereby assumed, the parties to this contract severally agree as follows:—

1. The Club hereby employs the Player as a skilled Hockey Player for the term of 3 year(s) commencing October 1st, 19 74 and agrees, subject to the terms and conditions hereof, to pay the Player a salary of

1974-75 FORTY THOUSAND AND NO.............................$40,000.00
1975-76 FORTY-FIVE THOUSAND AND NO......................$45,000.00
1976-77 FIFTY THOUSAND AND NO..............................Dollars (845,000.00) $50,000.00

BONUSES: FOR SIGNING THIS CONTRACT..$25,000; IF PLAYER IS PROTECTED OR DRAFTED
AFTER THREE YEARS AN ADDITIONAL $25,000 WILL BE PAID;
$5,000 BONUS IF PLAYER IS IN MINORS ON JAN. 1, 1975;
$5,000 BONUS ON JAN. 1, 1976 IF PLAYER PLAYS IN MINORS.
BONUSES NHL ONLY: FOR 2.95 AVERAGE $1,500; FOR 2.80 AVERAGE $2,000 ADDITIONAL;
FOR 2.90 AVERAGE $3,000 ADDITIONAL; FOR EACH SHUTOUT $250;
BONUSES CHL & AHL: FOR 2.75 AVERAGE $1,500; FOR 2.60 AVERAGE $1,500 ADDITIONAL;
THESE BONUSES ARE PROVIDING PLAYER PARTICIPATES IN OVER 25 GAMES.

Payment of such salary shall be in consecutive semi-monthly instalments following the commencement of the regular League Championship Schedule of games or following the date of reporting, whichever is later; provided, however, that if the Player is not in the employ of the Club for the whole period of the Club's games in the National Hockey League Championship Schedule, then he shall receive only that part of the salary for the number of days of actual employment to the number of days of the League Championship Schedule of games.

And it is further mutually agreed that if this Contract and rights to the services of the Player are assigned, exchanged, loaned or otherwise transferred to a Club in another League, the Player shall only be paid at the rate of

1974-75 FIFTEEN THOUSAND AND NO.............. Dollars in the MINORS
or 1975-76 FIFTEEN THOUSAND AND NO.............. Dollars in the MINORS League.
or 1976-77 FIFTY THOUSAND AND NO.............. Dollars in the MINORS League.
Dollars in the League.

2. The Player agrees to give his services and to play hockey in all League Championship, Exhibition, Play-Off and Stanley Cup games to the best of his ability under the direction and control of the Club for the said season in accordance with the provisions hereof.

The Player further agrees,

(a) to report to the Club training camp at the time and place fixed by the Club, in good physical condition,

(b) to keep himself in good physical condition at all times during the season,

(c) to give his best services and loyalty to the Club and to play hockey only for the Club unless his contract is released, assigned, exchanged or loaned by the Club,

(d) to co-operate with the Club and participate in any and all promotional activities of the Club and the League which will in the opinion of the Club promote the welfare of the Club or professional hockey generally,

(e) to conduct himself on and off the rink according to the best standards of honesty, morality, fair play and sportsmanship, and to refrain from conduct detrimental to the best interests of the Club, the League or professional hockey generally.

The Club agrees that in exhibition games played after the start of the regular schedule (except where the proceeds are to go to charity, or where the player has agreed otherwise) the player shall receive his pro rata share of the gate receipts after deduction of legitimate expenses of such game. This provision re exhibition games is applicable in the National Hockey League only.

3. In order that the Player shall be fit in proper condition for the performance of his duties as required by this contract the Player agrees to report for practice at such time and place as the Club may designate and participate in such exhibition games as may be arranged by the Club within thirty days prior to the first scheduled Championship game. The Club shall pay the travelling expenses and meals en route from the Player's home to the Club's training camp. In the event of failure of the player to report and participate in exhibition games a fine not exceeding Five Hundred Dollars may be imposed by the Club and be deducted from the compensation stipulated herein. At the conclusion of the season the Club shall provide transportation direct to the Player's home.

4. The Club may from time to time during the continuance of this contract establish rules governing the conduct and deportment of the Player, and such rules shall form part of this contract as fully as if herein written. For violation of any such rules or for any conduct impairing the thorough and faithful discharge of the duties incumbent upon the Player, the Club may impose a reasonable fine upon the Player and deduct the amount thereof from any money due or to become due to the Player. The Club may also suspend the Player for violation of any such rules. When the Player is fined or suspended he shall be given notice in writing stating the amount of the fine and/or the duration of the suspension and the reason therefor.

5. Should the Player be disabled or unable to perform his duties under this contract he shall submit himself for medical examination and treatment by a physician selected by the Club, and such examination and treatment, when made at the request of the Club, shall be at its expense unless made necessary by some act or conduct of the Player contrary to the terms and provisions of this contract or the rules established under Section 4.

If the Player, in the sole judgment of the Club's physician, is disabled or is not in good physical condition at the commencement of the season or at any subsequent time during the season (unless such condition is the direct result of playing hockey for the Club) so as to render him unfit to play skilled hockey, then it is mutually agreed that the Club shall have the right to suspend the Player for such period of disability or unfitness and no compensation shall be payable for that period under this contract.

If the Player is injured as the result of playing hockey for the Club, the Club will pay the Player's reasonable hospitalization until discharged from the hospital, and his medical expenses and doctor's bills, provided that the hospital and doctor are selected by the Club and provided further that the Club's obligation to pay such expenses shall terminate at a period not more than six months after the injury.

It is also agreed that if the Player's injuries resulting directly from playing for the Club render him, in the sole judgment of the Club's physician, unfit to play skilled hockey for the balance of the season or any part thereof, then during such time the Player is so unfit, but in no case beyond the end of the current season, the Club shall pay the Player the compensation herein provided for and the Player releases the Club from any and every additional obligation, liability, claim or demand whatsoever. However if upon joint consultation between the Player, the Club's physician and the Club General Manager, they are unable to agree as to the physical fitness of the Player to return to play, the Player agrees to submit himself for examination by an independent medical specialist and the Parties hereto agree to be bound by his decision. If the Player is declared to be unfit to play he shall continue to receive the full benefits of this Agreement. If the Player is declared to be physically able to play and refuses to do so he shall be liable to immediate suspension without pay.

If upon joint consultation between the Player, the Club's Physician and the Club General Manager, they are unable to agree upon the physical fitness of the Player to return to play following an injury not resulting directly from playing for the Club, the Player agrees to submit himself for examination by an independent medical specialist and the Parties hereto agree to be bound by his decision. If the Player is declared to be fit for play, he shall be entitled to receive the full benefits of this agreement. If he is declared to be not physically able to play, he shall not be entitled to the benefits of this agreement until he has been declared to be physically fit to play by the independent medical specialist.

6. The Player represents and agrees that he has exceptional and unique knowledge, skill and ability as a hockey player, the loss of which cannot be estimated with certainty and cannot be fairly or adequately compensated by damages. The Player therefore agrees that the Club shall have the right, in addition to any other rights which the Club may possess, to enjoin him by appropriate injunction proceedings from playing hockey for any other team and/or for any breach of any of the other provisions of this contract.

7. The Player and the Club recognize and agree that the Player's participation in other sports may impair or destroy his ability and skill as a hockey player. Accordingly the Player agrees that he will not during the period of this Contract and during any period when he is obligated under this contract to enter into a further contract with the Club engage or participate in football, baseball, softball, hockey, lacrosse, boxing, wrestling or other athletic sport without the written consent of the Club.

[right column, partially cut off]

and/or for any breach of any of the other provisions of this contract.

...agree that the Player's participation in other sports may impair or destroy his ability ...her agrees that he will not during the period of this Contract and during any period when ...her contract with the Club engage or participate in football, baseball, softball, hockey, ...without the written consent of the Club.

...to the Club during the period of this Contract and during any period when he is ...contract with the Club the exclusive right to permit or authorize any person, firm ...photograph, motion pictures or television of himself, and agrees that all rights in such ...exclusively and may be used, reproduced, distributed or otherwise disseminated by the ...

...the period of this Contract and during any period when he is obligated under this ...the Club he will not make public appearances, participate in radio or television programs, ...sor newspaper or magazine articles, or sponsor commercial products without the written ...withheld unreasonably. Where the Club grants its written consent to any of the activities ...his proper share of the proceeds of such activities.

...will not pay, and the Player will not accept from any person, any bonus or anything of ...of games except as authorized by the League By-Laws.

...period of this contract and during any period when he is obligated under this contract to ...will not tamper with or enter into negotiations with any player under contract or reserva...such player's current or future services, without the written consent of the Club with which ...to be imposed by the President of the League.

...shall have the right to sell, assign, exchange and transfer this contract, and to loan the ...key club, and the Player agrees to accept and be bound by such sale, exchange, assignment, ...and carry out this contract with the same purpose and effect as if it had been entered into by ...

...the event that this contract is assigned, or the Player's services are loaned, to another Club, ...personally to the Player or by mail to the address set out below his signature hereto advise ...Club to which he has been assigned or loaned, and specifying the time and place of reporting ...such other Club he may be suspended by such other Club and no salary shall be payable to ...

...expenses incurred by a player during the playing season when such move is directed by the ...

...payments to the Player provided for in Section 1 hereof or shall fail to perform any other ...Club hereunder, the Player may, by notice in writing to the Club, specify the nature of the ...days from receipt of such notice, this contract shall be termin...the default within fifteen (15) days from receipt of such notice, the obligation of the Club to pay the Player's ...all obligations of both parties shall cease, except the obligation of the Club to pay the Player's ...

...contract upon written notice to the Player (but only after obtaining waivers from all other ...any time:

...the Club's rules governing training and conduct of players,

...his services hereunder or in any other manner materially breach this contract.

...sub-section (a) or (b) the Player shall only be entitled to compensation due to him to the date ...date of the mailing of such notice to his address as set out below his signature hereto. ...terminated by the Club while the Player is "away" with the Club for the purpose of playing ...shall be paid on the first week-day after the return "home" of the Club.

...that the Club may carry out and put into effect any order or ruling of the League or its President ...or the Club, shall terminate forthwith.

...in the event of his suspension pursuant to any of the provisions of this contract, there shall be ...Section 1 hereof an amount equal to the exact proportion of such salary as the number of days' ...days of the League Championship Schedule of games.

...tion arising from a state of war or other cause beyond the control of the League or of the Club, it shall ...or the Club to suspend or cease or reduce operations, then:

...tion of operations, the Player shall be entitled only to the proportion of salary due at the date of ...of operations, the salary stipulated in Section 1 hereof shall be replaced by that mutually agreed upon ...the Player.

...later than August 10th of the final year of this contract, tender the Player a Player's Termination ...choice of executing said Player's Termination Contract and delivering it to the Club on or before September ...by being unconditionally released from any further obligation to provide services under this contract as of ...year. The Player's Termination Contract shall be on the same terms and conditions as this contract except ...additional season as a Player's Termination Contract and shall provide for the Player's unconditional release ...provide services under said Player's Termination Contract effective the following June 1st.

...not take the action permitted under subsection (a), it shall no later than September 1st of the final year ...if the Player is a "protected" player or played at least fifty NHL games in the preceding season), tender the ...Player's previous year's salary and conditions (including this Section 17) as this Standard Player's Contract ...number of years of its fixed term may be different.

...to any action taken by the Club under subsections (a) or (b), the Player may notify the Club no later than ...year of this contract that he wishes to sign a Player's Option Contract. If the Player gives such notice, the ...ember 25th of that year tender the Player a Player's Option Contract, and the Player shall forthwith enter ...Player's Option Contract shall be on the same terms and shall provide that effective the following June 1st the Player will be a ...other obligation to provide services under said Player's Option Contract, and as such will have the right, as ...the League By-Laws, the text of which Section is printed on the reverse side hereof, to negotiate and contract ...e, or with any other club.

...does not take the action permitted under subsection (a) and the Player does not give notice to the Club in ...here is attached to this contract a special option provision agreed to by the parties, in which case the phrase ...ract" means the last year which any exercised special option adds to the fixed term specified in Section 1 ...bargaining agreement is then in effect, the Player's salary shall be the same as his salary for the previous year.

...does not take the action permitted under subsection (a) and the Player does not give notice to the Club in ...(c), then the parties shall enter into a new Standard Player's Contract for the succeeding season upon the same terms and ...shall enter into a one-year Standard Player's Contract, except as to salary, which shall be determined by neutral ...Section 17) as this Standard Player's Contract, except as to salary, providing a mechanism for such arbitration, provided, however, ...bargaining agreement is then in effect, the Player's salary shall be the same as his salary for the previous year.

...this Section 17, the phrase "final year of this contract" means the final year of the term specified in Section 1 ...here is attached to this contract a special option provision agreed to by the parties, in which case the phrase ...ract" means the last year which any exercised special option adds to the fixed term specified in Section 1 ...d/or the proposed contract to the Player in person or on before the date set forth below his signature hereto. The ...rked no later than said deadline date or the Player hand delivers the required written ...ivery obligations under this Section 17 shall be deemed fulfilled if the Player hand delivers the required written ...cuted contract on or before the applicable deadline date or mails it by registered mail postmarked no later than ...the Club at its address set forth below.

...and the Player severally and mutually promise and agree to be legally bound by the Constitution and By-Laws of ...the terms and provisions thereof, a copy of which shall be open and available for inspection by Club, its directors ...the main office of the League and at the main office of the Club.

...Player, if the main office of the League and at the main office of the Club.

...the Player further agree that in case of dispute between them, except as to the compensation to be paid to the Player ...dispute shall be referred within one year from the date it arose to the President of the League as an arbitrator and ...accepted as final by both parties.

...the Player further agree that all fines imposed upon the Player under the Playing Rules, or under the provisions of ...s, shall be deducted from the salary of the Player and be remitted by the Club to the N.H.L. Players' Emergency ...

...rties agree that the rights provided in Section 17 and in any Addendum hereto and the promise of the Player to ...with the Club, or such other club as provided in Section 2 and Section 11, and the Club's right to take pictures of ...Player as provided in section 8 have all been taken into consideration in determining the salary payable to the Player ...thereof.

...severally and mutually agreed that the only contracts recognized by the President of the League are the Standard Player's ...Contracts, Player's Termination Contracts, and Player's Option Contracts which have been duly executed and filed in the League's office ...and approved by him, and that this Agreement contains the entire agreement between the Parties and there are no oral or written induce...ments, promises or agreements except as provided herein.

In Witness Whereof, the parties have signed this 8TH day

of AUGUST A.D. 19 74.

WITNESSES:

MAPLE LEAF GARDENS, LTD.,
60 CARLTON ST. TORONTO, ONTARIO   Club
_____   Address of Club

Howard Starkman   By _____ FOR THE   President

_____   Player

R. Gregory

_____   Home Address of Player

I hereby certify that I have, at this date, received, examined and noted of record the within Contract, and that it is in regular form.

Dated Mar 19th 1975   President NATIONAL HOCKEY LEAGUE

Randy Carlyle.

RANDY CARLYLE
APPENDIX "A"   29th May 1976

THE BONUS MONEY AND SALARY STATED ON CONTRACT MAYBE CHANGED IF DESIRED
BY CARLYLE, RANDY SO THAT HE MAY BUY ANNUITIES. IF CHANGED, MAPLE LEAFS
AGREE TO NOT UNREASONABLY WITHOLD CONSENT.

(a) Toronto Maple Leafs to purchase or lease a new car (Corvette) approx.
     $10,500.00 for 3 years.

(b) Leafs to pay $7,500.00 to Carlyle family, October 1976.

(c) If you play in NHL 80 games (except under emergency) in the last two (2)
     years of this contract, 1977/78 and 1978/79, you will receive an
     additional $10,000.00.

(d) If you play in NHL 120 games (except under emergency) in the last two (2)
     years of this contract, 1977/78 and 1978/79 you will receive an
     additional $20,000.00.

     NB: Either (c) or (d) to be paid not both.

(e) If you play as a regular in all 3 years of this contract (not under
     emergency) you will receive $30,000.00.

     NB: Either (c) or (d) or (e) to be paid not all.

(f) NHL Bonus Only: For being voted in top 3 Rookies, salary to be increased
                      by $2,500.00.
     (either/or)
                      For being voted in top 5 Rookies, salary to be increased
                      by $1,500.00.

     For ending 1st in our Division $1,500.00
     For ending 2nd in our Division $1,000.00   (only one to be paid)
     For each +1-10 $ 50.00
     For +10 $ 500.00
     For each + 11 and up $ 100.00
     For team average of 239 goals against
     or better (under 3.00 goals against
     team average) $1,000.00

Randy Carlyle's Double Deal

Before he was a Stanley Cup–winning coach with the Anaheim Ducks or charged with leading the Toronto Maple Leafs back to the promised land, Randy Carlyle was a rookie defenceman from the OHL's Sudbury Wolves looking to crack the Leafs lineup—though it was a surprise that Toronto took him at all in the amateur draft, in the second round, 30th overall, in May 1976. The entire NHL had been warned that Carlyle was the property of the WHA's Cincinnati Stingers, as they had penned the Sudbury native to a contract four months earlier. "Carlyle signed with Cincinnati Feb. 1," his agent Norm Kaplan said at the time. "It was a standard player contract and it called for a substantial bonus, which he received. The money wasn't spent, but held in his name." After a call to Carlyle, Leafs GM Jim Gregory was under the impression that he had only inked a letter of intent. "We talked him out of it," said Gregory, who hustled up to Sudbury with Marlies coach George Armstrong and assistant manager John McLellan to make a deal. At an introductory press conference, Carlyle said, "I didn't sign a [WHA] contract. It's not true. To my knowledge, I only initialled a letter of intent. I didn't initial a contract." The initial deal was a three-year term, with $50,000 a year, as well as a $50,000 signing bonus; the addendum includes money for his family and a Corvette. Gregory said the Leafs made a deal with a local car dealer for a great price: "He took it as part of his signing bonus." The Stingers and the WHA started to initiate a lawsuit. In August, the Stingers dropped the claim to Carlyle when the Leafs agreed to take Mike Pelyk off their hands.

NATIONAL HOCKEY LEAGUE

920 SUN LIFE BUILDING · MONTREAL, P.Q., H3B 2W2 · (514) 871-9220 · TWX 610-421-3260

PRESIDENT'S OFFICE   June 1, 1976.

Mr. Harold Ballard
Maple Leaf Gardens Limited
60 Carlton Street
Toronto, Ontario M5B 1L1

                    Re: Randy Carlyle

Dear Harold:

        Further to my telephone discussion just con-
cluded, concerning the above-named player, I enclose herewith the photocopy of the Agreement dated February 1, 1976,
between Cincinnati Hockey Club and Carlyle to enter into a
WHA standard players contract on or before June 15, 1976.
I obtained this from Norman Caplan after he obtained permission for its release from the Cincinnati Club.

        In the course of conversation with Caplan this
morning, he told me that there had been deposited to Randy
Carlyle's credit at the Royal Bank of Canada in Westmount
Square (Montreal) about the same date the sum of $15,000
which had been used to buy a deposit certificate which
matured sometime in May 1976 which had been rolled over
by Caplan with an interest deposit of $300 odd credited
to Carlyle's account.

        He also volunteered the information that after
the Sudbury team finished its season, Carlyle wanted to go
on holiday and rather than cash the deposit certificate, Caplan had advanced Carlyle $1,000 which he would repay when he
came into the office to sign the Cincinnati contract.

        I did not discuss any other aspect of the agree-
ment or Carlyle's relations with Caplan.

        I would like to confirm my opinion that Carlyle
should abstain from making any statements to anyone except
his own lawyer.

        With kind personal regards, I remain,

                            Yours sincerely,

                            C.S. Campbell
                            President

CSC:t
Encl.
cc - Mr. R.M. Sedgewick

Pelyk Comes Home

Mike Pelyk was more concerned about returning to the NHL than he was about the actual contents of his 1976–77 contract. After two years with the WHA's Vancouver Blazers and Cincinnati Stingers, the swift-skating defenceman headed back home to Toronto. "There was a lot of change going on. The WHA was basically dropping out of business for all intents and purposes," said Pelyk. "You go there with grand expectations." The bonuses in his contract with the Leafs, negotiated with GM Jim Gregory and Pelyk's agent, Alan Eagleson, were simple— all about the plus/minus. "I just wanted to get back." Pelyk's first contract, when he was drafted 17th overall in the 1964 NHL amateur draft from the Toronto Marlboros, was a different experience than dealing with Gregory, whom he'd known and trusted from the Marlies. Punch Imlach and King Clancy travelled to the Pelyk homestead, because Mike was still underage. "'This is what it's going to be. This is what you'll make in the minors, and here's what you'll make in the NHL.' That was it. It was up to you to make a decision," he recalled. For the 1978–79 season, Pelyk was in Buffalo and balked at going back to the AHL. "It's a tough decision when you quit," he said. "You think you could probably play some more, but you don't want to spend time in the minors." Pelyk ran a hockey school for 17 years and now sells real estate. He also suits up with the NHL alumni and the Leafs alumni squads. "I'm a lot slower now. But it's still fun to get out with the guys."

Mike Pelyk.

IMPORTANT NOTICE TO PLAYER

Before signing this contract you should carefully examine it to be sure that all terms and conditions
agreed upon have been incorporated herein, and if any has been omitted, you should insist upon having
it inserted in the contract before you sign.

NATIONAL HOCKEY LEAGUE
STANDARD PLAYER'S CONTRACT
(1974 FORM)

This Agreement

BETWEEN :

MAPLE LEAF GARDENS, LIMITED
hereinafter called the "Club",
a member of the National Hockey League, hereinafter called the "League"

—AND—

MICHEAL PELYK
hereinafter called the "Player"

of ....TORONTO........ in {Province} of ....ONTARIO........

Witnesseth :

That in consideration of the respective obligations herein and hereby assumed, the parties to this contract severally
agree as follows :

1.   The Club hereby employs the Player as a skilled Hockey Player for the term of **1** year(s) commencing October 1st, 19**76**.
and agrees, subject to the terms and conditions hereof, to pay the Player a salary of

1976/77 EIGHTY THOUSAND AND NO................................ Dollars ($ **80,000.00**)

BONUSES (NHL Jamboree)

For each plus to 10	$ 50.00
For plus 10	$250.00
For each plus 11 and up	$100.00

Payment of such salary shall be in consecutive semi-monthly instalments following the commencement of the regular League Championship Schedule of games or following the date of reporting, whichever is later ; provided, however, that if the Player is not in the employ
of the Club for the whole period of the Club's games in the National Hockey League Championship Schedule, then he shall receive only
part of the salary in the ratio of the number of days of actual employment to the number of days of the League Championship Schedule
of games.

And it is further mutually agreed that if the Contract and rights to the services of the Player are assigned, exchanged, loaned or
otherwise transferred to a Club in another League, the Player shall only be paid at the rate of

or .... Dollars in the .... League.
or .... Dollars in the .... League.
or .... Dollars in the .... League.

2.   The Player agrees to give his services and to play hockey in all League Championship, Exhibition, Play-Off and Stanley Cup
games to the best of his ability under the direction and control of the Club for the said season in accordance with the provisions hereof.
The Player further agrees,

(a) to report to the Club training camp at the time and place fixed by the Club, in good physical condition,

(b) to keep himself in good physical condition at all times during the season,

(c) to give his best services and loyalty to the Club and to play hockey only for the Club unless his contract is released, assigned,
exchanged or loaned by the Club.

(d) to co-operate with the Club and participate in any and all promotional activities of the Club and the League which will in
the opinion of the Club promote the welfare of the Club or professional hockey generally.

(e) to conduct himself on and off the rink according to the highest standards of honesty, morality, fair play and sportsmanship,
and to refrain from conduct detrimental to the best interests of the Club, the League or professional hockey generally.

The Club agrees that in exhibition games played after the start of the regular schedule (except where the proceeds are to go to
charity, or where the player has agreed otherwise) the player shall receive his pro rata share of the gate receipts after deduction of legitimate
expenses of such game. This provision re exhibition games is applicable in the National Hockey League only.

3.   In order that the Player shall be fit in proper condition for the performance of his duties as required by this contract the
Player agrees to report for practice at such time and place as the Club may designate and participate in such exhibition games as may be
arranged by the Club within thirty days prior to the first scheduled Championship game. The Club shall pay the travelling expenses
and meals en route from the Player's home to the Club's training camp. In the event of failure of the player to so report and participate
in exhibition games a fine not exceeding Five Hundred Dollars may be imposed by the Club and be deducted from the compensation
stipulated herein. At the conclusion of the season the Club shall provide transportation direct to the Player's home.

4.   The Club may from time to time during the continuance of this contract establish rules governing the conduct and conditioning of the Player, and such rules shall form part of this contract as fully as if herein written. For violation of any such rules or for
any conduct impairing the thorough and faithful discharge of the duties incumbent upon the Player, the Club may impose a reasonable
fine upon the Player and deduct the amount thereof from any money due to or become due to the Player. When the Player is fined or suspended he shall be given notice in writing stating the amount
the Player for violation of any such rules. When the Player is fined or suspended he shall be given notice in writing stating the amount
of the fine and/or the duration of the suspension and the reason therefor.

5.   Should the Player be disabled or unable to perform his duties under this contract he shall submit himself for medical examination and treatment by a physician selected by the Club, and such examination and treatment, when made at the request of the Club,
shall be at its expense unless made necessary by any act or conduct of the Player contrary to the terms and provisions of this contract
or the rules established under Section 4.

If the Player, in the sole judgment of the Club's physician, is disabled or is not in good physical condition at the commencement
of the season or at any subsequent time during the season (unless such condition is the direct result of playing hockey for the Club) so
as to render him unfit to play skilled hockey, then it is mutually agreed that the Club shall have the right to suspend the Player for such
period of disability or unfitness, and no compensation shall be payable for that period under this contract.

If the Player is injured as the result of playing hockey for the Club, the Club will pay the Player's reasonable hospitalization until
discharged from the hospital, and his medical expenses and doctor's bills, provided that the hospital and doctor are selected by the Club
and provided further that the Club's obligation to pay such expenses shall terminate at a period not more than six months after the
injury.

It is also agreed that if the Player's injuries resulting directly from playing for the Club render him, in the sole judgment of the
Club's physician, unfit to play skilled hockey for the balance of the season or any part thereof, then during such time the Player is so
unfit, but in no event beyond the end of the current season, the Club shall pay the Player the compensation herein provided for and the
Player releases the Club from any and every additional obligation, liability, claim or demand whatsoever. However if upon joint consultation between the Player, the Club's physician and the Club General Manager, they are unable to agree as to the physical fitness
of the Player to return to play, the Player agrees to submit himself for examination by an independent medical specialist and the Parties
hereto agree to be bound by his decision. If the Player is declared to be unfit for play he shall continue to receive the full benefits of this
Agreement. If he is declared to be physically able to play and refuses to do so he shall be liable to immediate suspension without
pay.

If upon joint consultation between the Player, the Club's Physician and the Club General Manager, they are unable to agree
upon the physical fitness to return to play following an injury not resulting directly from playing for the Club, then such time the Player is so
submit himself for examination by an independent medical specialist and the Parties hereto agree to be bound by his decision. If the
Player is declared to be fit for play, he shall be entitled to receive the full benefits of this agreement. If he is declared to be not
physically able to play, he shall not be entitled to the benefits of this agreement until he has been declared to be physically fit to play
by the independent medical specialist.

[right column]

...sician and the Club General Manager, they are unable to agree
...sulting directly from playing for the Club, the Player agrees to
...t and the Parties hereto agree to be bound by his decision. If he
... the full benefits of this agreement. If he is declared to be not
... agreement until he has been declared to be physically fit to play

...d and unique knowledge, skill and ability as a hockey player, the loss
... or adequately compensated by damages. The Player therefore agrees
...ich the Club may possess, to enjoin him by appropriate injunction
...y breach of any of the other provisions of this contract.

...Player's participation in other sports may impair or destroy his ability
... will not during the period of this Contract and during any period when
...th the Club engage or participate in football, baseball, softball, hockey,
...tten consent of the Club.

...provided during the period of this Contract and during any period when he is
... the Club the exclusive right to permit or authorize any person, firm
...tion pictures or television of himself, and agrees that all rights in such
...ay be used, reproduced, distributed or otherwise disseminated by the

...g this Contract and during any period when he is obligated under this
...not make public appearances, participate in radio or television programs,
...e magazine articles, or sponsor commercial products without the written
...bly. Where the Club grants its written consent to any of the activities
...of the Player will not accept from any person, any bonus or anything of
...s authorized by the League By-Laws.

...tract and during any period when he is obligated under this contract to
...with or enter into negotiations with any player under contract or reserva-
...t or future services, without the written consent of the Club with which
...nt by the President of the League.

...ight to sell, assign, exchange and transfer this contract, and to loan the
...Player agrees to accept and be bound by such sale, exchange, assignment,
...contract with the same purpose and effect as if it had been entered into by

...contract is assigned, or the Player's services are loaned, to another Club,
...Player or by mail to the address set out below his signature hereto advise
...as been assigned or loaned, and specifying the time and place of reporting
...me may be suspended by such other Club and no salary shall be payable to

...by a player during the playing season when such move is directed by the

...Player provided for in Section 1 hereof or shall fail to perform any other
...e Player may, by notice in writing to the Club, specify the nature of the
...in fifteen (15) days from receipt of such notice, this contract shall be termin-
...both parties shall cease, except the obligation of the Club to pay the Player's

...itten notice to the Player (but only after obtaining waivers from all other

...erning training and conduct of players,

(b) the Player shall only be entitled to compensation due to him to the date
...such notice to his address as set out below his signature hereto.
...Club while the Player is "away" with the Club for the purpose of playing
...first week-day after the return "home" of the Club.

...carry out and put into effect any order or ruling of the League or its President
...spension his salary shall cease for the duration thereof and that in the event of
...terminate forthwith.

...his suspension pursuant to any of the provisions of this contract, there shall be
...n amount equal to the exact proportion of such salary as the number of days'
...e Championship Schedule of games.

...ate of war or other cause beyond the control of the League or of the Club, it shall
...d or cease or reduce operations, then :
...Player shall be entitled only to the proportion of salary due at the date of

...salary stipulated in Section 1 hereof shall be automatically cancelled on the date of

...salary stipulated in Section 1 hereof shall be replaced by that mutually agreed upon

...of the final year of this contract, tender the Player a Player's Termination Contract
...Player's Termination Contract and delivering it to the Club on or before September
...y released from any further obligation to provide services under this contract as of
...rmination Contract shall be on the same terms and conditions as this contract except
...yer's previous year's salary and shall provide for the Player's unconditional release
...ayer's Termination Contract effective the following June 1st.
...aid Player's Termination Contract effective the following June 1st.
...rmitted under subsection (a), it shall no later than September 1st of the final year
...cted" player or played at least fifty NHL games in the preceding season), tender the
...terms and conditions (including this Section 17) as this Standard Player's Contract
...d term may be different.

...the Club under subsections (a) or (b), the Player may notify the Club no later than
...h he wishes to sign a Player's Option Contract. If the Player gives such notice, the
...tender the Player a Player's Option Contract, and the Player shall it shall be for only
...d be on the same terms and conditions as this contract except that 1st the Player will be a
...salary and shall provide that effective the following June 1st the Player will be a
...e services and said Player's Option Contract, and as such will have the right, as
...text of which Section is printed on the reverse side hereof, to negotiate and contract

...e permitted under subsection (a) and the Player does not give notice to the Club in
...all enter into a new Standard Player's Contract by mutual agreement or, failing
...one-year Standard Player's Contract for the succeeding season upon the same terms and
...tandard Player's Contract, except as to salary, which shall be determined by neutral
...ining agreement providing a mechanism for such arbitration, provided, however,
...then in effect, the Player's salary shall be the same as his salary for the previous year.
...he "final year of this contract" means the final year of the term specified in Section 1
...contract a special option provision agreed to by the parties, in which case the phrase
...which any exercised special option adds to the fixed term specified in Section 1.
...igations under this Section 17 shall be deemed fulfilled if the Club delivers the required
...ct to the Player in person on or before the applicable deadline date or mails same by
...deadline date to the Player at the address set forth below his signature hereto. The
...is Section 17 shall be deemed fulfilled if the Player hand delivers the required written
...re the applicable deadline date or mails it by registered mail postmarked no later than
...forth below.

...d mutually promise and agree to be legally bound by the Constitution and By-Laws of
...hereof, a copy of which shall be open and available for inspection by Club, its directors
...of the League and at the main office of the Club.
...in case of dispute between them, except as to the compensation to be paid to the Player
...within one year of dispute between them, except as to the President of the League as an arbitrator and
...parties.
...at all fines imposed upon the Player under the Playing Rules, or under the provisions of
...t the salary of the Player and be remitted by the Club to the N.H.L. Players' Emergency

...provided in Section 17 and in any Addendum hereto and the promise of the Player to
...er club as provided in Section 2 and Section 11, and the Club's right to take pictures of
...s 8 have all been taken into consideration in determining the salary payable to the Player

...the parties severally acknowledge and agree that the only contracts recognized by the President of the League are the Standard Player's
20.   It is severally and mutually agreed that the only contracts recognized by the President of the League are the Standard Player's
Contracts, Player's Termination Contracts, and Player's Option Contracts which have been duly executed and filed in the League's office
and approved by him, and that this Agreement contains the entire agreement between the Parties and there are no oral or written inducements, promises or agreements except as provided herein.

In Witness Whereof, the parties have signed this ....**19th**........... day

of ....**August**.......... A.D. 19**76**.

WITNESSES :   **MAPLE LEAF GARDENS, LIMITED**   Club

                                                                    60 Carlton Street, Toronto, Ontario   Address of Club

........*Gerald McNamara*........   By ....*[signature]*........   President

                                                                    ....*[signature]*........   for the

                                                                                                          Player

........*Gerald McNamara*........, Linstead Court, Weston Ontario   Home Address of Player

I hereby certify that I have, at this date, received, examined and noted of record the within Contract, and that it is in regular form.

Dated ....**Dec 3rd** 19**76**.   ....*[signature]*........   President NATIONAL HOCKEY LEAGUE

Turnbull Skates into Sponsorship

Sometimes, something good can come from an injury. In the case of Leafs defenceman Ian Turnbull, torn ankle ligaments resulted in an endorsement deal with Micron. In the summer of 1976, "Hawk" was working his way back into shape in his hometown of Montreal. Terry Harper, then of the Detroit Red Wings, was one of the locals on the ice as well. A couple of years earlier, Harper had been a part of the group that had come up with the "skate boot"—a harder shell rather than leather—and hooked Turnbull up with Lange skates. "I couldn't skate on my old Tackaberrys. There was no way with the rip in my ligaments that I could hold myself up," Turnbull said. "I tried the ski-boot skate, and it isolated it enough that I could go ahead and skate with marginal pain." Some of the people behind Lange ended up forming Micron, and Turnbull, Larry Robinson, and Scotty Bowman were some of its promoters. "Mostly I was just promoting it," recalled Turnbull, who would be asked to target some junior players. "What I would do is send them some skates, introduce them to them. I think I had to seek out permission from Harold [Ballard]," explained Turnbull. "I can't remember if it had to do with using the Leafs logo or not; something was amiss about it, and I had to get it all sorted out."

Marcel Dionne and Ian Turnbull battle.

A G R E E M E N T

AGREEMENT made as of the 29 day of *April* 1977.

BY AND BETWEEN:

LES PRODUITS SPORTIFS MICRON INC.-
MICRON SPORTS PRODUCTS INC.
a body corporate and politic
having its place of business at
5665 Paré Street, Town of Mount
Royal, District of Montreal,
Province of Quebec, (hereinafter
referred to as
"MICRON")

PARTY OF THE FIRST PART

A N D :

IAN TURNBULL ENTERPRISES LTD.,
a body corporate and politic
having its place of business in
the City of Toronto, Province
of Ontario, (hereinafter referred
to as "ENTERPRISES")

PARTY OF THE SECOND PART

A N D :

IAN TURNBULL, professional hockey
player, residing and domiciled
at

(hereinafter referred to as
"TURNBULL")

INTERVENING PARTY

W I T N E S S E T H :

WHEREAS TURNBULL, presently a member of the Toronto
Maple Leaf Hockey Team, is a professional hockey player of great
expertise and accomplishment, and is widely known as such; and

WHEREAS, TURNBULL has entered into a contract with
ENTERPRISES pursuant to which he agreed to render certain services to and granted certain rights to ENTERPRISES for at least
the full term of the contract hereinafter provided, and by the
terms of the said contract ENTERPRISES has the right to enter
into an agreement for the furnishing of TURNBULL's services
to MICRON and to grant MICRON the rights and licenses hereinafter set forth; and

WHEREAS, MICRON is engaged in the manufacture and sale
of hockey skates and accessory equipment and desires to acquire
certain services of TURNBULL in the promotion of sales of its
hockey skates and accessory equipment and the right and li-
cense to use TURNBULL's endorsement, (as such term is hereinafter defined), in connection with the sales of its hockey

2/-

---

11.   JOINT AND SEVERAL OBLIGATIONS.   All rights and
obligations arising to TURNBULL or ENTERPRISES in virtue of
the present Agreement shall be joint and several.

IN WITNESS WHEREOF, the Parties have signed this
Agreement as of the date first written above.

LES PRODUITS SPORTIFS MICRON INC.-
MICRON SPORTS PRODUCTS INC.
Per:

_____   _____
WITNESS   PARTY OF THE FIRST PART

                                IAN TURNBULL ENTERPRISES LTD.
                                Per:

_____   _____
WITNESS   PARTY OF THE SECOND PART

                                IAN TURNBULL

_____   _____
WITNESS   INTERVENING PARTY

Leaf stars of the past gather for
a goodbye to Maple Leaf Gardens
on February 13, 1999.

CHAPTER 6

THE 1980s and 1990s

All-Star Sittler

Over the years, the criteria for making the NHL All-Star Game have changed, but the honour remains the same. The 1980 game was Darryl Sittler's third. "It's always a thrill, any time you get invited," said Sittler. "You never know when the next one is, so when you have one, you enjoy it. It's a nice break in the season. It's an honour to play." The 32nd NHL All-Star Game was at the Detroit's Joe Louis Arena. Sittler especially remembers sharing the ice with a legend on the Wales Conference squad. "Detroit was special because Gordie Howe played in that game," he recalled. Sittler got one assist, on a Ron Stackhouse goal in the third period, as the Campbell Conference went down 6–3. The letter from Brian O'Neill, NHL executive vice-president, reminded players to bring their gear. "It's all your own equipment. You just wear their socks and maybe different colour pants, shell, and jersey. But the rest of it is stuff that you're comfortable with and play with." The one thing not provided? Something to wear to the black-tie dinner the night before at the Detroit Plaza Hotel. "Never owned a tux. I always rented."

NATIONAL HOCKEY LEAGUE
960 SUN LIFE BUILDING • MONTREAL, P.Q., H3B 2W2 • (514) 871-9220 • TWX 610-421-3260
PRESIDENT'S OFFICE

January 22, 1980

To: All-Star Players –
Prince of Wales Conference

Re: All-Star Game – Detroit, Michigan
February 5, 1980

Gentlemen:

This is to advise you that you have been selected to represent the Prince of Wales Conference in the Annual All-Star Game which will take place at the Joe Louis Arena in Detroit on Tuesday, February 5, 1980.

You are reminded that there will be a financial remuneration to the players participating in the All-Star Game on the basis of $1,000 to each player on the winning team and $750 to each player on the losing team. To qualify for payment a player must be dressed.

Your Club has agreed to your participation in the Game and will be responsible for your transportation and other expenses going to and from Detroit and while you are in Detroit.

The Coach of the Team, Scott Bowman, has requested that all players report to him at the Detroit Plaza Hotel prior to the Dinner on February 4th. Hotel accommodation has been reserved for you there.

Also, there are two tickets available for purchase by you to the All-Star Game but you are requested to notify the Detroit Club by January 30th whether or not you require these tickets.

..../2

To: All-Star Players   January 22, 1980
    Prince of Wales Conference

You will require full equipment, including sticks, but a set of uniforms including sweaters, stockings and pants, will be provided. These uniforms will be collected for use in future games. When helmets are worn, Clarence Campbell Conference players will wear black helmets and Prince of Wales Conference players will wear white helmets.

The special Dinner will be held at the Detroit Plaza Hotel in Detroit on Monday, February 4th, and you are invited to be a guest of the League and it is hoped that you will attend and sit at the Head Table when each participant will be presented with his personal memento, and representatives of the press, radio and television from all over the League will attend. The All-Star Dinner will be open to the general public and the proceeds will be turned over to a local charity. You are reminded that the Dinner is a black-tie affair.

The All-Star Game is our principal show-piece and it is essential that everyone invited to take part in any capacity should do everything in his power to make it a first-class presentation.

Yours sincerely,

NATIONAL HOCKEY LEAGUE

Brian O'Neill
Executive Vice-President

Sittler's Infamous No-Trade Clause

No-trade clauses are fairly standard in today's NHL, at least to the point that a player can limit the teams to which he will accept a trade. But in the 1970s, the no-trade clause was pretty rare. In April 1974, the Leafs agreed to give Darryl Sittler one. Represented by Alan Eagleson, Sittler was the star of an up-and-coming squad. Eagleson was not one to leave a pot unstirred. "It is somewhat disturbing to Darryl to know that he is not the highest paid member of the Leaf Team, but he accepts the reality of it in a very mature manner," assured Eagleson in an October 1976 letter to Jim Gregory. When Punch Imlach returned as GM in 1979, he thought it was time for Sittler to go. He felt that a revised contract from 1978, made by Gregory and owner Harold Ballard to increase Sittler's pay "constituted a new contract and did not mention the no-trade clause," Imlach wrote in *Heaven and Hell in the NHL*. "I thought there was a loophole there and I intended to use it." Eagleson warned other NHL teams of the no-trade clause. In the end, Imlach was thwarted and traded Sittler's best friend, Lanny McDonald, instead. Jim Gregory was called upon to make a statuary declaration in a Toronto court in regards to the no-trade clause, making note that "Mr. Harold Ballard was advised of the condition and approved the condition." It wasn't until January 1982, when Gerry McNamara was the GM, that Sittler agreed to a trade to Philadelphia. "I inherited the problem, and I traded him," said McNamara. "He wanted more money. I couldn't give him any more money."

Darryl Sittler.

TO DARRYL SITTLER & DARRYL SITTLER ENTERPRISES:

Dear Sir:

      Darryl Sittler will be playing out his present
year ($145,000.00 plus $5,000.00), with the following terms.

      Although not expressed as a term of that '77-'78
to '83-'84 contract we wish to confirm to you the understanding reached
between our Company and each of you that during the term of the contract
the right to the services of DARRYL SITTLER as a professional hockey
player would not be traded to any other professional hockey club
without his consent.

1978/79	One hundred and seventy thousand and no.—————	$170,000.00
1979/80	One hundred and seventy thousand and no.—————	$170,000.00
1980/81	One hundred and seventy thousand and no.—————	$170,000.00
1981/82	One hundred and seventy thousand and no.—————	$170,000.00
1982/83	One hundred and seventy thousand and no.—————	$170,000.00
1983/84	Option.	

NHL BONUSES

- For 60 points - 1st or 2nd ALL STAR - $5,000.00
  (or in the opinion of management, a good year.)

- For winning the Stanley Cup - $25,000.00
  (This bonus can only be paid once during this contract.)

- Two Red Seats to be put under name D. Sittler and paid for
  by him and will try for 2 Golds as well.
  (These seats are his but cannot be assigned to anyone without
  first offering them to Maple Leaf Gardens.)

- Sittler to do 2 personal appearances per year for Maple Leaf
  Gardens.

_____
DARRYL SITTLER, Player

_____
JIM GREGORY, General Manager

_____
Witness

_____
Witness

_____
Date

Dye & Durham Co. Limited, 160 Bartley Drive, Toronto
Law and Commercial Stationers
Form No. 141

Canada
PROVINCE OF ONTARIO

Judicial District
of York

In the Matter of

A no trade clause in the contract between
Darryl Sittler and Maple Leaf Gardens Hockey
Club.

TO WIT:

I, JAMES GREGORY

of the   City   of   Toronto   in the Municipality of
Metropolitan Toronto

SOLEMNLY DECLARE THAT

1. That on July 25, 1977, I was the General Manager of the Toronto
   Maple Leaf Hockey Club.

2. That on July 25, 1977, negotiations for the services of Darryl
   Sittler Enterprises Ltd. and Darryl Sittler, were finalized.

3. That attached hereto as Schedule "A" is a copy of the agreement
   reached on that date.

4. That during the month of August 1978, the contract was amended in
   order to accomplish two objectives:

   (a) to increase the amount of compensation paid by Maple Leaf
       Gardens because of the high performance level of Sittler,
       as set out in Schedule "B" attached; and

   (b) to acknowledge the change in name from Darryl Sittler
       Enterprises Ltd. to Jay Anne Limited.

5. That the contracts referred to herein were based on one major
   condition, namely, that the services of Darryl Sittler would not
   be traded to any other professional hockey club without the
   consent of Sittler.

6. That because National Hockey League offices will not accept
   contracts with a no trade clause included therein, a separate
   letter agreement was structured, a copy of which is attached
   hereto as Schedule "A".

7. That ~~I was instructed to accept the no-trade condition by~~
   Mr. Harold Ballard. _was advised of the condition_
   and approved the condition.

8. That, in accordance with our agreement reached in 1977 and
   amended in 1978, Darryl Sittler has a no trade contract with
   the Toronto Maple Leaf Hockey Club through the 1983/84 hockey
   season.

AND I make this solemn Declaration conscientiously believing it to be true, and knowing
that it is of the same force and effect as if made under oath.

DECLARED before me at the City

of Toronto

in the Municipality of
Metropolitan Toronto

this day of ~~January~~ February 19 80

_____
A Commissioner, etc.

_____
JAMES GREGORY

Zanussi Sent Home

The trade deadline was noon on March 10, 1981—noon in *each* time zone across the continent. Ron Zanussi had just finished practice at the Met Center, thinking he was safe. But in the dressing room, the chalkboard read: "Zoo, go see Louie." Zanussi learned from North Stars GM Lou Nanne that he had been dealt to the Leafs. "I went, 'Okay, that's great. It's my hometown.' It was my childhood dream to play for Toronto," said Zanussi. Interestingly, his agent was Brent Imlach, son of Leafs GM Punch Imlach. "I think with Brent being my agent, it was a plus, just to get things moving contract-wise," he said. The passionate Toronto fans were a plus too, but there were hassles. "You're playing in front of all your family and friends on a consistent basis, [and] the phone calls for tickets interrupt your daily routine," said "Zoo," who got his nickname from his junior days with the London Knights. The right winger got into 12 games for the Buds before the playoffs, where the team lost to Minnesota— and the North Stars subsequently marched right to the Stanley Cup finals, losing to the Islanders. "That left a bitter taste in my mouth. But what can you do? Losing to my old team, I didn't like that." The following year, with 43 games, was Zanussi's last in the NHL. He moved back to Minnesota, and has worked for Northwest Airlines/ Delta ever since, on the tarmac.

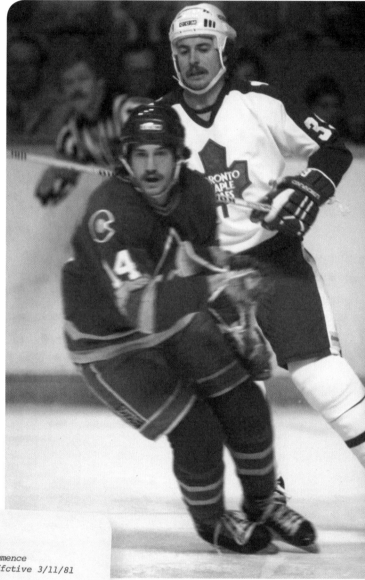

Steve Tambellini of the Colorado Rockies and Ron Zanussi of the Leafs.

```
                    CC: ACCOUNTING 3/10/81

                    PLEASE NOTE:  Toronto will commence
                    paying Ron Zanussi's salary effctive 3/11/81


   NHL STAR MSP

   NHL LEAFS TOR

   MARCH 10/81      12:10 P.M.   E.S.T.

   ATTN: LOU NANNE

   THIS T IS TO CONFIRM THAT THE TORONTO MAPLE LEAFS TRADE THEIR SECOUND
   ROUND SELECTION IN THE 1981 ENTRY DRAFT TO THE MINNESOTA NORTH STARS
   IN EXCHANGE FOR PLAYER RON ZANUSSI AND THE NORTH STARS' THIRD-ROUND
   SELECTION IN THE 1981 ENTRY DRAFT.

   PLEASE CONFIRM SAME BY TWX.

   THANKS AND REGARDS

   GEORGE "PUNCH" IMLACH
   GENERAL MANAGER


   NHL LEAFS TOR

   NHL STAR MSP
```

(Read instructions for completion and registration on reverse side.)

STANDARD ASSIGNMENT AGREEMENT

(Uniform agreement for assignment of the rights to services of a player,
amateur or professional, to or by a club.)

This Agreement made and entered into this _____10th_____ day of _____March_____ 19__81__,

BETWEEN : _____NORTHSTAR HOCKEY PARTNERSHIP (Minnesota North Stars)_____ ✓
(Corporate name of the Company, Club or Association) PARTY OF THE FIRST PART

and : _____MAPLE LEAF GARDENS, LTD (Toronto Maple Leafs)_____
(Corporate name of the Company, Club or Association) PARTY OF THE SECOND PART

WITNESSETH : The party of the First Part hereby assigns to the Party of the Second Part
its rights to services of

PLAYER(S) _____Ron Zanussi_____

under { Standard Contract / ~~Unsigned Draft Choice~~ } upon the following terms and conditions

Strike out inappropriate parts
*Minnesota trades their 3rd round selection in the 1981 Entry Draft
and player Ron Zanussi to Toronto for Toronto's 2nd round
selection in the 1981 Entry Draft*

WAIVER CERTIFICATE :

The transferor hereby certifies : *(strike out (1) or (2) below)*

(1) The Player(s) is a (n) ~~amat~~ prof. player for whom League waivers are not required.

(2) ~~The Player(s) has been waived out of the League and has not played in six (6) League~~
~~or Play-off games since the waivers were obtained.~~

IN WITNESS WHEREOF the parties hereto have subscribed through our respective Presidents
or authorized agents, witnessed on the date set out above.

Northstar Hockey Partnership
CLUB

_____[signature]_____   By _____[signature]_____
WITNESS   (Party of the First Part)
                                                      Mr. Lou Nanne, General Manager

Maple Leaf Gardens, Ltd
CLUB

_____[signature]_____   By _____[signature]_____
WITNESS   (Party of the Second Part)
                                                      Mr. George Imlach, General Manager

CENTRAL REGISTRY
REC'D | SEEN
MAR 20 11 20 '81

ACTION
Bull 789

Instructions for Completion

(1) Fill in the **correct** date and the **correct** corporate names of the parties to the Agreement, as well as the correct **full** names of the players involved. Except in cases of trades, separate assignments should be prepared for **each** player.

(2) Strike out the inapplicable kinds of agreement and the inapplicable clause of the waiver certificate at the bottom.

(3) Have Agreements signed by authorized officers and each signature should be witnessed.

Instructions for Registration

(1) Write to Central Registry, 920 Sun Life Building, Montreal, Canada H3B 2W2; advising of the transaction and enclosing all copies of the Agreement, with instructions for registration. Send a copy of **this letter** for each league affected by the transaction except the National Hockey League and for each Club affected.

(2) Central Registry must be advised immediately by TWX of this transaction by both Clubs concerned. Copies of this agreement should be initiated by the Club transferring the player and forwarded to the Club receiving the player for completion and subsequent filing with Central Registry as described in (1) above.

(3) Sufficient copies of the Agreement should be prepared and sent to the Central Registry for the following purposes :

    (a) Central Registry
    One copy (signed) for **each** player involved.

    (b) Each affected League
    One copy.

    (c) Each club involved
    One copy (signed).

Send **all** copies of the Agreement to the Central Registry.

(4) Central Registry will report transaction in the first regular Bulletin after notice is received, which will serve as acknowledgment of receipt of the notice.

(5) Central Registry will record, time-stamp and distribute by mail, copies of Agreement received to the Leagues and Clubs affected, which will serve as acknowledgment of receipt of documents,—no other acknowledgment will be sent.

T.V.B. 5M-9-74

Ihnacak's Great Escape

With the team's third-round pick in the 1982 NHL draft in June, the Leafs selected Peter Ihnacak of Czechoslovakia. But in a story worthy of the Cold War at the height of Communism, the Leafs had already signed him in April after his daring defection, leaving his national team during the 1982 World Championships in Helsinki, Finland. Leafs coach Mike Nykoluk and GM Gerry McNamara were en route to the tournament when they were approached in the airport in New York City. It was John Ihnacak, one of Peter's three siblings who had fled Czechoslovakia years before. That family history had meant hell for Peter, as the ruling parties distrusted him and he was repeatedly denied the opportunity to represent his homeland in non–Eastern Bloc countries. By the 1982 World Championships, he and John had hatched a plan to escape, and the Leafs brass were offered first crack at him. "We knew when they were going to do this, and we ran into Peter on the elevator. I could see Peter was nervous," recalled Nykoluk. Peter and John went over to Sweden on a party boat, and the Leafs brass followed. "I went over there and talked him into signing with the Toronto Maple Leafs," said Nykoluk. The draft pick, obtained from the Flyers in the Darryl Sittler trade, formalized things. Peter Ihnacak would play seven seasons with the Leafs, including a couple playing alongside another brother, Miroslav, who had also escaped Czechoslovakia. He is now a Leafs scout in Europe. "I wanted to play hockey, yes," Ihnacak told the *National Post* in 2006. "But I wanted to play hockey somewhere where I was going to be free."

Peter Ihnacak.

ADDENDUM TO NATIONAL HOCKEY LEAGUE STANDARD PLAYER'S CONTRACT

PETER IHNACAK

I REVISIONS TO N.H.L. SALARY

The following levels of achievement, if attained, will be added to the base level of N.H.L. salary, for each ramining season of this N.H.L. Contract, including Option Year.

a) If Player Scores 20 Goals and 40 Points..............$5,000.00 (additional)
b) If Player Scores 25 Goals and 50 Points..............$10,000.00 (additional)
c) If Player Scores 30 Goals and 60 Points..............$5,000.00 (additional)
d) If Player Scores 30 Goals or 70 Points..............$10,000.00 (additional)
e) If Player Scores 35 Goals or 80 Points..............$10,000.00 (additional)

NOTE: Once Player has attained particular salary revision level (a to e), he cannot attain that particular level again for purposes of salary revision. Maximum base salary that Player may attain through revision to salary is $175,000.00.

II ANNUAL N.H.L. BONUSES

If Player Scores 20 Goals and 40 Points..............$5,000.00 (additional)
If Player Scores 25 Goals and 50 Points..............$5,000.00 (additional)
If Player Scores 30 Goals and 60 Points..............$10,000.00 (additional)
If Player Scores 30 Goals or 70 Points..............$5,000.00 (additional)
If Player Scores 35 Goals or 80 Points..............$10,000.00 (additional)
If Team Qualifies for Playoffs...$2,500.00 For Each Playoff Round Won...$2,500.00

NOTE: Team must qualify for N.H.L. Playoffs in order for Player to attain any of the above revisions to N.H.L. salary or annual N.H.L. bonuses.

III N.H.L. CONTRACT EXTENSION

It is agreed that this N.H.L. Contract shall be extended for an additional season if: a) Team Qualifies for the N.H.L. Playoffs in both the 1984-85 and 1986 seasons AND b) Player Plays in 50 N.H.L. Games in both the 1984-85 and 1985-86 seasons or is on the N.H.L. roster for 80 Games in both the 1984-85 and 1985-86 seasons.

This Contract will be extended at the following N.H.L. Salary:

1986-87: $140,000.00 (Plus Salary Revisions to a Maximum of $175,000.00)
(Option Year) 1987-88: $140,000.00 (Plus Salary Revisions to a Maximum of $175,000.00)

NOTE: The Revisions to N.H.L. Salary and Annual N.H.L. Bonuses as listed above are to be included in the extension of this N.H.L. Contract.

_____
WITNESS

GERRY McNAMARA
General Manager, Toronto Maple Leafs

_____
WITNESS

PETER IHNACAK

SEPTEMBER 17, 1984
DATED

IMPORTANT NOTICE TO PLAYER
Before signing this contract you should carefully examine it to be sure that all terms and conditions agreed upon have been incorporated herein, and if any has been omitted, you should insist upon having it inserted in the contract before you sign.

NATIONAL HOCKEY LEAGUE
STANDARD PLAYER'S CONTRACT
(1982 FORM)

BETWEEN MAPLE LEAF GARDENS LTD.
hereinafter called the "Club,"
a member of the National Hockey League, hereinafter called the "League"

AND PETER IHNACAK
hereinafter called the "Player"

of POPRAD in [Province/State] of CZECHOSLOVAKIA

1. In consideration of the respective obligations herein and hereby assumed, the parties to this contract severally agree as follows:—
The Club hereby employs the Player as a skilled Hockey Player for the term of TWO year(s) commencing October 1st, 19 84 and agrees, subject to the terms and conditions hereof, to pay the Player a salary of

1984-85 ONE HUNDRED AND FORTY THOUSAND———————— Dollars ($ 140,000.00).
1985-86 ONE HUNDRED AND FORTY THOUSAND————————
OPTION YEAR $140,000.00
1986-87 ONE HUNDRED AND FORTY THOUSAND———————— $140,000.00

SEE: ATTACHED ADDENDUM RE: BONUSES & SALARY REVISION

Payment of such salary shall be in consecutive semi-monthly installments following the commencement of the regular League Championship Schedule of games or following the dates of reporting, whichever is later; provided, however, that if the Player is not in the employ of the Club for the whole period of the Club's games in the National Hockey League Championship Schedule, then he shall receive only part of the salary in the ratio of the number of days of actual employment to the number of days of the League Championship Schedule of Games.

And it is further mutually agreed that if the Contract and rights to the services of the Player are assigned, exchanged, loaned or otherwise transferred to a Club in another League, the Player shall only be paid at an annual salary rate of

.... Dollars in the .... League.
.... Dollars in the .... League.
.... Dollars in the .... League.

The Player agrees to give his services and to play hockey in all League Championship, All Star, International, Exhibition, Play-Off and Stanley Cup games to the best of his ability under the direction and control of the Club in accordance with the provisions hereof.

The Player further agrees,
(a) to report to the Club training camp at the time and place fixed by the Club, in good physical condition.
(b) to keep himself in good physical condition at all times during the season.
(c) to give his best services to the Club and to play hockey only for the Club unless his contract is released, assigned, exchanged or loaned by the Club.
(d) to co-operate with the Club and participate in any and all reasonable promotional activities of the Club which will in the opinion of the Club promote the welfare of the Club and to cooperate in the promotion of the League and professional hockey generally.
(e) to conduct himself on and off the rink according to the highest standards of honesty, morality, fair play and sportsmanship, and to refrain from conduct detrimental to the best interest of the Club, the League or professional hockey generally.

2. The Club agrees that in exhibition games played after the start of the regular schedule (except where the proceeds are to go to charity, or where the player has agreed otherwise) the player shall receive his pro rata share of the gate receipts after deduction of legitimate expenses of such game. This provision re exhibition games is applicable in the National Hockey League only.

3. In order that the Player shall be fit in proper condition for the performance of his duties as required by this contract, the Player agrees to report for practice at such time and place as the Club may reasonably designate and participate in such exhibition hockey only with the Club, or such other club as provided in Sections 2, 11 and 12, and the Club's right to televise the Player as provided in Section 8 have all been taken into consideration in determining the salary payable to the Player under Section 1 hereof.

19. ... quired written notific... later than said deadli...
The Club a... League and by any C... NHLPA, and by all o... officers, and the Play...

The Club and... a new contract, the d... decision shall be acc... Bargaining Agreemen...

The Club and... the League By-Laws,... Fund.

20. The parties agree that the rights provided ...

21. It is severally and mutually agreed that the only contracts recognized by the President of the League are the Standard Player's Contracts, Player's Termination Contracts, Player's Option Contracts, Post-Option Year Termination Contracts (Corporate), Standard Termination Contracts (Corporate), Standard Option Contracts (Corporate) and Post-Option Year Termination Contracts (Corporate) which have been duly executed and filed in the League's office and approved by him (or his designated representative), and that this Agreement contains the entire agreement between the Parties and there are no oral or written inducements, promises or agreements except as provided herein.

In Witness Whereof, the parties have signed this 17TH day of SEPTEMBER A.D. 19 84

WITNESSES:

MAPLE LEAF GARDENS LTD.
Club

60 CARLTON ST., TORONTO, ONTARIO
Address of Club

By _____
President

X Peter Ihnacak
Player

_____
Home Address of Player

I hereby certify that I have, at this date, received, examined and noted of record the within Contract and that it is in regular form.

Dated OCT 23 1984 19........

_____
for the National Hockey League

Contract Demands Get Stumpy Shipped Out

According to Gerry McNamara, the Leafs GM at the time, the counter-proposal submitted by Don Meehan, the agent for Steve Thomas, is a perfect example of how to get one's client shipped out of town. McNamara read the demands from the 1987 negotiation and began to laugh. "He'd never get that from me!" said McNamara. "Stumpy" Thomas had a great 1986–87, second on the team in goals with 35 goals, as well as 27 assists. With an idea of what every player was worth, McNamara didn't see Thomas fitting into the Leafs' financial structure, so the GM dealt him to Chicago with Rick Vaive and Bob McGill for Al Secord and Ed Olczyk on September 3, 1987. "Stevie Thomas wouldn't sign and he got traded," said McNamara, praising the speedy 5-foot-11 left winger, who went undrafted before McNamara signed him as a free agent in May 1984. "He was a great player for us." Complicating the issue was Thomas' dislike of Leafs coach John Brophy. "Stevie never told me this, but somebody that was a really good friend of his came and told me that he didn't want to play for John Brophy. He wouldn't sign the contract, so he went to Chicago." Thomas would play another 17 years, including two stints each with the Leafs and Hawks, and as a valuable, speedy asset on the Isles, Devils, Mighty Ducks, and Red Wings.

Steve Thomas in his second go-round in Toronto.

NEWPORT SPORTS

Donald E. Meehan B.A. LL.B.
Patrick J. Morris B.A. LL.B.

Newport Sports Management Inc.
SUITE 601, 201 CITY CENTRE DRIVE
MISSISSAUGA, ONTARIO L5B 2T4
TELEPHONE (416) 275-2800

June 3rd, 1987.

Maple Leaf Gardens Limited,
60 Carlton Street,
Toronto, Ontario, M5B 1L1.

Attention: Mr. Gerry McNamara.

Dear Gerry:

Re: Steve Thomas

I have now had the opportunity of meeting with Steve, concerning my most recent meeting with you. I have related the nature of our discussions to Steve and the salary figures relating to a new Contract, that you have conveyed to me.

We are prepared to accept and sign a Contract based on the following terms and conditions:

1. SALARY:
   1987/88   - $ 260,000.00
   1988/89   -   270,000.00
   1989/90   -   280,000.00
   1990/91 (Option Year)   -   290,000.00

2. TEAM BONUSES:
   If Club finishes a Season first in its division   -   5,000.00
   If Club finishes a Season second in its division -   4,000.00
   If Club finishes a Season third in its division   -   3,000.00

   If Club wins first round of playoffs   -   3,000.00
   If Club wins second round of playoffs -   4,000.00
   If Club wins third round of playoffs   -   5,000.00
   If Club wins the Stanley Cub   - 10,000.00

3. PERSONAL BONUSES:

   If player wins any Major League Award   - 25,000.00
   If player is second in voting for any Major League
   Award   - 15,000.00
   If player is voted to First All-Star Team
   (end of Season)   - 25,000.00
   If player is voted to Second All-Star Team
   (end of Season)   - 15,000.00

   If player scores 35 goals   -   5,000.00
   If player scores 40 goals   -   5,000.00
   If player scores 45 goals   -   5,000.00
   If player scores 50 goals   - 10,000.00

I look forward to hearing from you at your convenience.

Yours very truly,

DONALD E. MEEHAN

DEM/t
E. & O. E.

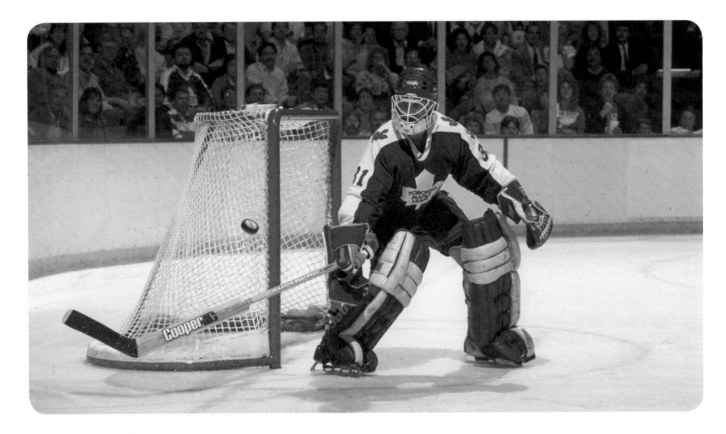

Ken Wregget and the Friendly Confines of the Gardens

Ken Wregget.

Ken Wregget learned through the years to not get too upset when his last name was spelled incorrectly—there's only one "T" at the end, though some of his Victoriaville sticks and his initial contract might tell you differently. "I always laugh about that," said Wregget, who was an easy-going sort as a Leafs goaltender. He was chosen 45th overall in the 1982 draft, from the Western Hockey League's Lethbridge Broncos, a Toronto draft class that included Gary Nylund, Gary Leeman, and Peter Ihnacak. He found the Leafs brass of GM Gerry McNamara and his right-hand man Gord Stellick to be excellent people, and Wregget would often sit in their office, having a cigarette. "We'd sit down and just shoot the breeze with him after practice—I can't say every day, but quite a few days," said Wregget. "We'd go up and sit in the office, and they were very open." As McNamara was a former netminder too, he and Wregget would sometimes settle in the stands at Maple Leaf Gardens and study the action. Wregget had his agent, Bill Watters, handle most of the negotiations. "When you were a kid, you dreamed about winning the Stanley Cup—it's not about bonuses," said Wregget, who did win a Cup as a part of the 1992 Pittsburgh Penguins. Wregget has been an occasional guest of Gord Stellick's radio shows. "I always bust him for trading me," said Wregget of the March 1989 deal. "I met Gord in the office, and I remember going down the escalators and looking around, because I wanted to build something there, be a part of something. They weren't doing real well at that point. But it gave me the opportunity, and I felt honoured to be a part of it. They really made me feel warm and welcomed."

ADDENDUM TO N.H.L. STANDARD PLAYER'S CONTRACT

KEN WREGGET

N.H.L. BONUSES:

If Player Wins 20 Games in Regular Season........$7,500.00
If Player Wins 25 Games in Regular Season........$7,500.00 (additional)
If Player Wins 30 Games in Regular Season.......$10,000.00 (additional)

If Team Wins First Round of Playoffs (must play
in 1 Game of Round)....................................$5,000.00
If Team Wins Second Round of Playoffs (must play
in 1 Game of Round)....................................$5,000.00 (additional)
If Team Wins Third Round of Playoffs (must play
in 1 Game of Round)....................................$7,500.00 (additional)
If Team Wins Fourth Round of Playoffs (must play
in 1 Game of Round)...................................$10,000.00 (additional)

N.H.L. SALARY REVISION:

If Player is goaltender of record for 62 Points during the Regular
Season than the sum of 50% of his Bonuses attained (for Games Won)
shall be added to his base N.H.L. salary for each subsequent season
of this N.H.L. Contract, including Option Year.

_____
WITNESS

GERRY McNAMARA
General Manager, Toronto Maple Leafs

_____
WITNESS (Middlemaugh)

KEN WREGGET
Goaltender, Toronto Maple Leafs

JULY 27, 1987
DATE

NATIONAL HOCKEY LEAGUE

STANDARD PLAYER'S CONTRACT
(1982 FORM — AMENDED 1984)

BETWEEN **MAPLE LEAF GARDENS LTD.**
hereinafter called the "Club,"
a member of the National Hockey League, hereinafter called the "League"

AND **KEN WREGGET**
hereinafter called the "Player"

of **BRANDON** in Province of **MANITOBA**

In consideration of the respective obligations herein and hereby assumed, the parties to this contract severally agree as follows:
The Club hereby employs the Player as a skilled Hockey Player for the term of ...one... year(s) commencing October ... 19 86
and agrees, subject to the terms and conditions hereof, to pay the Player a salary of

1986-87 ONE HUNDRED AND TWENTY THOUSAND---------------------Dollars ($ 120,000.00).

OPTION YEAR

1987-88 ONE HUNDRED AND TWENTY THOUSAND--------------------- $120,000.00

NOTE: Player is guaranteed a minimum salary of $35,000.00 per Season

SEE: ATTACHED ADDENDUM RE: N.H.L. BONUSES

Payment of such salary shall be in consecutive semi-monthly installments following the commencement of the regular League Championship Schedule of games or following the dates of reporting, whichever is later; provided, however, that if the Player is not in the employ of the Club for the whole period of the Club's games in the National Hockey League Championship Schedule, then he shall receive only part of the salary in the ratio of the number of days of actual employment to the number of days of the League Championship Schedule of Games.

And it is further mutually agreed that if the Contract and rights to the services of the Player are assigned, exchanged, loaned or otherwise transferred to a Club in another League, the Player shall only be paid at an annual salary rate of

1986-87 ($30,000.00) THIRTY THOUSAND---------Dollars in the **Minor** League.
or 1987-88 ($30,000.00) THIRTY THOUSAND---------Dollars in the **Minor** League.
or ---------Dollars in the --------- League.

2. The Player agrees to give his services and to play hockey in all League Championship, Play-Off and Stanley Cup games to the best of his ability under the direction and control of the Club in accordance with the provisions hereof.

The Player further agrees,
(a) to report to the Club training camp at the time and place fixed by the Club, in good physical condition,
(b) to keep himself in good physical condition at all times during the season,
(c) to give his best services to the Club and to play hockey only for the Club unless his contract is released, assigned, exchanged or loaned by the Club,
(d) to co-operate with the Club and participate in any and all reasonable promotional activities of the Club which will in the opinion of the Club promote the welfare of the Club and to cooperate in the promotion of the League and professional hockey generally.
(e) to conduct himself on and off the rink according to the highest standards of honesty, morality, fair play and sportsmanship, and to refrain from conduct detrimental to the best interest of the Club, the League or professional hockey generally.

The Club agrees that in exhibition games played after the start of the regular schedule (except where the proceeds are to go to charity, or where the player has agreed otherwise) the player shall receive his pro rata share of the gate receipts after deduction of legitimate expenses of such game. This provision re exhibition games is applicable in the National Hockey League only.

3. In order that the Player shall be fit in proper condition for the performance of his duties as required by this contract, the Player agrees to report for practice at such time and place as the Club may reasonably designate and participate in such exhibition games as may be arranged by the Club.

4. The Club may from time to time during the continuance of this contract establish reasonable rules governing the conduct and conditioning of the Player, and such reasonable rules shall form part of this contract.

The Club and the Player further agree that in case of dispute between them, except as to the compensation to be paid to the Player on a new contract, the dispute shall be referred within one year from the date it arose to the President of the League, as an arbitrator and his decision shall be accepted as final by both parties, unless, and to extent that, other arbitration procedures are provided in any Collective Bargaining Agreement between the member clubs of the League and the NHLPA to cover such dispute.

The Club and the Player further agree that all fines imposed upon the Player under the Playing Rules, or under the provisions of the League By-Laws, shall be deducted from the salary of the Player and be remitted by the Club to the N.H.L. Players' Emergency Fund.

20. The parties agree that the rights provided in Section 18 and in any Addendum hereto and the promise of the Player to play hockey only with the Club, or such other club as provided in Sections 2, 11 and 12, and the Club's right to take pictures of and televise the Player as provided in Section 8 have all been taken into consideration in determining the salary payable to the Player under Section 1 hereof.

21. It is severally and mutually agreed that the only contracts recognized by the President of the League are the Standard Player's Contracts, Player's Termination Contracts, Player's Option Contracts, Post-Option Year Termination Contracts, Standard Contracts (Corporate), Standard Termination Contracts (Corporate), Standard Option Contracts (Corporate) and Post-Option Year Termination Contracts (Corporate) which have been duly executed and filed in the League's office and approved by him (or his designated representative), and that this Agreement contains the entire agreement between the Parties and there are no oral or written inducements, promises or agreements except as provided herein.

In Witness Whereof, the parties have signed this ...29TH... day
of ...AUGUST... A.D. 19 86

WITNESSES:

MAPLE LEAF GARDENS LTD.
60 CARLTON ST., TORONTO, ONTARIO
Address of Club

By _Gerry McNamara_
President

Ken Wregget
Player

Home Address of Player

I hereby certify that I have, at this date, received, examined and noted of record the within Contract, and that it is in regular form.

Dated ...MAR 10 1987... 19......

_____
for the National Hockey League

Thornton Finds Success

Scott Thornton was selected third overall in the 1989 NHL amateur draft, and the Leafs also took two other teammates from his Belleville Bulls team, all in the first round: Rob Pearson (12th) and Steve Bancroft (21st). "I guess I won't have to look for a roommate," quipped Thornton at the draft. Of the three, Thornton had the most success, playing 941 NHL games—though only 33 were with Toronto before the odyssey that took the centreman to Edmonton, Montreal, Dallas, San Jose, and Los Angeles. More recently, he won the 2013 version of the CBC's *Battle of the Blades*. Perhaps there was a hint of his future success in figure skating with his comments to the *Toronto Star*'s Mark Harding at the draft: "I'm not sure I'll be a dominant scorer, but I feel I can be consistent. I like to think of myself as an all-around player. I'm not afraid to use my body, but I also like the finesse style of game." Of the three times he was traded, the first, on September 19, 1991, was the biggest: Vincent Damphousse, Peter Ing, Luke Richardson, Thornton, and cash went to Edmonton for Grant Fuhr, Glenn Anderson, and Craig Berube. The *Edmonton Journal* was uncertain what to make of Thornton, calling him "the unknown factor." Damphousse promised good things from his teammate: "He's a hard worker. He's more of a checking centre. He's very good defensively." The player taken first overall that year by the Quebec Nordiques ended up being the most important Leaf of the 1990s and 2000s: Mats Sundin.

Scott Thornton.

cc: BM
BF
KP

MEMORANDUM

TO: Cliff Fletcher
           Central Registry

FROM: Glen Sather

DATE: September 20, 1991

RE: **SEPTEMBER 19th, 1991 TRADE**

This will confirm Cliff Fletcher's memo of September 20th, 1991 that:

Edmonton trade players Grant Fuhr, Glenn Anderson and Craig Berube to Toronto in exchange for players Vincent Damphousse, Peter Ing, Luke Richardson and Scott Thornton.

Toronto will also give Edmonton a 1993, 2nd Round Entry Draft Choice plus $125,000.00 if player Glenn Anderson scores a total of 60 goals during the 1991/92 and 1992/93 regular season and playoffs - OR - a 1993, 1st Round Entry Draft Choice plus $250,000.00 if Glenn Anderson scores a total of 70 goals during the 1991/92 and 1992/93 regular season and playoffs.

Glen Sather

Glen Sather

GS/bd

NORTHLANDS COLISEUM, 7424 - 118 AVENUE, EDMONTON, ALBERTA, T5B 4M9 ● TEL (403) 474-8561 ● TICKETING (403) 471-2191 ● ADMIN FAX (403) 477-9625

STANLEY
CUP
CHAMPIONS
1983-1984
1984-1985
1986-1987
1987-1988
1989-1990

Wayne Gretzky.

Watch Out for that 99 Guy

Each NHL team has its own way to recap a game. The Leafs of the mid-1990s used a legal-sized page to record the lineups for each team and make notes about penalty killing and the power play. Usually, the handwritten page is followed by an official game sheet that further breaks down things—numbers on the backs of the players, who the referees were, shots per period, and penalties—and a video file page. Toronto, coached by Pat Burns, won the game detailed here 5–3 over Los Angeles. Apparently, some player wearing #99 was dangerous from behind the net. Who knew?

LINEUPS

Toronto vs L.A. Date: MAR.18/95

Score: 5-3 (w)

Visiting Team: TORONTO

		DND
RHODES		- BAUMGARTNER (SHOULDER)
POTVIN		- ELLETT (FOOT)
		- CRAIG (FINGER)
MACOUN	JONSSON	- GARTNER (FOOT)
MIRONOV	BUTCHER	- GILL (SHOULDER)
MARTIN	BEREHOWSKY	- JABLONSKI

SUNDIN GILMOUR RYCHEL   99 PP
ANDREYCHUK RIDLEY WOOD   M 92
BERG EASTWOOD SUTTER   17
BORSCHEVSKY MANDERVILLE YAKE 77 33

Penalty Killing:
- FC - DOWN QUICK
  - BACK AT YOU IN N.Z.
- CROSSCOURT DUMP TO SPEED?
- STATIC → HARD ROTATION
- Ⓑ RUN UP HIGH - LOW + OUTNUMBER
- F IS OUT HARD AT PTS - "CHANGE FOCUS"

Power Play:
- BO - ALL 5 BACK
- SHOOT-INS - MAKE CONTACT
- 99 BEHIND NET - 92 IN FRONT
- 17 GETS AVAILABLE (PICKS)
- UMBRELLA - WATCH OUT 22
- BACKDOOR ⚹ F MUST DROP DOWN TO HELP

Comments:
- WE ATTACKED THEM w/ PUCK.
- ALL KINDS OF SHOTS @ HRUDEY (BAD ANGLE WRIST LONG) MANY REBOUNDS
- UP ICE PLAYS + ZOO!

Home Team: L.A.

		DND
32 HRUDEY		- TODD (KNEE)
31 FUHR		- BOUCHER (WRIST)
		- JOHNSON
		- WATTERS (GROIN)
25 SYDOR	24 PETIT	- BLAKE (GROIN)
77 COWIE	33 MCSORLEY	- SHUCHUK
29 SNELL	3 TSYGUROV	

		DND
		- CRAIG (FINGER)
MACOUN	JONSSON	- GARTNER (FOOT)
MIRONOV	BUTCHER	- GILL (SHOULDER)
MARTIN	BEREHOWSKY	- JABLONSKI

SUNDIN GILMOUR RYCHEL   99 PP
ANDREYCHUK RIDLEY WOOD   M 92
BERG EASTWOOD SUTTER   17
BORSCHEVSKY MANDERVILLE YAKE 77 33

Penalty Killing:
- FC - DOWN QUICK
  - BACK AT YOU IN N.Z.
- CROSSCOURT DUMP TO SPEED?
- STATIC → HARD ROTATION
- Ⓑ RUN UP HIGH - LOW + OUTNUMBER
- F IS OUT HARD AT PTS - "CHANGE FOCUS"

Power Play:
- BO - ALL 5 BACK
- SHOOT-INS - MAKE CONTACT
- 99 BEHIND NET - 92 IN FRONT
- 17 GETS AVAILABLE (PICKS)
- UMBRELLA - WATCH OUT 22
- BACKDOOR ⚹ F MUST DROP DOWN TO HELP

Comments:
- WE ATTACKED THEM w/ PUCK.
- ALL KINDS OF SHOTS @ HRUDEY (BAD ANGLE WRIST LONG) MANY REBOUNDS
- UP ICE PLAYS + ZOO!

Home Team: L.A.

		DND
32 HRUDEY		- TODD (KNEE)
31 FUHR		- BOUCHER (WRIST)
		- JOHNSON
		- WATTERS (GROIN)
25 SYDOR	24 PETIT	- BLAKE (GROIN)
77 COWIE	33 MCSORLEY	- SHUCHUK
29 SNELL	3 TSYGUROV	

21 GRANATO	99 GRETZKY	17 KURRI
7 QUINN	13 LANG	22 TOCCHET
44 BURRIDGE	39 PERREAULT	19 DRUCE
28 LACROIX	15 CONACHER	55 CROWDER

Comments: ⚹ DZFO - CONACHER GOING FWD ON F.O +
SYDOR JUMPING

Felix Potvin.

Gold Stars for Potvin

How does a team determine the worth of a player? His specific contributions? His leadership? His overall abilities? For the Maple Leafs of 1995–96, there was a Player Evaluation Report. During the regular season, they were compiled on a 10-game basis, with a 1 to 4 rating system, where 1 is poor and 4 is excellent. Flipping through the files, there are only occasional perfect ratings: Felix Potvin got a whopping 16 top ratings for his play, and his backup, Damian Rhodes, got one; as far as skaters go, Mats Sundin and Larry Murphy were each perfect once, Doug Gilmour twice, and Kirk Muller got gold stars upon his Leafs debut on January 24, 1996, and again in game #68. For the last 17 games of the season, Nick Beverly was the Leafs coach on an interim basis, replacing the fired Pat Burns. In the playoffs, the Leafs fell to the Blues in six games, and Mike Gartner's 3.8 was the highest rating.

Player Evaluation Report
1996 Western Conf. Quarter-Finals vs St. Louis

Rating	
1 -	Poor
2 -	Average
3 -	Good
4 -	Excellent

GP	W	L
6	2	4

Game by Game Coaches' Rating

	Apr. 16 vs St. Louis	Apr. 18 vs St. Louis	Apr. 21 @ St. Louis	Apr. 23 @ St. Louis	Apr. 25 vs St. Louis	Apr. 27 @ St. Louis	TOTALS (TOR./StL.)
Date	Apr. 16	Apr. 18	Apr. 21	Apr. 23	Apr. 25	Apr. 27	
Opposition	vs St. Louis	vs St. Louis	@ St. Louis	@ St. Louis	vs St. Louis	@ St. Louis	
Result	L 1-3	W 5-4 OT	L 2-3 OT	L 1-5	W 5-4 OT	L 1-2	15 - 21
Shots	34 - 29	39 - 34	21 - 40	42 - 34	40 - 39	24 - 35	200 - 211
Scoring Chances	14 - 15	19 - 17	11 - 19	13 - 16	17 - 17	8 - 12	82 - 96
							Avg.
Goalies							
29 Potvin, F	2.3	3.3	3.0	2.6	2.1	3.3	2.8
33 Beaupre, D				2.9			2.9
Defence							
2 Zettler, R					2.0	2.3	2.2
4 Ellett, D	2.6	1.8	2.0	2.3	2.8	2.6	2.4
23 Gill, T	2.8	3.1	2.8	2.6	2.8	1.3	2.6
26 Yushkevich, D	1.5	1.3	1.3	1.5			1.4
34 Macoun, J	2.5	2.9	2.8	3.0	3.5	3.5	3.0
55 Murphy, L	2.1	3.0	0.8	0.0	2.4	2.4	1.8
72 Schneider, M	2.6	3.4	1.8	0.6	2.4	2.5	2.2
Right Wing							
9 Craig, M	1.9	2.8	1.8	2.5	2.4	2.1	2.3
11 Gartner, M	1.1	2.0	1.2	0.3	3.8	1.6	1.7
18 Presley, W	1.9	1.6	1.7	1.5		1.4	1.6
28 Domi, T	2.3	3.0	2.0	2.4	2.8	1.9	2.4
Left Wing							
8 Warriner, T	2.3	3.1	1.0	1.6	3.3	1.8	2.2
17 Clark, W	1.8	1.1	0.7	0.3	2.6	2.0	1.4
21 Muller, K	1.5	3.1	3.2	2.1	2.5	1.9	2.4
32 Kypreos, N				3.1	2.9	2.5	2.6
37 Kolesar, M			1.8	2.0	1.9		1.9
Centre							
12 Convery, B	1.8	1.1	1.0		0.9	0.5	1.1
13 Sundin, M	2.5	3.1	1.2	1.0	2.8	2.6	2.2
15 Gagner, D	1.4	1.9	1.0	0.9	1.6	0.5	1.2
93 Gilmour, D	2.4	3.0	1.0	2.3	3.0	2.8	2.4
Team Average per Game	2.1	2.5	1.7	1.8	2.6	2.1	2.1

An Easy Night for the Video Guy

In a digital world where players can watch specific plays on their iPads, it is quaint to look back on a simpler time, way back in 1997, when video tape ruled the day. Following a game, such as this December 27, 1997 classic, where the Red Wings—on their way to a second straight Stanley Cup—shellacked the Maple Leafs 8–1, a video technician would watch the game again and make note of the number on the counter so that the specific clip could be found again. Many of the video file sheets in the collection are two or three pages, but when things don't go your way, there isn't a lot to highlight apparently....

Acknowledgements

Thanks to Michael Holmes at ECW Press for the introduction to Allan Stitt, setting in motion this whole fascinating book.

Near the top of the acknowledgements list has to be Leslie Campbell, Allan's long-time executive assistant at ADR Chambers | Stitt Feld Handy Group. Not only was Leslie lovely and accommodating on every visit, she also was the gatekeeper of the documents and, perhaps most impressively, has the puzzle-like mind (and patience) to put them all back after a day poring through them. Thanks as well to Radek Cecha for the photography and to Zachary Kozak for helping with everything from photo-copying to moving desks.

The Hockey Hall of Fame has been behind this project the entire way, from Ron Ellis contacting a few players on our behalf, to Phil Pritchard and Craig Campbell providing stories and photos. Kelly Gallagher, the municipal curator at Hockey Heritage North, deserves a shout-out as well; the Shep Mayer piece here is one of my favourites, and I owe it all to her help.

Mike Wyman introduced me to Al Shaw, the caretaker of the NHL old-timers luncheons at Shopsy's, and for that I am eternally grateful. I've been able to sit and listen to Brian MacFarlane tell stories at lunch and to my old friend Toronto historian extraordinaire Mike Filey crack bad jokes, just like he used to all those years ago in the *Toronto Sun* library.

My friends at the Society for International Hockey Research that I told about the project were enthusiastic, as I am about the "obscure" group of passionate people who care so much about the game. Bob Visser's personal project/obsession of an all-time Maple Leafs Registry was referenced along the way. Join us at sihrhockey.org—I would be a member even if it wasn't a tax write-off.

Like the historians, Jeff Tyson and the hockey card autograph collectors are a fanatical bunch, but wonderful and giving as well. It has been fun adding to my collection as I meet some of these players in person. (Thanks to my wife, Meredith, for allowing me out of the house!)

And I have been fortunate to have a great research assistant in my son, Quinn, who loves hockey when baseball isn't in season. Before his first hockey practice of the winter of 2013–14, he got a personal message of encouragement from Paul Henderson; who else could say that?

References

The world is blessed with many books about the Toronto Maple Leafs. Here are a few that were referenced:

Imlach, Punch with Scott Young. *Heaven and Hell in the NHL.* Toronto: McClelland & Stewart, 1982.

Imlach, Punch with Scott Young. *Hockey Is a Battle: Punch Imlach's Own Story.* Toronto: Macmillan Company of Canada, 1969.

O'Malley, Martin. *Gross Misconduct: The Life of Spinner Spencer.* Toronto: Viking Canada, 1988.

Shea, Kevin with Paul Patskou, Roly Harris, and Paul Bruno. *Toronto Maple Leafs: Diary of a Dynasty, 1957–1967.* Richmond Hill, ON: Firefly Books, 2010.

Sittler, Darryl and Chris Goyens, with Allan Turowetz. *Sittler.* Toronto: Macmillan Canada, 1991.

Smythe, Thomas Stafford with Kevin Shea. *Centre Ice: The Smythe Family, the Gardens and the Toronto Maple Leafs Hockey Club.* Toronto: HB Fenn and Company, 2000.

Smythe, Conn and Scott Young. *Conn Smythe: If You Can't Beat 'Em in the Alley.* Toronto: McClelland & Stewart, 1981.

of the season or at any subsequent time during the season (unless such condition is the direct result of playing hockey for the Club) so as to render him unfit to play skilled hockey, then it is mutually agreed that the Club shall have the right to suspend the Player for such period of disability or unfitness, and no compensation shall be payable for that period under this contract.

If the Player is injured as the result of playing hockey for the Club, the Club will pay the Player's reasonable hospitalization until discharged from the hospital, and his medical expenses and doctor's bills, provided that the hospital and doctor are selected by the Club and provided further that the Club's obligation to pay such expenses shall terminate at a period not more than six months after the injury.

It is also agreed that if the Player's injuries resulting directly from playing for the Club render him, in the sole judgment of the Club's physician, unfit to play skilled hockey for the balance of the season or any part thereof, then during such time the Player is so unfit, but in no event beyond the end of the current season, the Club shall pay the Player the compensation herein provided for and the Player releases the Club from any and every additional obligation, liability, claim or demand whatsoever. However the player shall, in the first instance, be the sole judge of his own fitness to resume play following an injury sustained while playing hockey for the Club.

6. The Player represents and agrees that he has exceptional and unique knowledge, skill and ability as a hockey player, the loss of which cannot be estimated with certainty and cannot be fairly or adequately compensated by damages. The Player therefore agrees that the Club shall have the right, in addition to any other rights which the Club may possess, to enjoin him by appropriate injunction proceedings from playing hockey for any other team and/or for any breach of any of the other provisions of this contract.

7. The Player and the Club recognize and agree that the Player's participation in other sports may impair or destroy his ability and skill as a hockey player. Accordingly the Player agrees that he will not during the period of this Contract and of the option of renewal thereof engage or participate in football, baseball, softball, hockey, lacrosse, boxing, wrestling, or other athletic sport without the written consent of the Club.

8. (a) The Player hereby irrevocably grants to the Club during the period of this Contract and of the option of renewal thereof the exclusive right to permit or authorize any person, firm or corporation to take and make use of any still photograph, motion pictures or television of himself, and agrees that all rights in such pictures and television shall belong to the Club exclusively and may be used, reproduced, distributed or otherwise disseminated by the Club directly or indirectly in any manner it desires.

(b) The Player further agrees that during the period of this Contract and of the option of renewal thereof he will not make public appearances, participate in radio or television programs, or permit his picture to be taken, or write or sponsor newspaper or magazine articles, or sponsor commercial products without the written consent of the Club. Where the Club grants its written consent to any of the activities recited in this sub-section the Player shall receive his proper share of the proceeds of such activities.

9. It is mutually agreed that the Club will not pay, and the Player will not accept from any person, any bonus or anything of value for winning any particular game or series of games except as authorized by the League By-Laws.

10. The Player agrees that during the currency of this agreement he will not tamper with or enter into negotiations with any player under contract or reservation to any Club of the League for or regarding such player's current or future services, without the written consent of the Club with which such player is connected under penalty of a fine to be imposed by the President of the League.

11. It is mutually agreed that the Club shall have the right to sell, assign, exchange and transfer this contract, and to loan the Player's services to any other professional hockey club, and the Player agrees to accept and be bound by such sale, exchange, assignment, transfer or loan, and will faithfully perform and carry out this contract with the same purpose and effect as if it had been entered into by the Player and such other Club.

It is further mutually agreed that in the event that this contract is assigned, or the Player's services are loaned, to another Club, the Club shall, by notice in writing delivered personally to the Player or by mail to the address set out below his signature hereto advise the Player of the name and address of the Club to which he has been assigned or loaned, and specifying the time and place of reporting to such club. If the Player fails to report to such other Club he may be suspended by such other Club and no salary shall be payable to him during the period of such suspension.

The Club shall pay the actual moving expenses incurred by a player during the playing season when such move is directed by the Club and is not part of disciplinary action.

12. If the Club shall default in the payments to the Player provided for in Section 1 hereof or shall fail to perform any other obligation agreed to be performed by the Club hereunder, the Player may, by notice in writing to the Club, specify the nature of the default, and if the Club shall fail to remedy the default within fifteen (15) days from receipt of such notice, this contract shall be terminated, and upon the date of such termination all obligations of both parties shall cease, except the obligation of the Club to pay the Player's compensation to that date.

13. The Club may terminate this contract upon written notice to the Player (but only after obtaining waivers from all other League clubs) if the player shall at any time:

(a) fail, refuse or neglect to obey the Club's rules governing training and conduct of players,

(b) fail, refuse or neglect to render his services hereunder or in any other manner materially breach this contract,

(c) fail, in the opinion of the Club's management, to exhibit sufficient skill or competitive ability to warrant further employment as a member of the Club's team.

In the event of termination under sub-section (a) or (b) the Player shall only be entitled to compensation due to him to the date such notice is delivered to him or the date of the mailing of such notice to his address as set out below his signature hereto.

In the event of termination under sub-section (c) it shall take effect thirty days from the date upon which such notice is delivered to the Player, and the Player shall only be entitled to the compensation herein provided to the end of such thirty-day period.

In the event that this contract is terminated by the Club while the Player is "away" with the Club for the purpose of playing games the instalment then falling due shall be paid on the first week-day after the return "home" of the Club.

14. The Player further agrees that the Club may carry out and put into effect any order or ruling of the League or its President for his suspension or expulsion and that in the event of suspension his salary shall cease for the duration thereof and that in the event of expulsion this contract, at the option of the Club, shall terminate forthwith.

15. The Player further agrees that in the event of his suspension pursuant to any of the provisions of this contract, there shall be deducted from the salary stipulated in Section 1 hereof an amount equal to the exact proportion of such salary as the number of days' suspension bears to the total number of days of the League Championship Schedule of games.

16. If because of any condition arising from a state of war or other cause beyond the control of the League or of the Club, it shall be deemed advisable by the League or the Club to suspend or cease or reduce operations, then:

(a) in the event of suspension of operations, the Player shall be entitled only to the proportion of salary due at the date of suspension,

(b) in the event of cessation of operations, the salary stipulated in Section 1 hereof shall be automatically cancelled on the date of cessation, and

(c) in the event of reduction of operations, the salary stipulated in Section 1 hereof shall be replaced by that mutually agreed upon between the Club and the Player.